The
DINNER &
SUPPER Cookbook

The
DINNER & SUPPER Cookbook

Complete Menus, Recipes, & Tips

Jean Wickstrom

Oxmoor House, Inc., Birmingham

Library of Congress Catalog Number: 77-75686
ISBN: 0-8487-0476-2
Manufactured in the United States of America
First Printing 1977
Second Printing, 1978

The Dinner & Supper Cookbook

Managing Editor: Ann H. Harvey
Editor: Karen Phillips Irons
Assistant Food Editors: Sandra Day, Marilyn Wyrick
Production Manager: Robert L. Nance

Mechanical Art: Barbara Exum
Illustrations: John Anderson
Photographs: Jerome Drown (cover, pages 25, 94, 195, 264);
Taylor Lewis (pages 59, 60, 93, 161, 162, 229, 230, 263);
Kent Kirkley (pages 26, 196);
Phillip Kretchmar (page 127); Bert O'Neal (page 128).

Cover:
*Chicken Marengo adds elegance to any party scene. The
recipe for this classic dish is on page 120.*

CONTENTS

INTRODUCTION

Dedicated to people who enjoy eating, *The Dinner & Supper Cookbook* is a guide to the tastiest meals on your table. Since food has long been a symbol of hospitality in the South, even the plainest food when enjoyed with family and friends can take on a feeling of elegance and sophistication.

This cookbook is our proud collection of dinner and supper menus that we hope will make the cooking and eating in your home just a little easier and a lot more fun.

From our *Southern Living*® test kitchens come recipes that are traditionally served on holidays or anticipated at Sunday dinners, as well as those that are enjoyed at elaborate dinner parties or casual cookouts. And we have included many familiar everyday menus, all having that extra touch which makes them delicious family surprises.

Think of the many carefully selected and tested menus here as ingredients in themselves; pick and choose; and create your own unique blend of hospitality from our *Southern Living*® kitchen.

Jean Wickstrom

FAMILY SUPPERS

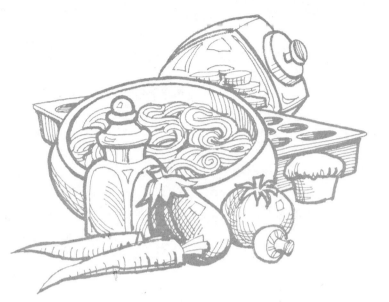

Serve Beef — Plain or Fancy

Soup for Hearty Appetites

Stir Up a Casserole

Family-Pleasing Tuna Supper

Sweet and Sour and Appetizing

Chicken with a Flair

Simple-to-Make Family Fare

Turkey Makes an Encore

Have Soup and Sandwiches

Supper Olé

Serve Pork Tonight

Chicken Pie, a Family Favorite

A New Way with Venison

Favorite Spaghetti Supper

When you're cooking for a family day after day, new ideas can be rather hard to come up with, especially if you're trying to consider cost. So we've put together some nutritious family menus featuring delicious, yet low-cost, dishes to serve families of all sizes. All of the favorites are here—from Italian spaghetti, to chicken pot pie, to beef stroganoff, to a steak sandwich. They are dishes that your family will request again and again and again.

Serve Beef—Plain or Fancy

(Supper for Six to Eight)

Tasty Beef Stroganoff or Dutch Meat Loaf
Pickled Brussels Sprouts or Sautéed Green Peppers
Creamy Carrot Salad
Quick Rolls
Cherry Pudding
Iced Tea   Coffee

TASTY BEEF STROGANOFF

3 pounds round steak, ½ inch thick
1 large onion, sliced
¼ cup melted margarine
¼ cup all-purpose flour
1 (10½-ounce) can consommé, undiluted
1 (10¾-ounce) can tomato soup, undiluted
1 (4-ounce) can sliced mushrooms, drained
1½ teaspoons monosodium glutamate
  Salt and pepper to taste
½ cup commercial sour cream
  Hot cooked noodles

Cut meat diagonally into strips about ¼ inch wide and 2 inches long. Brown meat and onion in margarine; sprinkle with flour, blending well. Gradually add consommé and tomato soup; cook, stirring constantly, until smooth and thick.

Add mushrooms, monosodium glutamate, salt, and pepper to meat mixture; mix well. Cover and cook over low heat 1½ hours or until meat is tender, stirring occasionally. When ready to serve, stir in sour cream. Serve over noodles. Yield: 6 to 8 servings.

DUTCH MEAT LOAF

1½ pounds ground beef
1 cup breadcrumbs
1 medium onion, finely chopped
1½ teaspoons salt
¼ teaspoon pepper
1½ cups tomato sauce, divided
1 cup water
1 tablespoon prepared mustard
2 tablespoons vinegar
2 tablespoon brown sugar or molasses
  Hot cooked noodles
  Parsley

Combine beef, breadcrumbs, onion, salt, pepper, and ½ cup tomato sauce; press into a 9- x 5- x 3-inch loafpan.

Combine 1 cup tomato sauce, water, mustard, vinegar, and brown sugar; blend well. Pour half of sauce over loaf; bake at 350° for 1 hour.

Unmold loaf and place on noodles. Heat remaining sauce, and spoon over meat loaf. Garnish with parsley. Yield: 6 to 8 servings.

PICKLED BRUSSELS SPROUTS

1 (10-ounce) package frozen brussels
    sprouts
2 (8-ounce) jars pearl onions, drained
2 (6-ounce) cans mushroom caps, drained
1½ cups white vinegar
¼ cup salt
1 cup sugar
1 teaspoon celery seeds
1 teaspoon turmeric
½ teaspoon dry mustard
1 teaspoon mustard seeds

Pour boiling water over brussels sprouts; cover
and set aside for 10 minutes. Drain. Add onions
and mushroom caps; mix gently.

Combine remaining ingredients in a saucepan;
bring to a boil and cook 3 minutes. Pour hot
vinegar mixture over vegetables; toss gently.
Cover and store in refrigerator at least a week
before serving. Yield: 6 to 8 servings.

Note: Marinade may be saved and used again.

SAUTÉED GREEN PEPPERS

1 cup sliced onion
1 tablespoon salad oil
3 large green peppers, seeded and sliced
    into rings
½ pound fresh mushrooms, sliced
1 teaspoon salt
⅛ teaspoon red pepper
⅛ teaspoon oregano

Sauté onion in oil until golden. Add remaining
ingredients, stirring gently to mix. Cover and
cook over medium heat about 5 minutes or until
all vegetables are tender, stirring occasionally.
Yield: 6 to 8 servings.

CREAMY CARROT SALAD

1 (8¼-ounce) can crushed pineapple
24 marshmallows
1 (5-ounce) jar cream cheese with
    pineapple
1 (3-ounce) package lemon-flavored
    gelatin
1½ cups boiling water
¾ cup grated carrot

Drain pineapple, reserving juice. Heat pineapple
juice over low heat; add marshmallows, stirring
until melted. Add cream cheese, and blend until
smooth.

Dissolve gelatin in boiling water; cool. Combine marshmallow mixture and gelatin; chill until
consistency of unbeaten egg white. Stir in pineapple and carrot; pour into an 8-inch square pan.
Chill until firm. Cut into squares to serve. Yield:
8 to 10 servings.

QUICK ROLLS
(see Index)

CHERRY PUDDING

1 (16-ounce) can red tart pitted cherries,
    undrained
1½ cups sugar, divided
½ cup milk
1 teaspoon baking powder
1 cup all-purpose flour
2 tablespoons butter or margarine

Combine cherries and 1 cup sugar; stir until sugar
is dissolved. Combine ½ cup sugar, milk, baking
powder, and flour; blend until smooth.

Melt butter in an 8-inch baking pan. Spoon
in batter, spreading well. Pour cherry mixture
over batter. Bake at 350° for 45 to 55 minutes
or until done. Yield: 6 to 8 servings.

Soup for Hearty Appetites
(Supper for Six)

Delicious Seafood Chowder or Ham 'n Corn Soup
Green Salad   French Salad Dressing
Lemon Muffins or Jiffy Cheese Biscuits
Cranberry Cream Pie
Coffee   Tea

DELICIOUS SEAFOOD CHOWDER

  1 medium potato, peeled and diced
  1 medium onion, chopped
  1 pint oysters, drained
  ¼ cup melted butter or margarine
  2 tablespoons all-purpose flour
    Salt and pepper to taste
  1 teaspoon Worcestershire sauce
    Dash of hot sauce
  1 (8-ounce) can minced clams, drained
  2 (4½-ounce) cans shrimp, drained and
    chopped
  1 quart milk, scalded
    Chopped parsley

Place potato and onion in a saucepan; cook in water to cover until tender. Drain.

Cook oysters in butter 2 to 3 minutes over low heat or until edges of oysters curl. Combine flour, salt, pepper, Worcestershire sauce, and hot sauce in a large saucepan; blend until smooth.

Add potatoes, onion, and remaining ingredients except parsley; let stand, covered, for 15 minutes. Heat and serve. Sprinkle each serving with parsley. Yield: 6 servings.

HAM 'N CORN SOUP

  3 quarts water
  2 pounds cooked ham, cubed
  2 medium onions, chopped
  1 (16-ounce) can stewed tomatoes
  1 large green pepper, chopped
  1 (10-ounce) package frozen corn
  ½ teaspoon pepper
  ½ teaspoon sugar
    Salt to taste

Combine water, ham, onions, tomatoes, and green pepper in a large saucepan; simmer about 1 hour. Add corn, pepper, sugar, and salt; simmer 10 to 15 minutes. Yield: 6 servings.

FRENCH SALAD DRESSING

1 (10¾-ounce) can tomato soup,
    undiluted
1½ cups salad oil
½ cup sugar
1 teaspoon salt
1 teaspoon pepper
⅔ cup vinegar
½ teaspoon whole oregano
    Dash of onion salt
    Dash of garlic salt

Combine all ingredients in blender; cover and blend well. Yield: 1 quart.

LEMON MUFFINS

1 cup shortening
1 cup sugar
4 eggs, separated
2 cups all-purpose flour
2 teaspoons baking powder
1 teaspoon salt
½ cup lemon juice
2 teaspoons grated lemon rind

Cream shortening and sugar until light and fluffy; add egg yolks, beating well. Combine flour, baking powder, and salt; add to creamed mixture alternately with lemon juice, beginning and ending with dry ingredients. Beat well after each addition.

Fold stiffly beaten egg whites into batter, and stir in lemon rind. Fill greased muffin cups three-fourths full. Bake at 375° for 20 to 25 minutes or until done. Yield: 1½ dozen muffins.

JIFFY CHEESE BISCUITS

½ cup shortening
2½ cups self-rising flour
1 cup coarsely shredded Cheddar cheese
¾ cup milk

Cut shortening into flour with pastry blender or 2 knives. Add cheese, and gradually stir in milk; knead lightly.

Turn dough out onto a lightly floured board; roll to ½-inch thickness. Cut into small biscuits. Place on a greased baking sheet, and bake at 425° for 10 to 12 minutes. Yield: 20 biscuits.

CRANBERRY CREAM PIE

1 cup whole-berry cranberry sauce
½ cup firmly packed brown sugar
1 (3-ounce) package orange-flavored
    gelatin
½ pint whipping cream, whipped
½ cup finely chopped pecans or walnuts
1 baked 9-inch pastry shell or graham
    cracker crust
    Whipped cream

Combine cranberry sauce and brown sugar in a saucepan; bring to a boil. Remove from heat. Add gelatin, stirring until dissolved; cool. Fold in whipped cream and nuts. Pour into pastry shell; chill several hours or until set. Garnish with additional whipped cream. Yield: one 9-inch pie.

Keep staples—such as sugar, flour, rice, and spices—in tightly covered containers at room temperature. Staples that are frequently replenished should be rotated so that the oldest is always used first.

New cast-iron cookware should always be seasoned before using. Rub the interior of the utensil with oil or shortening, and place in a 250° or 300° oven for several hours. Wipe off oily film, and store. If scouring is necessary after using the utensil, re-season the surface immediately to prevent rusting.

Stir Up a Casserole

(Supper for Four to Six)

Sausage-Macaroni Casserole or Creamy Tuna-Macaroni Casserole
Italian-Fried Eggplant
Flavorful Tomatoes
Pineapple-Cheese Pie
Iced Tea

SAUSAGE-MACARONI CASSEROLE

  1 pound bulk sausage
  1 medium onion, chopped
  ½ green pepper, chopped
  2 tablespoons all-purpose flour
  ½ teaspoon salt
1½ cups milk
  1 (8-ounce) package elbow macaroni,
     cooked and drained
  2 cups shredded Cheddar cheese, divided

Sauté sausage, onion, and green pepper in a skillet; pour off drippings. Add flour and salt, blending well. Gradually add milk; cook over low heat, stirring constantly, until thickened. Stir in macaroni and 1 cup cheese.

Spoon mixture into a lightly greased 1½-quart casserole; sprinkle remaining cheese on top of casserole. Bake at 400° for 25 to 30 minutes. Yield: 4 to 6 servings.

CREAMY TUNA-MACARONI CASSEROLE

  1 (6½-ounce) can tuna, drained and
     flaked
  1 teaspoon parsley flakes
  1 (10¾-ounce) can cream of mushroom
     soup, undiluted
  ¼ cup pasteurized process cheese spread
  1 tablespoon dried green pepper
  ½ teaspoon celery salt
  ¼ teaspoon black pepper
  ⅛ teaspoon crushed red pepper
  2 cups shell macaroni, cooked
  ½ cup water
  3 slices pasteurized process American
     cheese slices
  ½ cup crushed potato chips

Combine all ingredients except sliced cheese and potato chips. Spoon mixture into a greased 1½-quart casserole; top with cheese slices and potato chips. Bake at 350° for 30 minutes. Yield: 4 to 6 servings.

ITALIAN-FRIED EGGPLANT

1 medium eggplant
2 teaspoons salt, divided
1 cup all-purpose flour
1 teaspoon baking powder
2 teaspoons Italian seasoning
1 teaspoon onion powder
  Dash of red pepper
  Dash of garlic powder
2 eggs, beaten
⅔ cup milk
1 tablespoon salad oil
  Hot salad oil

Peel eggplant, and cut into finger-size strips. Sprinkle with 1 teaspoon salt; cover with water, and soak 1 hour. Drain and pat dry with absorbent towels.

Combine flour, 1 teaspoon salt, baking powder, and remaining seasonings in a mixing bowl. Add eggs, milk, and 1 tablespoon salad oil; beat until smooth. Dip eggplant strips in batter, and sauté in hot oil until golden brown. Yield: 4 to 6 servings.

Note: Cauliflower or zucchini may be substituted for eggplant.

FLAVORFUL TOMATOES

4 ripe tomatoes
1 Spanish onion, sliced and separated
   into rings
¼ teaspoon sugar
½ teaspoon salt
  Freshly ground pepper
1 tablespoon chopped fresh chives
1 tablespoon basil
1 tablespoon dillweed
1 teaspoon celery seeds
¼ cup commercial French dressing
  Lettuce leaves

Slice tomatoes into ½-inch-thick slices. Arrange tomato slices and onion rings in a shallow dish; sprinkle with sugar and seasonings. Pour French dressing over tomatoes. Cover and refrigerate overnight. Serve on lettuce leaves. Yield: 4 to 6 servings.

PINEAPPLE-CHEESE PIE

¼ cup cold milk
1 envelope (1 tablespoon) unflavored
   gelatin
½ cup milk, scalded
⅔ cup sugar
⅛ teaspoon salt
1 (8-ounce) package cream cheese,
   softened and cut into pieces
1 tablespoon lemon juice
1 teaspoon vanilla extract
1 cup commercial sour cream
1 (8¼-ounce) can crushed pineapple
1 (9-inch) graham cracker crust

Combine cold milk and gelatin in blender; blend on lowest speed to soften gelatin. Add scalded milk and blend until gelatin dissolves. Scrape sides of blender with spatula.

Add sugar, salt, cream cheese, lemon juice, vanilla, and sour cream; blend until smooth.

Drain pineapple and reserve 3 tablespoons syrup. Add pineapple and reserved syrup to blender mixture; blend until smooth. Pour into crust. Chill about 3 to 4 hours or until firm. Yield: one 9-inch pie.

Family-Pleasing Tuna Supper
(Supper for Four)

Tuna Patties
Potatoes in Mustard Sauce or Herb Fried Potatoes
Creole Okra
Green Salad   Celery Seed Dressing
Buttermilk Biscuits
Fruit Rhapsody
Iced Tea   Coffee

TUNA PATTIES

1 (6-ounce) package chicken-flavored
    stuffing mix
½ cup hot water
1 (10¾-ounce) can cream of chicken
    soup, undiluted and divided
2 eggs, beaten
1 (9¼-ounce) can tuna, drained and
    flaked
3 tablespoons melted butter or margarine
¼ cup milk

Remove vegetable seasoning packet and stuffing crumbs from package. Combine vegetable seasoning and water; stir until well blended. Add stuffing crumbs, half of soup, eggs, and tuna; blend well. Form into 6 patties, and brown in butter.

Combine remaining soup and milk; heat thoroughly. Serve as a sauce with patties. Yield: 6 servings.

POTATOES IN MUSTARD SAUCE

3 medium potatoes, cooked and diced
½ medium onion, chopped
3 tablespoons butter or margarine
1½ tablespoons all-purpose flour
1 chicken bouillon cube
¾ cup boiling water
½ teaspoon salt
½ teaspoon pepper
1 tablespoon prepared mustard
1 tablespoon breadcrumbs
1 tablespoon grated Parmesan cheese

Place potatoes in a greased 1-quart casserole, and set aside. Sauté onion in butter until limp; stir in flour until smooth. Dissolve bouillon cube in boiling water, and gradually stir into flour mixture. Cook over low heat, stirring constantly, until sauce bubbles. Stir in salt, pepper, and mustard; simmer 10 minutes.

Pour sauce over potatoes. Combine breadcrumbs and cheese; sprinkle over casserole. Bake at 375° for 15 to 20 minutes. Yield: 4 servings.

HERB FRIED POTATOES

    3 tablespoons butter or margarine
    3 medium potatoes, pared and cut in
        ⅛-inch strips
    ½ teaspoon ground oregano
    2 tablespoons chopped parsley
    ½ teaspoon instant minced onion
    ½ teaspoon salt
        Pepper to taste

Melt butter in a 10-inch skillet; add potatoes. Cover and cook over medium heat 10 minutes. Turn potatoes carefully; cook, uncovered, 10 minutes more, turning occasionally to brown all sides. Sprinkle with remaining ingredients during last 5 minutes of cooking. Yield: 4 servings.

CREOLE OKRA

    ½ cup minced onion
    ½ cup finely chopped green pepper
    3 tablespoons bacon drippings
    3 cups sliced okra
    3 cups chopped tomatoes
    ¼ cup chopped fresh parsley
    4 teaspoons sugar
    1½ teaspoons salt
    ¾ teaspoon pepper

Sauté onion and green pepper in bacon drippings until tender. Add okra; cook over medium heat 5 minutes, stirring constantly. Stir in remaining ingredients. Simmer, uncovered, 15 minutes; add a small amount of water, if necessary. Yield: 4 servings.

CELERY SEED DRESSING

    ½ cup sugar
    1 teaspoon dry mustard
    1 teaspoon salt
    2 teaspoons celery seeds
    2 teaspoons grated onion
    ⅓ cup cider vinegar
    2 teaspoons horseradish
    1 cup salad oil

Combine all ingredients in container of electric blender; cover and blend well. Chill. Yield: 1½ cups.

BUTTERMILK BISCUITS

    1 cup self-rising flour
    ½ teaspoon salt
    2½ tablespoons shortening
    ½ cup buttermilk

Combine flour and salt; cut in shortening. Add buttermilk, and stir until well blended.
    Roll out dough to ½-inch thickness on a floured surface; cut with a 2-inch biscuit cutter. Place on lightly greased baking sheet, and bake at 425° for 15 to 20 minutes. Yield: about 1 dozen biscuits.

FRUIT RHAPSODY

    1 (16-ounce) can seedless grapes, drained
    1 (11-ounce) can mandarin orange
        sections, drained
    1 (15½-ounce) can pineapple chunks,
        drained
    1 cup miniature marshmallows
    1 cup commercial sour cream
    1 cup flaked coconut

Combine all ingredients; chill at least 6 hours before serving. Yield: 8 servings.

Sweet and Sour and Appetizing

(Supper for Six)

Sweet-and-Sour Pork   Rice
Oriental Salad
Egg Rolls
Hot Mustard Sauce and Sweet-and-Sour Sauce
Almond Angels
Tea

SWEET-AND-SOUR PORK

1½ to 2 pounds boneless lean pork
    shoulder or loin, sliced ½ inch thick
1 to 2 tablespoons melted shortening
1 (20-ounce) can pineapple chunks
¾ cup water
¼ cup vinegar
1 tablespoon soy sauce
¼ cup firmly packed dark brown sugar
½ teaspoon salt
2 tablespoons cornstarch
2 tablespoons water
⅓ cup thinly sliced onion
1 green pepper, cut into thin strips
1½ to 2 cups hot cooked rice

Cut meat into strips about 3 to 4 inches long and 1 inch wide. Sauté in shortening over moderate heat until lightly browned; drain.

Drain pineapple, reserving juice. Combine pineapple juice, ¾ cup water, vinegar, soy sauce, brown sugar, and salt; pour over meat. Cover and simmer 1 hour or until meat is tender.

Combine cornstarch and 2 tablespoons water; add to meat. Cook over low heat, stirring constantly, until thickened; add pineapple chunks, onion, and green pepper. Cover and simmer 10 to 15 minutes or until vegetables are tender. Serve over rice. Yield: 6 servings.

ORIENTAL SALAD

1 pound fresh spinach
1 (8-ounce) can water chestnuts, drained
    and sliced
1 (16-ounce) can bean sprouts, drained
6 slices bacon, cooked and crumbled
½ cup sugar
⅓ cup catsup
⅓ cup vinegar
1 cup salad oil
5 tablespoons Worcestershire sauce
1 small onion, quartered

Wash spinach thoroughly, and tear into bite-size pieces. Combine spinach, water chestnuts, and bean sprouts in a large bowl. Sprinkle with bacon.

Combine remaining ingredients in blender; blend well. When ready to serve, pour dressing over salad; toss lightly. Yield: 6 to 8 servings.

EGG ROLLS
(see Index)

HOT MUSTARD SAUCE
(see Index)

SWEET-AND-SOUR SAUCE
(see Index)

ALMOND ANGELS

  4 egg whites
¼ teaspoon cream of tartar
¼ teaspoon salt
1½ cups sugar
½ teaspoon vanilla extract
½ teaspoon almond extract
  1 cup blanched slivered almonds

Combine egg whites, cream of tartar, and salt; beat until mixture holds soft peaks. Gradually beat in sugar, then flavorings; fold in almonds.

Grease cookie sheets well. Line with unglazed brown paper, and grease paper well. Drop mixture by teaspoonfuls onto greased paper. Bake at 250° for 50 minutes. Remove from cookie sheets immediately, and cool on wire racks. Yield: 3½ to 4 dozen cookies.

Fall is the time to check your spices to see if they have lost their aroma. The spice should smell strong and clear as soon as you open the container. If it doesn't, now is the time to replace it. This is the peak time of year for using spices, and you'll want to get the most in flavor and aroma.

Tinted coconut makes a child's cake more festive. Fill a pint jar a third to half full of coconut. Add a few drops of cake coloring to 1 to 2 tablespoons water, and add to coconut; cover jar, and shake well to distribute color evenly.

Chicken with a Flair
(Supper for Six)

Sesame Chicken or Baked Parmesan Chicken
Potato Casserole
Brussels Sprouts Piquant
Blueberry Salad
Commercial French Rolls   Butter
Lemon-Buttermilk Pound Cake
Iced Tea   Coffee

SESAME CHICKEN

    1 (10¾-ounce) can golden mushroom
       soup, undiluted
    ¾ cup milk
    ¼ teaspoon poultry seasoning
    2 cups round buttery cracker crumbs
    3 tablespoons sesame seeds
    6 chicken breasts
    2 tablespoons melted margarine

Combine soup, milk, and poultry seasoning; blend well, and set aside half of mixture. Combine cracker crumbs and sesame seeds.

Dip chicken in half of soup mixture, and coat with crumb mixture Arrange chicken in a single layer in a lightly greased 13- x 9- x 2-inch baking dish; drizzle with margarine. Bake at 400° for 40 to 50 minutes or until tender.

Heat reserved soup mixture, and serve as a gravy. Yield: 6 servings.

BAKED PARMESAN CHICKEN

    1 cup dry breadcrumbs
    ⅓ cup grated Parmesan cheese
    ¼ teaspoon ground oregano
    ¼ teaspoon pepper
       Salt to taste
    1 clove garlic, minced
    ¾ cup melted butter or margarine,
       divided
    1 (3-pound) chicken, cut up

Combine breadcrumbs, cheese, oregano, pepper, and salt; set aside. Lightly sauté garlic in 2 tablespoons butter; stir in remaining butter. Dip chicken in garlic butter; roll each piece in breadcrumb mixture.

Place chicken in a 13- x 9- x 2-inch pan; sprinkle with remaining breadcrumb mixture, and pour on remaining garlic butter. Bake at 350° for 55 minutes or until golden brown. Yield: 6 servings.

POTATO CASSEROLE

6 medium potatoes, cooked and grated
1½ teaspoons salt
1 cup commercial sour cream
6 to 8 green onions, chopped
1 cup shredded Cheddar cheese
½ cup butter or margarine, melted

Combine all ingredients except butter; spoon into a 2-quart casserole. Pour butter over top, and bake at 400° about 25 minutes or until lightly browned on top. Yield: 6 to 8 servings.

BRUSSELS SPROUTS PIQUANT

½ medium onion, sliced
2 tablespoons melted butter or margarine
2 tablespoons all-purpose flour
1 cup tomato juice
1 teaspoon sugar
   Salt and pepper to taste
1 pound fresh brussels sprouts or
      2 (10-ounce) packages frozen brussels
      sprouts, cooked and drained
¼ cup shredded Cheddar cheese

Sauté onion in butter in a small skillet; remove onion, reserving drippings. Add flour to drippings, blending well; gradually add tomato juice. Cook over low heat, stirring constantly until smooth and thickened. Stir in sugar, salt, pepper, and onion.
   Place brussels sprouts in a 1½-quart casserole; pour tomato sauce over top. Sprinkle with cheese. Bake at 350° for 15 minutes. Yield: 6 servings.

BLUEBERRY SALAD

1 (8¼-ounce) can crushed pineapple
2 (3-ounce) packages blackberry-flavored
      or black raspberry-flavored gelatin
3 cups boiling water
1 (15-ounce) can blueberries, drained
1 (8-ounce) carton commercial sour cream
1 (8-ounce) package cream cheese, softened
½ cup sugar
   Chopped pecans

Drain pineapple, reserving juice. Dissolve gelatin in boiling water; stir in pineapple juice. Chill until consistency of unbeaten egg white. Stir in pineapple and blueberries. Pour into a 10- x 6- x 1¾-inch pan. Chill until firm.
   Combine sour cream, cream cheese, and sugar; mix until smooth and well blended. Spread over salad, and top with pecans. Yield: 6 to 8 servings.

LEMON-BUTTERMILK POUND CAKE

1 cup shortening
½ cup butter or margarine, softened
2½ cups sugar
4 eggs
½ teaspoon soda
1 tablespoon hot water
½ teaspoon salt
1 teaspoon lemon extract
3½ cups all-purpose flour
1 cup buttermilk
   Lemon Sauce

Cream shortening, butter, and sugar until light and fluffy; add eggs, one at a time, beating well after each addition.
   Dissolve soda in hot water, and add salt and lemon extract; stir into creamed mixture. Add flour to creamed mixture alternately with buttermilk, beginning and ending with flour; beat well after each addition.
   Pour batter into a well-greased and floured 10-inch tube pan or Bundt pan. Bake at 325° for 1 hour and 15 minutes. While still warm, punch holes in cake with a toothpick; spoon Lemon Sauce over cake. Yield: one 10-inch cake.

Lemon Sauce:

1 cup sugar
½ cup hot water
   Juice and grated rind of 2 lemons

Combine all ingredients in a small saucepan; bring to a boil. Reduce heat, and simmer 10 to 12 minutes. Yield: 1½ cups.

Simple-to-Make Family Fare
(Supper for Six)

Frankfurter Hash or Seafood-Stuffed Green Peppers
Harvest Golden Salad
Cheese-Rice Fritters
Coconut Snack Cake
Iced Tea   Coffee

FRANKFURTER HASH

  2 tablespoons salad oil
  4 small boiled potatoes, peeled and diced
  3 medium onions, sliced
  3 medium-size green peppers, sliced
12 frankfurters, cut into 1-inch slices
  3 tomatoes, diced
  1 teaspoon salt
  ¼ teaspoon white pepper

Pour oil into an electric wok (or an electric skillet); heat to 350°. Place potatoes and onion in oil, and stir-fry until lightly browned; push vegetables up sides of wok. Add green pepper and franks, and stir-fry 2 minutes; push up sides of wok. Reduce heat and add tomatoes, salt, and white pepper; cook 1 minute. Gently stir all foods together. Yield: 6 servings.

SEAFOOD-STUFFED GREEN PEPPERS

  6 medium-size green peppers
  ½ pound shrimp, peeled and deveined
  1 (6-ounce) package frozen crabmeat,
     thawed and drained
1½ cups cooked rice
  ½ cup chopped celery
  ½ cup chopped onion
  2 tablespoons chopped pimiento
  ¾ cup mayonnaise
  1 teaspoon curry powder
  ½ teaspoon salt
    Dash of pepper
    Breadcrumbs
    Butter or margarine

Cut top off each pepper; remove seeds and membrane. Cook in boiling salted water 5 minutes; drain well, and set aside.

Combine shrimp, crabmeat, rice, celery, onion, and pimiento. Combine mayonnaise, curry powder, salt, and pepper; stir into crabmeat mixture, mixing thoroughly.

Stuff peppers with seafood mixture; sprinkle each with breadcrumbs, and dot with butter. Place in a 1½-quart baking dish; add hot water to a depth of ½ inch. Bake at 350° for 30 minutes. Yield: 6 servings.

HARVEST GOLDEN SALAD

1 (3-ounce) package orange-flavored
   gelatin
1 cup boiling water
1 (8-ounce) can crushed pineapple
1 cup grated carrot
⅓ cup shredded Cheddar cheese
⅓ cup mayonnaise or salad dressing
¼ cup chopped pecans
   Lettuce leaves

Dissolve gelatin in 1 cup boiling water. Drain pineapple, reserving juice. Add enough water to pineapple juice to make ¾ cup liquid; stir in gelatin mixture. Chill until consistency of unbeaten egg white.

Fold pineapple and carrot into thickened gelatin.

Pour into a 10- x 6- x 1¾-inch pan, and chill until firm. Combine cheese and mayonnaise; spread over gelatin, and sprinkle with pecans. Serve on lettuce leaves. Yield: 6 to 8 servings.

CHEESE-RICE FRITTERS

1 cup cottage cheese, sieved
1 egg, slightly beaten
½ cup milk
1 cup cooked rice
1 tablespoon prepared mustard
½ cup all-purpose flour
½ teaspoon baking powder
¼ teaspoon salt
½ cup drained whole kernel corn
   Mint jelly

Combine cottage cheese and egg; stir in milk, rice, and mustard. Combine flour, baking powder, and salt. Add to cottage cheese mixture; stir until smooth. Stir in corn.

Drop by heaping tablespoonfuls onto a hot, greased griddle; cook until brown on both sides. Serve with mint jelly. Yield: About 2 dozen fritters.

COCONUT SNACK CAKE

⅔ cup shortening
1 cup firmly packed brown sugar
2 eggs
1 teaspoon vanilla extract
2 cups all-purpose flour
1 teaspoon soda
2 teaspoons ground cinnamon, divided
½ teaspoon salt
1 cup buttermilk
1 cup flaked coconut
1 cup sugar
½ teaspoon ground nutmeg
¼ cup half-and-half

Cream shortening and brown sugar until light and fluffy. Add eggs and vanilla; blend thoroughly. Combine flour, soda, 1 teaspoon cinnamon, and salt. Add to creamed mixture alternately with buttermilk, beginning and ending with dry ingredients; beat well after each addition. Spoon batter into a greased and floured 13- x 9- x 2-inch pan.

Combine coconut, 1 cup sugar, 1 teaspoon cinnamon, nutmeg, and half-and-half; spoon over batter. Bake at 350° for 35 minutes or until cake tests done. Yield: one 13- x 9- x 2-inch cake.

Turkey Makes an Encore
(Supper for Six to Eight)

Turkey Chow Mein or Turkey Delicious
Glazed Squash
Molded Cranberry Waldorf
Commercial Crescent Rolls   Butter
Nutmeg Cake
Iced Tea   Coffee

TURKEY CHOW MEIN

  1 (4-ounce) can sliced mushrooms
½ cup coarsely chopped onion
½ cup sliced celery
    Salad oil
  1 green pepper, cut into strips
  2 cups chopped, cooked turkey
  1 cup drained bean sprouts
  1 (10¾-ounce) can cream of chicken
    soup, undiluted
½ teaspoon salt
¼ teaspoon pepper
  1 tablespoon soy sauce
  3 tablespoons sherry
    Chow mein noodles

Drain mushrooms, reserving liquid; set aside.
Lightly sauté onion and celery in a small amount of oil 3 minutes. Add green pepper, turkey, bean sprouts, and mushrooms; cook 2 to 3 minutes, stirring occasionally. Add soup and mushroom liquid; cook, stirring constantly, until thoroughly heated. Stir in salt, pepper, soy sauce, and sherry. Serve over noodles. Yield: 6 to 8 servings.

TURKEY DELICIOUS

1½ cups turkey or chicken broth
  1 tablespoon chopped onion
  1 tablespoon chopped carrot
  1 stalk celery, chopped
  1 teaspoon parsley flakes
  3 peppercorns
  1 bay leaf
¼ cup butter or margarine
¼ cup chopped green pepper (optional)
¼ cup all-purpose flour
  1 cup milk
  1 egg yolk, slightly beaten
  1 (8-ounce) package pasteurized process
    cheese spread, cut into cubes
  1 (2-ounce) jar pimiento, chopped
    (optional)
    Salt to taste
  6 to 8 slices of turkey breast
  2 (10-ounce) packages frozen broccoli
    spears, cooked and drained

Combine broth, onion, carrot, celery, parsley, peppercorns, and bay leaf; bring to a boil. Cover and simmer 20 minutes; strain broth and set aside.

Melt butter in a saucepan; if desired, sauté green pepper until tender. Blend in flour and gradually stir in milk and strained broth. Cook and stir until thickened. Add a small amount of thickened sauce to egg yolk, stirring well; blend egg yolk into remaining sauce. Add cheese and stir until melted; add pimiento, if desired, and salt.

Place a layer of turkey in the bottom of each of 6 to 8 individual baking dishes; top with broccoli spears. Pour sauce over all and bake at 350° for 15 minutes. Yield: 6 to 8 servings.

GLAZED SQUASH

2 large butternut or acorn squash
½ cup sugar
½ cup firmly packed brown sugar
½ cup water
  Dash of ground allspice
2 tablespoons butter or margarine

Parboil whole squash about 15 minutes or until tender; drain. Peel squash, and halve crosswise; remove seeds and membrane, and cut into ½-inch thick slices. Place in an 11¾- x 7½- x ¾-inch baking dish.

Combine sugar, water, and allspice; pour over squash. Dot with butter. Bake at 350° for 25 to 30 minutes, basting frequently until glazed. Yield: 6 to 8 servings.

MOLDED CRANBERRY WALDORF

2 cups cranberry juice cocktail, divided
1 (3-ounce) package lemon-flavored gelatin
¼ teaspoon salt
1 cup chopped, unpeeled apple
½ cup chopped celery
¼ cup chopped walnuts
  Mayonnaise or salad dressing (optional)

Pour 1 cup cranberry juice in a saucepan, and bring to a boil; add gelatin, stirring until dissolved. Stir in remaining cranberry juice and salt. Chill until slightly thickened.

Fold apple, celery, and nuts into gelatin mixture. Pour into a 4-cup mold; chill until firm. Unmold, and top with mayonnaise, if desired. Yield: 6 to 8 servings.

NUTMEG CAKE

1 (8-ounce) carton commercial sour cream
¾ teaspoon soda
2 cups loosely packed brown sugar
2 cups all-purpose flour
½ cup shortening
1 egg
1 teaspoon ground nutmeg
½ cup chopped walnuts or pecans

Combine sour cream and soda; set aside.

Combine sugar, flour, and shortening; blend with pastry blender until crumbly. Spoon half the mixture into a greased 9-inch square pan.

Combine remaining crumb mixture with sour cream mixture, egg, and nutmeg; mix well. Spoon batter over crumb mixture; sprinkle with nuts. Bake at 350° for 35 to 40 minutes. Yield: one 9-inch square cake.

To keep pasta from sticking together, add 1 or 2 tablespoons salad oil to the cooking water.

To reheat cooked pasta or rice, place it in a strainer over a pan of boiling water. Cover and steam 10 to 15 minutes.

Have Soup and Sandwiches
(Supper for Six)

Creamy Asparagus Soup
Hot Brown Sandwiches or Sicilian Steak Sandwiches
Apple Slaw
Date-Filled Bars
Iced Tea

CREAMY ASPARAGUS SOUP

1 (10-ounce) package frozen cut asparagus
½ cup chicken broth
2 egg yolks
1¼ cups milk
½ teaspoon salt
¼ teaspoon white pepper
2 drops of hot sauce
Parsley
Paprika

Combine asparagus and chicken broth; bring to a boil and cook, uncovered, for 8 minutes. Put in blender, and blend until smooth; add egg yolks, and blend well.

Return asparagus mixture to saucepan; stir in milk, salt, pepper, and hot sauce. Heat well, but do not boil. Top each serving with parsley and paprika. Yield: 6 small servings.

HOT BROWN SANDWICHES

6 tablespoons butter or margarine
¾ cup all-purpose flour
½ teaspoon salt
⅛ teaspoon white pepper
1½ cups turkey broth or chicken broth
1½ cups milk
¾ cup grated Parmesan cheese
12 slices bread, toasted
Sliced turkey or chicken
Paprika
12 slices tomato
12 slices bacon, cooked
Parsley

Melt butter, and stir in flour; cook over low heat, blending until smooth. Stir in salt and pepper. Gradually add broth and milk; cook, stirring constantly, until smooth and thickened. Add cheese; simmer about 10 minutes. (Sauce will be thick.)

Place 2 slices toast on each of 6 ovenproof plates. Place turkey on each slice of toast; cover with sauce, and sprinkle with paprika. Top each with 1 slice tomato and 1 slice bacon. Bake at 400° for 10 minutes or until sauce is bubbly. Garnish with parsley. Yield: 6 servings.

SICILIAN STEAK SANDWICHES

6 medium-size cubed steaks
2 tablespoons melted margarine
  All-purpose flour
1 large green pepper, sliced
¼ cup commercial Italian salad dressing
1 large onion, sliced
2 medium tomatoes, sliced
3 small loaves French bread, split
  lengthwise
  Mozzarella cheese slices, cut into
  quarters

Sauté steaks in margarine to desired doneness, reserving drippings for gravy. Sprinkle a small amount of flour into pan drippings; cook until slightly thickened, stirring constantly.

In another pan, sauté green pepper in salad dressing 5 minutes. Add onion and tomatoes; cook an additional 5 minutes or until tender. Cover each bread half with a steak; spoon on vegetables and gravy. Top with cheese; broil until cheese melts. Yield: 6 servings.

APPLE SLAW

6 small apples, grated
  Juice of 1 lemon
1 head cabbage, shredded
⅔ cup mayonnaise
½ cup sugar
⅓ teaspoon salt
¼ cup raisins (optional)

Combine apples and lemon juice in a large mixing bowl; add cabbage, mayonnaise, sugar, and salt, mixing well. Stir in raisins, if desired. Yield: 6 servings.

DATE-FILLED BARS

¾ cup shortening or margarine
1 cup firmly packed brown sugar
1¾ cups all-purpose flour
1 teaspoon salt
½ teaspoon soda
1½ cups quick-cooking oats, uncooked
  Date Filling

Cream shortening and sugar until light and fluffy. Combine flour, salt, and soda; add to creamed mixture. Stir in oats, blending well.

Pat half of mixture into a lightly greased 13- x 9- x 2-inch pan, and spread with Date Filling; top with remaining oat mixture, patting lightly to smooth top crust. Bake at 400° for 30 minutes. While warm, cut into bars and remove from pan. Yield: 32 bars.

Date Filling:

1½ pounds dates, chopped
¼ cup sugar
1½ cups water

Combine dates, sugar, and water in saucepan; cook over low heat until smooth and thickened (5 to 10 minutes). Cool slightly before spreading on crust. Yield: about 3 cups.

Don't throw away cheese that has dried out or any small leftover pieces. Grate the cheese; cover and refrigerate for use in casseroles or other dishes.

To store leftover egg yolks, put them in a small jar, cover with cold water, and refrigerate. Drain and use within a couple of days.

Supper Olé
(Supper for Four)

Quickie Tacos or Sour Cream Enchiladas
Relish Hot Sauce
Mexican Avocado Salad
Ice Cream   Apple Ice Cream Sauce
Iced Tea

QUICKIE TACOS

½ pound ground beef
½ (9-ounce) package tortilla chips
1 (8-ounce) jar taco sauce
⅔ cup shredded Cheddar cheese
⅓ cup chopped onion
⅓ head lettuce, chopped

Sauté ground beef until brown; drain. Place tortilla chips in a 8- x 8- x 2-inch pan, and bake at 200° about 5 to 10 minutes. Heat taco sauce in a small saucepan.

Arrange tortilla chips on 4 serving plates; sprinkle with meat, cheese, onion, and lettuce. Top with taco sauce. Yield: 4 servings.

SOUR CREAM ENCHILADAS

1 (8-ounce) carton commercial sour cream
2 cups shredded Monterey Jack cheese
1 medium onion, chopped
1 (3½-ounce) can ripe olives, chopped and drained
¾ cup salad oil
8 to 10 tortillas
1 (14-ounce) can enchilada sauce
½ cup shredded Cheddar cheese

Combine sour cream, Monterey Jack cheese, onion, and olives in a small bowl; mix well.

Heat oil in a deep skillet. Fry tortillas just until limp, turning once. Drain on paper towels.

Spoon enchilada sauce on opposite sides of each tortilla. Place about 2 tablespoons sour cream mixture in center of each. Roll up and place, seam side down, in a 13- x 9-inch baking dish.

Spoon any remaining sauce over enchiladas; sprinkle with shredded Cheddar cheese. Bake at 350° for 15 to 20 minutes. Yield: 4 servings.

RELISH HOT SAUCE
(see Index)

MEXICAN AVOCADO SALAD

¾ cup olive oil
1 teaspoon curry powder
2 teaspoons salt
¼ cup cider vinegar
1 clove garlic, crushed
1 teaspoon sugar
½ cup chopped onion
1 (15-ounce) can garbanzo beans, drained
1 cup sliced pitted black olives
1 cup chopped avocado
  Lettuce

Combine oil, curry powder, salt, vinegar, garlic, and sugar; blend well. Add remaining ingredients except lettuce; stir gently. Let stand at room temperature 1 hour; chill. Drain and serve on lettuce. Yield: 4 servings.

APPLE ICE CREAM SAUCE

½ cup firmly packed brown sugar
1 tablespoon cornstarch
½ teaspoon ground cinnamon
¼ teaspoon ground nutmeg
½ teaspoon grated lemon rind
¾ cup water
1 (20-ounce) can pie-sliced apples, undrained
1 quart vanilla ice cream

Combine brown sugar, cornstarch, cinnamon, nutmeg, lemon rind, and water; blend well. Stir in apple slices; cook over medium heat, stirring constantly, until thickened. Serve hot over ice cream. Yield: 4 to 6 servings.

To add egg yolks to a hot sauce, beat the egg yolks in a small bowl; warm them by stirring in a little of the hot sauce. Add yolks to hot sauce, stirring constantly as mixture heats and thickens.

Use the store's comparative pricing information for good buys. The unit-price data allows you to compare the cost of similar products of different sizes by weight, measure, or count.

Do not thaw fish at room temperature or in warm water; it will lose moisture and flavor. Instead, place in refrigerator to thaw; allow 18 to 24 hours for thawing a 1-pound package. Do not refreeze thawed fish.

Shop alone and after you have eaten. Studies show that people tend to buy more when hungry or when accompanied by others.

Serve Pork Tonight
(Supper for Six)

Pork Chops Cacciatore or Honey Ham Loaf
Sour Cream Noodles
Savory Green Beans
Spiced Peaches
Melt Aways
Iced Tea   Coffee

PORK CHOPS CACCIATORE

  6 (½-inch-thick) pork chops
    Salt and pepper to taste
    Hot salad oil
  1 medium onion, sliced
  2 tablespoons firmly packed brown sugar
  1 (1½-ounce) envelope spaghetti sauce
    mix
  2 (16-ounce) cans tomatoes, undrained
    and chopped

Season pork chops with salt and pepper; brown on both sides in hot oil in a large skillet. Place chops in a shallow 2-quart casserole; top each with onion slice. Sprinkle with brown sugar.

Sprinkle spaghetti sauce mix over drippings in skillet; blend well. Add tomatoes, stirring well. Simmer over low heat 5 minutes. Spoon sauce over chops and onions.

Cover and bake at 350° for 1 hour; uncover and bake an additional 15 minutes or until chops are tender. Yield: 6 servings.

HONEY HAM LOAF

  1½ cups fine breadcrumbs
  ¼ cup milk
  1 pound cooked ham, ground
  ½ pound ground pork
  1 egg
  2 tablespoons honey
  ¼ teaspoon ground cinnamon
  ⅛ teaspoon ground cloves
  2 tablespoons firmly packed light brown
    sugar
  2 tablespoons honey
  1 tablespoon vinegar

Soak breadcrumbs in milk. Combine breadcrumbs, ham, pork, egg, 2 tablespoons honey, cinnamon, and cloves; mix well. Shape mixture into a loaf in a greased 2-quart shallow baking dish.

Combine brown sugar, 2 tablespoons honey, and vinegar. Spoon one-third of this mixture over the loaf. Bake at 350° for 1 hour. Spoon remaining honey mixture over ham twice during baking. Yield: 6 servings.

SOUR CREAM NOODLES

1 (8-ounce) package fine noodles
1 cup cottage cheese
1 (8-ounce) carton commercial sour
   cream
⅛ teaspoon garlic salt
1 onion, finely grated
1 tablespoon Worcestershire sauce
   Grated Parmesan cheese

Cook noodles according to package directions; drain. Combine noodles and remaining ingredients except Parmesan, mixing gently. Spoon mixture into a lightly greased 2-quart casserole; sprinkle with Parmesan cheese. Bake at 350° for 45 minutes. Yield: 6 to 8 servings.

SAVORY GREEN BEANS
(see Index)

SPICED PEACHES

2 (29-ounce) cans cling peach halves
1⅓ cups sugar
1 cup cider vinegar
4 cinnamon sticks
2 teaspoons whole cloves

Drain peaches, reserving syrup. Combine peach syrup, sugar, vinegar, cinnamon sticks, and cloves in a saucepan; bring to boiling; lower heat and simmer 10 minutes. Pour hot syrup over peach halves and let cool. Chill thoroughly before serving. Store in refrigerator. Yield: about 4 pints.

MELT AWAYS

1 cup margarine, softened
1 cup sugar
1 egg, separated
1 teaspoon vanilla extract
2 cups all-purpose flour
1 cup chopped pecans, divided

Cream margarine and sugar until light and fluffy; blend in egg yolk, vanilla, and flour. Stir in ½ cup pecans. Spread dough evenly in a lightly greased 15- x 10- x 1-inch jellyroll pan.

Beat egg white until frothy; brush over dough. Sprinkle with remaining pecans. Bake at 350° for 25 to 30 minutes or until lightly browned. Cool slightly and cut into bars. Yield: about 3½ dozen bars.

When making hot chocolate, dissolve the cocoa in a small amount of cold water; place over low heat, stirring constantly until smooth. Add cold milk, stirring constantly. Beat with a rotary beater when mixture starts to foam to prevent the formation of scum.

Plan your menus for the week, but stay flexible enough to substitute good buys when you spot them. By planning ahead, you can use leftovers in another day's meal.

Chicken Pie, A Family Favorite
(Supper for Six)

Chicken Pot Pie
Fresh Asparagus Spears
Celestial Salad
Pecan Pie Surprise Bars
Iced Tea   Coffee

CHICKEN POT PIE

1 (3-pound) broiler-fryer chicken
3½ cups water
   Leaves of 2 stalks celery
4 peppercorns
1½ teaspoons salt
5 slices bacon
½ cup chopped green onion
½ cup chopped celery
½ cup all-purpose flour
3 hard-cooked eggs, sliced
1 (10-ounce) package frozen peas and
   carrots, thawed
1 (2-ounce) jar diced pimiento
1 teaspoon salt
⅛ teaspoon white pepper
⅛ teaspoon thyme
   Uncooked biscuits

Combine chicken, water, celery leaves, peppercorns, and 1½ teaspoons salt in a Dutch oven. Bring to a boil; cover, and simmer 1½ hours or until done. Remove chicken from broth; cool, and cut into 1-inch cubes. Strain broth, reserving 3 cups; set aside.

Cook bacon; reserve 3 tablespoons bacon drippings. Drain bacon on absorbent paper towels; crumble. Sauté onion and celery in reserved bacon drippings 5 minutes. Gradually add flour, stirring until blended well. Add reserved broth; stir constantly until mixture is bubbly and thickens. Add chicken, bacon, eggs, peas and carrots, pimiento, 1 teaspoon salt, pepper, and thyme; stir until blended well. Spoon into a 3-quart casserole; top with biscuits. Bake at 450° for 10 to 15 minutes or until biscuits are golden. Yield: 6 to 8 servings.

Chicken Pot Pie topped with light, flaky biscuits will bring your family to the dinner table in a hurry.

FRESH ASPARAGUS SPEARS

2½ to 3 pounds fresh asparagus
1 cup boiling water
¼ cup melted butter
  Pimiento

Select asparagus with tight tips and unwrinkled stem bottoms. Break off tough ends of stems at the point where they are brittle. Wash thoroughly to dislodge soil in the tips. Loosely tie asparagus into serving-size bundles of 6 to 7 spears, or tie all spears together. Stand bundles upright in bottom of double boiler, add water, and cover with top part of double boiler. Cook over medium heat 12 to 15 minutes or until tender. Steam will cook the tip ends. To serve, cut away string, and arrange on warmed serving bowl or platter. Pour butter over asparagus; garnish with pimiento. Yield: 6 to 8 servings.

CELESTIAL SALAD

1 head lettuce
1 (11-ounce) can mandarin orange
    sections, drained
1 cup halved green grapes
½ cup chopped green onions
½ cup sliced toasted almonds, divided
⅔ cup salad oil
⅓ cup orange juice
¼ cup sugar
3 tablespoons vinegar
  Salt to taste
  Dash of dry mustard
1 teaspoon celery seeds
2 tablespoons chopped parsley

Wash lettuce and tear into bite-size pieces. Combine lettuce, orange sections, grapes, onion, and half of almonds in a large salad bowl.

Combine remaining ingredients except parsley in a covered container; shake well. Pour over salad, and toss well. Sprinkle with parsley and remaining almonds. Yield: 6 to 8 servings.

PECAN PIE SURPRISE BARS

1 (18½-ounce) package yellow cake mix
½ cup melted butter or margarine
4 eggs, divided
½ cup firmly packed brown sugar
1½ cups dark corn syrup
1 teaspoon vanilla extract
1 cup chopped pecans

Set aside ⅔ cup cake mix. Combine remaining cake mix, butter, and 1 egg in a large mixing bowl; mix with a fork until crumbly. Press crumbs in a greased 13- x 9- x 2-inch baking dish. Bake at 350° for 15 to 20 minutes or until light golden brown.

Combine reserved cake mix, 3 eggs, brown sugar, corn syrup, and vanilla in a mixing bowl; beat at medium speed of electric mixer 1 to 2 minutes. Pour over partially baked crust, and sprinkle with pecans. Bake at 350° for 30 to 35 minutes. Cool and cut into bars. Yield: 3 to 4 dozen bars.

Wild game dishes like these will win a trophy for the cook as well as the hunter: Venison with Sour Cream (page 28), Quail in Red Wine (page 41), and Stuffed Wild Duck (page 41).

A New Way with Venison
(Supper for Six to Eight)

Venison with Sour Cream   Noodles
Italian Zucchini or Zesty Broccoli Casserole
Beet Pickles
Squash Fritters
Rhubarb Crunch à la Mode
Iced Tea   Coffee

VENISON WITH SOUR CREAM

  2 pounds venison, cut in 2-inch cubes
  1 clove garlic, minced
  ¼ cup shortening, melted
  1 cup diced celery
  ½ cup chopped onion
  1 cup diced carrots
  2 cups water
  1 teaspoon salt
    Dash of pepper
  1 bay leaf
  4 tablespoons melted butter or margarine
  4 tablespoons all-purpose flour
  1 cup commercial sour cream
    Parsley
    Hot cooked noodles (optional)

Place venison, garlic, and shortening in a skillet; brown meat on all sides over medium heat. Remove meat to a shallow 2½-quart baking dish.

Add celery, onion, and carrots to drippings in skillet; sauté 2 minutes. Stir in water, salt, pepper, and bay leaf; pour over venison. Bake at 350° for 30 minutes; remove from oven. Drain, reserving broth.

Combine butter and flour in a skillet; cook over low heat, stirring until smooth. Add reserved broth; cook until thickened, stirring constantly. Stir in sour cream. Pour sauce over venison and vegetables. Garnish with parsley. Serve over noodles, if desired. Yield: 6 to 8 servings.

ITALIAN ZUCCHINI

  2 pounds zucchini, sliced
  3 tablespoons salad oil
  2 tablespoons olive oil
  1 (8-ounce) can tomato sauce
  1 clove garlic, minced
    Dash of crushed basil
  ½ cup red wine
  ¼ pound Monterey Jack cheese, sliced
  3 tablespoons grated Parmesan cheese

Sauté zucchini in salad oil until lightly browned; drain. Combine olive oil, tomato sauce, garlic, basil, and wine in a saucepan; simmer over low heat 2 to 3 minutes.

Layer zucchini, tomato sauce mixture, and Monterey Jack cheese in a lightly greased 2-quart casserole. Sprinkle with Parmesan cheese. Bake at 350° for 30 to 40 minutes or until bubbly. Yield: 6 to 8 servings.

ZESTY BROCCOLI CASSEROLE

    2 (10-ounce) packages frozen chopped
        broccoli
    1 (10¾-ounce) can cream of mushroom
        soup, undiluted
1½ cups shredded Cheddar cheese
    1 egg, beaten
    ¼ cup milk
    ¼ cup mayonnaise
    1 tablespoon horseradish
    2 tablespoons melted butter or margarine
    ¼ cup cracker crumbs

Cook broccoli according to package directions; drain. Combine soup, cheese, egg, milk, mayonnaise, and horseradish; stir into broccoli. Spoon into a greased 2-quart casserole.

Combine melted butter and cracker crumbs; sprinkle over broccoli mixture. Bake at 350° for 45 minutes. Yield: 6 to 8 servings.

BEET PICKLES
(see Index)

SQUASH FRITTERS

⅓ cup biscuit mix
¼ cup grated Parmesan or shredded
    Cheddar cheese
½ teaspoon salt
½ teaspoon pepper
2 eggs, slightly beaten
2 cups grated raw yellow squash
2 to 4 tablespoons butter or margarine

Combine all ingredients except butter, blending well. Melt butter in skillet over medium heat. Drop batter by tablespoonfuls into skillet. Cook fritters 2 to 3 minutes on each side or until golden brown. Yield: 6 to 8 servings.

RHUBARB CRUNCH À LA MODE

    1 cup all-purpose flour
    ¾ cup uncooked oats
    1 cup firmly packed brown sugar
    1 teaspoon ground cinnamon
    ½ cup melted butter or margarine
    4 cups chopped rhubarb
    1 cup sugar
    2 tablespoons cornstarch
    1 cup water
    1 teaspoon vanilla extract
      Ice cream

Combine flour, oats, brown sugar, cinnamon, and butter; blend well. Pat half of crumb mixture into a 9-inch baking pan; cover with rhubarb.

Combine sugar and cornstarch; slowly add water, blending well. Cook over low heat, stirring constantly, until smooth and slightly thickened. Stir in vanilla.

Pour sauce over rhubarb, and sprinkle with remaining crumbs. Bake at 350° for 40 minutes or until rhubarb is tender. Serve warm with ice cream. Yield: 6 to 8 servings.

Favorite Spaghetti Supper
(Supper for Six to Eight)

Italian Spaghetti
Fresh Garden Salad   Green Goddess Salad Dressing
Garlic Bread
Pink Fruit Freeze or Peach-Banana Freeze
Iced Tea   Coffee

ITALIAN SPAGHETTI

3 medium onions, chopped
1 large green pepper, chopped
3 to 4 stalks celery, chopped
4 cloves garlic, minced
1 (2-ounce) bottle olive oil
1 pound ground round steak
1 (14½-ounce) can tomatoes, undrained and chopped
1 (6-ounce) can tomato paste
Salt and pepper to taste
Chili powder to taste
Dash of cayenne
Dash of ground cinnamon
1 (4-ounce) can sliced mushrooms, drained
⅔ cup water
Hot cooked spaghetti

Sauté onion, green pepper, celery, and garlic in olive oil. Brown meat separately; drain well. Add meat and remaining ingredients except spaghetti to onion mixture; simmer 30 minutes, stirring occasionally. Serve over spaghetti. Yield: 6 to 8 servings.

FRESH GARDEN SALAD

½ pound fresh spinach, torn into bite-size pieces
½ head cauliflower, broken into flowerets
1 small green pepper, thinly sliced
6 to 8 radishes, thinly sliced
1 medium tomato, coarsely chopped
¼ head lettuce, torn into bite-size pieces
1 medium cucumber, sliced
1 hard-cooked egg, chopped
Green Goddess Salad Dressing

Toss all ingredients. Top with Green Goddess Salad Dressing. Yield: 6 to 8 servings.

Green Goddess Salad Dressing:

3 cups mayonnaise
1 (2-ounce) can anchovy fillets, drained and rinsed
4 green onions, chopped
¼ cup lemon juice
1 tablespoon chopped parsley
¼ cup vinegar

Combine all ingredients in blender; cover and blend until smooth. Chill well. Yield: 4 cups.

GARLIC BREAD
(see Index)

PINK FRUIT FREEZE

   1 (8-ounce) package cream cheese,
      softened
   1 quart strawberry ice cream, softened
   ½ cup mayonnaise
   2 (16-ounce) cans fruit cocktail, drained
   ⅓ cup chopped pecans
      Mint leaves (optional)
      Cherries (optional)

Combine cream cheese, ice cream, and mayonnaise; blend well. Fold in fruit cocktail and pecans; pour into a 9-inch square pan. Freeze until firm.

   To serve, place in refrigerator for 15 minutes; cut into squares. Garnish with mint and cherries, if desired. Yield: 6 to 8 servings.

PEACH-BANANA FREEZE

   1 (17-ounce) can peach slices, drained
   2 bananas, sliced
   1 (6-ounce) can frozen lemonade
      concentrate, partially thawed and
      undiluted
   ½ pint whipping cream
   1 teaspoon sugar

Mash peach and banana slices until mushy; stir in lemonade concentrate.

   Combine whipping cream and sugar; whip until thick and creamy. Fold into peach mixture. Pour into an 8-inch square dish, and freeze until firm. Cut into squares to serve. Yield: 8 servings.

With today's rising food prices, homemakers are focusing more attention on economical ways to shop. Remember that a good buy for one family may not be a good buy for another family.

Check newspaper food ads for weekly specials and menu ideas. You can save money on sale items, but don't buy something just because it's on sale; it's no bargain if your family won't eat it. Clip discount coupons in newspapers and magazines; remember to cash them when you purchase that item.

During the week, keep a shopping list handy to write down items as you need them. This will eliminate unnecessary trips to the store. Before your weekly shopping trip, make a complete shopping list. If the list is arranged according to the layout of the store, you'll save time and steps.

SUNDAY DINNERS

Sunday Roast Beef Dinner

Family-Pleasing Pork
   Chop Dinner

A Summer Delight

After-the-Hunt Feast

Sensational Baked Snapper

Gourmet Chicken with Rice

Serve Steak-in-the-Round

Slow Cooking Roast Dinner

Springtime Sunday Special

Southern Sunday Dinner

Sunday dinners are an event in the South. They are often small-scale family reunions as well as the most special meal of the week. Favorite dishes like fried chicken and roast are reserved for Sunday. Eating in the dining room, using a linen tablecloth, and bringing out the good china make it even more of an occasion. Keeping in mind treasured favorites, we have created menus that will draw your family home.

Sunday Roast Beef Dinner
(Dinner for Eight)

Cucumber Soup
Easy Oven Roast
Mashed Potatoes
Asparagus with Lemon Sauce
Red Raspberry Ring
Onion Rolls
Milky Way Cake or Peaches 'n Cream Pie
Coffee

CUCUMBER SOUP

  1 to 1½ cups grated cucumber
  1 quart buttermilk
  2 tablespoons chopped green onion
  1 teaspoon salt
    Cucumber slices
    Chives

Combine grated cucumber, buttermilk, onion, and salt; mix well. Cover and chill at least 2 or 3 hours. Mix again before serving in chilled cups. Garnish with cucumber slices and chives. Yield: 8 servings.

  Note: Scoop out and discard seeds before grating cucumber.

EASY OVEN ROAST

  1 (4- to 5-pound) boneless pot roast
    (bottom round, chuck, or rump)
    Salt and pepper to taste
  1 (10¾-ounce) can cream of mushroom
    soup, undiluted
  1 cup red wine
  1 cup small whole onions
  ½ cup sliced mushrooms
  2 tablespoons capers

Sprinkle roast with salt and pepper, and place in a Dutch oven. Combine soup and wine, blending well; add onions, mushrooms, and capers. Pour over roast.

  Cover tightly, and bake at 350° for 2½ to 3 hours for medium-well. Yield: 8 servings.

MASHED POTATOES

3 pounds potatoes
About 5 cups water
Salt
½ to ¾ cup milk
6 tablespoons butter or margarine,
softened
¾ teaspoon salt
Dash of pepper

Peel potatoes and cut into large pieces. Cook
in boiling salted water 15 to 20 minutes or until
tender. Drain.

Mash potatoes until no lumps remain. Add
milk in small amounts, beating after each addition. (Amount of milk needed to make potatoes
smooth depends on kind of potatoes.) Add butter, ¾ teaspoon salt, and pepper; beat vigorously
until potatoes are light and fluffy. Yield: 8 servings.

ASPARAGUS WITH LEMON SAUCE

¼ cup melted butter or margarine
¼ cup all-purpose flour
2 cups milk
2 egg yolks, beaten
2 tablespoons lemon juice
1 teaspoon salt
¼ teaspoon pepper
2 pounds asparagus, cooked

Combine butter and flour; cook over low heat
until bubbly, stirring constantly. Combine milk,
egg yolks, and lemon juice; beat well and gradually stir into flour mixture. Cook over low heat,
stirring constantly, until smooth and thickened.
Season with salt and pepper. Serve over hot
asparagus. Yield: 8 servings.

Note: To cook fresh asparagus, refer to page
27.

RED RASPBERRY RING

1 (10-ounce) package frozen red
raspberries, thawed
2 (3-ounce) packages red
raspberry-flavored gelatin
1½ cups boiling water
1 pint vanilla ice cream, softened
1 (6-ounce) can frozen pink lemonade
concentrate, thawed and undiluted
½ cup chopped pecans

Drain berries, reserving juice. Dissolve gelatin
in boiling water; add ice cream by spoonfuls,
stirring until melted. Stir in lemonade and
reserved juice. Chill until slightly thickened.

Add berries and pecans to gelatin mixture.
Pour into 6-cup ring mold; chill until firm. Yield:
8 servings.

ONION ROLLS
(see Index)

MILKY WAY CAKE

6 (1 11/16-ounce) chocolate-covered
   malt-caramel candy bars
½ cup butter or margarine
2 cups sugar
1 cup shortening
4 eggs
2½ cups all-purpose flour
1 teaspoon salt
1½ cups buttermilk
½ teaspoon soda
1 teaspoon vanilla extract
   Chocolate-Marshmallow Frosting

Combine candy bars and butter in a heavy
saucepan; place over low heat until melted, stirring constantly.

Combine sugar and shortening; beat until
creamy. Add eggs, and continue beating until
light and fluffy. Combine flour and salt; combine
buttermilk and soda. Add dry ingredients to
creamed mixture alternately with buttermilk
mixture, beating well after each addition. Stir
in vanilla and candy bar mixture.

Pour batter into 3 greased and floured 9-inch
cakepans. Bake at 350° for 30 minutes or until
done. When layers are completely cool, frost
with Chocolate-Marshmallow Frosting. Yield:
one 9-inch layer cake.

Chocolate-Marshmallow Frosting:

2 cups sugar
1 (13-ounce) can evaporated milk
½ cup butter or margarine
1 (6-ounce) package semisweet chocolate
   pieces
1 cup marshmallow cream

Combine sugar, milk, and butter in a heavy
saucepan; cook over medium heat until a small
amount dropped in cold water forms a soft ball.
Remove from heat, and add chocolate pieces
and marshmallow cream; stir until melted. Yield:
enough for one 3-layer cake.

PEACHES 'N CREAM PIE

1 unbaked 9-inch pastry shell
⅓ cup sugar
2 tablespoons all-purpose flour
¼ teaspoon ground nutmeg
¼ teaspoon grated lemon rind
1 cup commercial sour cream
5 to 6 medium peaches, peeled and thinly
   sliced

Bake pie shell at 400° for 7 minutes; set aside.
Combine remaining ingredients, mixing well.
Spoon into pastry shell. Bake at 400° for 10
minutes. Reduce heat to 350°, and bake 25 to
30 additional minutes. Yield: one 9-inch pie.

After removing a roast from the oven, let it rest
at least 15 minutes for easier carving.

To prevent a soggy crust in custard pies, brush
egg white on the uncooked pie shell; bake at
425° for 5 to 10 minutes. Add filling, and bake
according to recipe directions.

Family-Pleasing Pork Chop Dinner
(Dinner for Six)

Apple-Smothered Pork Chops
Sweet Potato Casserole or Golden Rice Casserole
Fresh Asparagus Spears
Spinach and Mushroom Salad
Onion Rolls
Carrot Cake
Iced Tea   Coffee

APPLE-SMOTHERED PORK CHOPS

6 loin pork chops
Salt
1½ teaspoons rubbed sage, divided
Hot salad oil
3 tart apples
3 tablespoons molasses
3 tablespoons all-purpose flour
2 cups hot water
1 tablespoon vinegar
⅓ cup seedless raisins

Season each chop with ¼ teaspoon salt and ¼ teaspoon sage; slowly brown on both sides in a small amount of hot oil. Place chops in a shallow baking dish; reserve drippings.

Peel, core, and slice apples ¼ inch thick; arrange on pork chops. Pour molasses over apples.

Sprinkle flour over drippings in skillet; cook until brown, stirring occasionally. Slowly add water, stirring constantly until smooth; bring to a boil. Stir in vinegar, ½ teaspoon salt, and raisins; pour over chops. Cover and bake at 350° for 1 hour. Yield: 6 servings.

SWEET POTATO CASSEROLE

3 cups mashed, cooked sweet potatoes
1 cup sugar
½ cup melted butter or margarine
2 eggs, well beaten
1 teaspoon vanilla extract
⅓ cup milk
Topping

Combine sweet potatoes, sugar, butter, eggs, vanilla, and milk; mix well. Spoon into a 2-quart casserole. Cover with Topping. Bake at 350° for 25 minutes. Yield: 6 to 8 servings.

Topping:

½ cup firmly packed brown sugar
¼ cup all-purpose flour
2½ tablespoons melted butter or margarine
½ cup chopped pecans

Combine all ingredients, mixing well; sprinkle on top of potato mixture before baking. Yield: about 1 cup.

GOLDEN RICE CASSEROLE

    3 cups cooked regular rice
1¼ cups shredded Cheddar cheese
    2 tablespoons finely chopped pimiento
    2 eggs, beaten
1¼ cups milk
    1 teaspoon salt
    1 cup bread cubes
    2 tablespoons melted margarine

Alternate layers of rice, cheese, and pimiento in a lightly greased 2-quart casserole. Combine eggs, milk, and salt; pour over rice mixture.

Toss bread cubes in margarine; spoon over mixture in casserole. Bake at 350° about 45 minutes or until set and lightly browned. Yield: 6 servings.

FRESH ASPARAGUS SPEARS
(see Index)

SPINACH AND MUSHROOM SALAD

1½ pounds fresh spinach
½ pound fresh mushrooms
    1 teaspoon salt
    1 clove garlic
¾ teaspoon dry mustard
    Several dashes of hot sauce
    3 tablespoons lemon juice
½ cup olive oil
    Freshly ground black pepper
    Cherry tomatoes, halved
    3 hard-cooked eggs, cut into wedges

Remove stems from spinach; wash well and pat dry. Tear into bite-size pieces. Quickly rinse mushrooms in cold water; drain well and slice thin.

Place salt and garlic in a large salad bowl. Mash garlic into salt with a wooden spoon until all that remains of garlic is a shred; discard it. Add mustard, hot sauce, lemon juice, oil, and pepper, stirring until well blended.

Add spinach and mushrooms to salad bowl; toss until well coated. Garnish with tomato halves and eggs. Yield: 6 servings.

ONION ROLLS

    1 (14½-ounce) package hot roll mix
⅓ cup instant minced onion
    1 cup water
    3 tablespoons melted butter or margarine

Prepare hot roll mix according to directions on package. Combine onion and water, and set aside for 5 minutes; drain.

Roll dough ½ inch thick on a lightly floured board. Brush with butter; sprinkle with onion. Roll up dough in jelly-roll fashion. Cut into ½-inch-thick slices. Place on a baking sheet. Cover and let rise; bake according to directions on package. Yield: 20 rolls.

CARROT CAKE

    2 cups sugar
1½ cups salad oil
    4 eggs, beaten
    3 cups self-rising flour
    2 teaspoons ground cinnamon
    2 cups grated carrot
1½ cups chopped pecans

Combine sugar, oil, and eggs; beat well. Blend in flour and cinnamon. Add carrots and nuts, mixing well. Pour into a well-greased and lightly floured 10-inch tube pan or Bundt pan. Bake at 350° for 1 hour or until cake tests done. Yield: one 10-inch cake.

A Summer Delight
(Dinner for Eight to Ten)

Asparagus Soup Marseilles
Ham Steak with Orange Rice Stuffing
Baked Vegetable Macedoine
Beet Relish Cups
Light and Tender Rolls
Fresh Fruit Sherbet and Bachelor Buttons
Iced Tea   Coffee

ASPARAGUS SOUP MARSEILLES

  1 pound fresh asparagus spears
2½ cups milk
  1 teaspoon instant minced onion
  1 teaspoon salt
  1 teaspoon dry mustard
  ½ teaspoon capers
  ½ teaspoon juice from capers
    Dash of pepper
    Shredded lemon peel or chopped
      hard-cooked egg and pimiento strips

Cook asparagus; drain well, and chop. Combine asparagus, milk, and next 6 ingredients in blender; blend at high speed until smooth.

Pour asparagus soup into a 2-quart saucepan; heat to serving temperature. Garnish with lemon peel. Yield: 5 cups.

Note: To cook fresh asparagus, refer to page 27.

HAM STEAK WITH ORANGE RICE STUFFING

  ½ cup seedless raisins
  2 cups cooked rice
  3 tablespoons frozen orange juice
    concentrate, undiluted
  ⅛ teaspoon pepper
  ½ teaspoon ground nutmeg
  1 egg, beaten
  2 (1-inch-thick) slices smoked, cooked
    ham (about 4 pounds)
  2 tablespoons firmly packed brown sugar
    Parsley

Cover raisins with boiling water and simmer 10 minutes; drain. Combine raisins, rice, orange juice concentrate, pepper, nutmeg, and egg.

Place 1 ham slice in a baking dish; spoon rice stuffing evenly over the top. Cover with remaining ham slice; sprinkle with brown sugar. Bake at 350° about 1 hour. Garnish with parsley. Yield: 8 to 10 servings.

BAKED VEGETABLE MACEDOINE

1 (10-ounce) package frozen cauliflower,
   thawed
1 (10-ounce) package frozen mixed
   vegetables, thawed
1 yellow squash, thinly sliced
1 zucchini squash, thinly sliced
1 potato, peeled and diced
1 cup cherry tomatoes, halved
½ cup chopped red onion
1 beef bouillon cube
1 cup water
¼ cup salad oil
2 tablespoons Worcestershire sauce
1 clove garlic, crushed
½ teaspoon Italian seasoning

Place vegetables in an ungreased, shallow 2-quart casserole; gently toss. Combine remaining ingredients in a small saucepan; bring to a boil, and pour over vegetables.

Cover and bake at 350° for 1 hour or until vegetables are tender; stir once. Yield: 8 to 10 servings.

BEET RELISH CUPS

1 (3-ounce) package lemon-flavored
   gelatin
1¼ cups boiling water
¾ cup beet liquid
2 tablespoons vinegar
½ teaspoon salt
1 teaspoon prepared horseradish
1 teaspoon Worcestershire sauce
1 teaspoon grated onion
4 drops hot sauce
1½ cups diced beets
½ cup diced celery

Dissolve gelatin in boiling water; stir in next 7 ingredients, and chill until partially set. Fold in beets and celery. Spoon into individual molds or a 4-cup mold. Chill until firm. Yield: 10 servings.

LIGHT AND TENDER ROLLS
(see Index)

FRESH FRUIT SHERBET

3 cups water
   Juice of 3 lemons
   Juice of 3 oranges
2 cups sugar
1 (8-ounce) can crushed pineapple,
   undrained
3 ripe bananas, mashed
2 egg whites, beaten

Combine water, fruit juices, and sugar; heat, stirring until sugar is dissolved. Cool, and stir in pineapple and banana. Pour into freezer trays, and freeze to a thick mush. Remove from trays, and fold in egg whites.

Pour mixture into freezer can of a 1-gallon hand-turned or electric freezer. Freeze according to manufacturer's instructions. Yield: 1 gallon.

BACHELOR BUTTONS

¾ cup butter, softened
1 cup firmly packed dark brown sugar
1 egg
2 cups all-purpose flour
1 teaspoon soda
¼ teaspoon ground ginger
¼ teaspoon ground cinnamon
¼ teaspoon salt
1 teaspoon vanilla extract
1 cup chopped nuts
⅓ cup sugar

Cream butter and brown sugar until light and fluffy; add egg, beating well. Combine flour, soda, ginger, cinnamon, and salt; add to creamed mixture, and mix well. Stir in vanilla and nuts; chill several hours.

Shape dough into 1-inch balls; dip each in sugar. Place on greased cookie sheets 2 inches apart; gently press each cookie flat with a fork. Bake at 350° for 17 minutes. Let cookies cool 2 minutes before removing from cookie sheets. Yield: 3½ dozen cookies.

After-the-Hunt Feast

(Dinner for Six)

Stuffed Wild Duck or Quail in Red Wine
Wild Rice-Sausage Casserole
Spinach Supreme
Strawberry-Grapefruit Salad
Commercial Hard Rolls   Butter
Sour Cream Pound Cake
Chocolate Sauce Supreme or Rhubarb Sauce
Coffee

STUFFED WILD DUCK

2 young, plump wild ducks, cleaned
  Salt
⅔ cup chopped celery
1 cup unpeeled chopped apple
2 small onions, chopped
6 tablespoons melted shortening or bacon
  drippings
1⅓ cups water
⅔ cup orange juice
  Parsley, grapes, apple wedges

Rub cavity of each duck with 1 teaspoon salt. Combine celery, apple, and onion; stuff into cavity of each duck. Close cavity with skewers.

Brown ducks in shortening in a heavy Dutch oven; add water, orange juice, and ½ teaspoon salt. Cover tightly; cook over low heat 45 minutes to 1 hour or until tender. (Cooking time depends on age of duck.) Baste 2 or 3 times during cooking. Garnish with parsley, grapes, and apple. Yield: 6 servings.

QUAIL IN RED WINE

6 quail, cleaned
  Brandy
  All-purpose flour
6 tablespoons butter or margarine
2 cups sliced mushrooms
¼ cup melted butter or margarine
1 cup consommé
1 cup dry red wine
1 stalk celery, quartered
  Salt and pepper
  Juice of 2 oranges, strained

Rub quail with a cloth soaked in brandy, and dust with flour. Melt 6 tablespoons butter in a heavy skillet; add quail, and sauté 10 minutes.

Sauté mushrooms in ¼ cup butter; pour over quail. Add consommé, wine, celery, salt, and pepper. Cover and simmer 20 to 30 minutes or until quail is tender. Discard celery, if desired; stir in orange juice. Heat thoroughly. Yield: 6 servings.

WILD RICE-SAUSAGE CASSEROLE

½ pound bulk sausage
1 medium onion, chopped
1 medium-size green pepper, chopped
½ cup chopped celery
1 (6-ounce) package long grain and wild
  rice mix
1 (4-ounce) package wild rice, rinsed
1 (10¾-ounce) can cream of chicken
  soup, undiluted
1 (10¾-ounce) can cream of mushroom
  soup, undiluted
1 cup shredded sharp Cheddar cheese
1 (4-ounce) can sliced mushrooms,
  drained

Brown sausage in a skillet; drain, reserving drippings. Sauté onion, green pepper, and celery in drippings until done.

Combine sausage, sautéed vegetables, long grain and wild rice mix (including seasoning packet), wild rice, soups, cheese, and mushrooms; mix well. Spoon into a shallow 2-quart casserole. Cover and bake at 325° for 1 hour or until done. Yield: 8 servings.

SPINACH SUPREME

2 (10-ounce) packages frozen chopped
  spinach
3 slices bacon, cooked and crumbled
1 (6-ounce) can sliced mushrooms,
  drained
¼ teaspoon marjoram
1 (8-ounce) carton commercial sour
  cream
½ cup shredded sharp Cheddar cheese

Cook spinach according to package directions; drain. Combine all ingredients except cheese.

Spoon mixture into a lightly greased 1½-quart casserole. Bake at 325° for 20 to 25 minutes. Sprinkle with cheese and return to oven for 5 minutes or until cheese is melted. Yield: 6 servings.

STRAWBERRY-GRAPEFRUIT SALAD

1 (3-ounce) package strawberry-flavored
  gelatin
1½ cups boiling water
⅓ cup grapefruit juice
1 cup strawberries, quartered
1 cup diced, drained grapefruit sections
6 whole strawberries
1 avocado, sliced
  Whipped Cream Salad Dressing

Dissolve gelatin in boiling water; add grapefruit juice. Chill until slightly thickened; fold in 1 cup strawberries and grapefruit. Pour into a 4-cup mold; chill until firm. Unmold and garnish with whole strawberries and avocado slices. Serve with Whipped Cream Salad Dressing. Yield: 6 servings.

Whipped Cream Salad Dressing:

1 egg, beaten
2 tablespoons sugar
1 tablespoon vinegar
1 tablespoon margarine
1 cup whipping cream, whipped

Combine egg, sugar, vinegar, and margarine; cook over low heat, stirring constantly, until smooth and thickened. Cool. Fold in whipped cream. Yield: about 1 cup.

SOUR CREAM POUND CAKE

1½ cups butter, softened
2 cups sugar
8 eggs
4 cups sifted self-rising flour
1 cup commercial sour cream
　Powdered sugar

Cream butter and sugar until light and fluffy; add eggs, one at a time, beating well after each addition.

Blend flour into creamed mixture alternately with sour cream, beginning and ending with flour; beat well after each addition.

Pour batter into a greased and floured 10-inch Bundt pan. Bake at 350° for 1 hour or until cake tests done. Cool in pan 10 minutes; invert on wire rack to cool completely. Sprinkle with powdered sugar. Yield: one 10-inch cake.

CHOCOLATE SAUCE SUPREME

1 (6-ounce) package semisweet chocolate
　morsels
¼ cup butter or margarine
1 cup sifted powdered sugar
　Dash of salt
½ cup light corn syrup
¼ cup hot water
¼ cup creme de cacao liqueur
1 teaspoon vanilla extract
　Pound cake or ice cream

Combine chocolate morsels, butter, sugar, salt, corn syrup, and water in a heavy saucepan. Place over low heat; stir until chocolate melts. Remove from heat, and add liqueur and vanilla.

Serve immediately, or pour hot mixture into hot, sterilized half-pint jars.

Cool and store in refrigerator. Serve over pound cake or ice cream. Yield: about 2 cups.

RHUBARB SAUCE

1 pound rhubarb, sliced
1 to 1¼ cups sugar
1 tablespoon cornstarch
　Red food coloring
　Pound cake or ice cream

Place rhubarb in a saucepan; add water to a depth of ½ inch. Add sugar, and bring to a boil; lower heat, and simmer 10 to 15 minutes or until tender. Spoon mixture into blender; blend until smooth. Add cornstarch and a few drops of red food coloring; mix well.

Return sauce to saucepan; cook until slightly thickened. Serve hot or cold over pound cake or ice cream. Yield: 3 cups

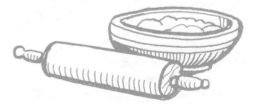

To get maximum volume when beating egg whites, have them at room temperature and beat in a deep glass or metal bowl—not plastic. Tip the bowl to determine if whites have reached the proper consistency. The whites will not slide when they've reached the "stiff but not dry" stage called for in many recipes.

All-purpose flour can be substituted for cake flour: 1 cup minus 2 tablespoons of all-purpose flour equals 1 cup cake flour.

Save lemon and orange rinds. Store in the freezer, and grate as needed for pies, cakes, breads, and cookies. Or the rinds can be candied for holiday uses.

Sensational Baked Snapper
(Dinner for Four)

Cold Quick Borscht
Tangy Baked Snapper
Sausage-Zucchini Boats
Baked Corn in Sour Cream or New-Fashioned Corn Relish
Grapefruit Soufflé Salad
Commercial French Rolls   Butter
Summer Peach Pie
Iced Tea   Coffee

COLD QUICK BORSCHT

1 (16-ounce) can whole beets, undrained
1 (10¾-ounce) can chicken broth
1 (8-ounce) carton commercial sour
   cream
¾ teaspoon salt
⅛ teaspoon white pepper
1½ teaspoons lemon juice
2 tablespoons chopped chives

Drain beets, reserving liquid. Put beets through a sieve, or puree in electric blender. Combine all ingredients except chives with beet liquid; mix well. Chill. When ready to serve, sprinkle with chives. Yield: 4 servings.

TANGY BAKED SNAPPER

6 tablespoons tomato sauce
1 tablespoon lemon juice
2 tablespoons melted margarine
   Dash of herb-seasoned salt
2 (1½- to 2-pound) dressed snappers
   Parsley
   Lemon slices

Combine tomato sauce, lemon juice, margarine, and salt. Place in a lightly greased baking pan. Brush fish with sauce, inside and out.

  Bake at 350° for 1 hour or until fish flakes easily when tested with a fork. Garnish with parsley and lemon slices. Yield: 4 servings.

SAUSAGE-ZUCCHINI BOATS

 4 medium zucchini squash
¼ pound bulk sausage
¼ cup chopped onion
½ to ¾ cup fine cracker crumbs
    Dash of garlic powder
    Pepper to taste
 1 egg, slightly beaten
½ teaspoon monosodium glutamate
¼ teaspoon salt
¼ teaspoon thyme
½ cup grated Parmesan cheese, divided
    Dash of paprika

Trim stem and blossom ends off zucchini. Cook zucchini in boiling salted water for 7 to 10 minutes or until tender. Drain.

Cut each squash in half lengthwise. Carefully scoop out pulp, leaving shells intact. Mash pulp, and drain off any liquid.

Brown sausage and onion; drain. Combine zucchini pulp, sausage, onion, cracker crumbs, garlic powder, pepper, egg, monosodium glutamate, salt, thyme, and 6 tablespoons cheese; mix well.

Stuff zucchini shells with pulp mixture. Place in a lightly greased baking dish. Sprinkle with remaining cheese and paprika. Bake at 350° for 25 to 30 minutes. Yield: 8 servings.

BAKED CORN IN SOUR CREAM

 6 slices bacon
 2 tablespoons chopped onion
 2 tablespoons butter or margarine
 2 tablespoons all-purpose flour
½ teaspoon salt
 1 cup commercial sour cream
 2 (12-ounce) cans whole kernel corn, drained
 1 tablespoon chopped parsley

Fry bacon; drain and crumble. Set aside.

Sauté onion in butter; blend in flour and salt. Gradually add sour cream, stirring until mixture is smooth. Heat just to boiling; add corn, and heat thoroughly. Fold in half of bacon.

Spoon into a greased 2-quart casserole; top with parsley and remaining bacon. Bake at 350° for 30 to 45 minutes. Yield: 6 servings.

NEW-FASHIONED CORN RELISH

 1 small onion, chopped
½ cup vinegar
½ cup sugar
 2 tablespoons celery seeds
½ teaspoon mustard seeds
 1 (12- or 16-ounce) can whole kernel corn, drained
¼ cup sweet pickle relish
¼ cup diced pimiento
½ cup chopped celery

Combine onion, vinegar, sugar, celery seeds, and mustard seeds; bring to a boil. Reduce heat and simmer for 10 minutes. Combine corn, pickle relish, pimiento, and celery; pour hot vinegar mixture over corn mixture, and mix well. Cool. Chill at least 24 hours to allow flavors to blend. Yield: about 3 cups.

GRAPEFRUIT SOUFFLÉ SALAD

1 (3-ounce) package lime-flavored gelatin
1 cup boiling water
½ cup grapefruit juice
1 tablespoon vinegar
½ cup mayonnaise
1 cup drained grapefruit sections
¼ cup chopped celery
    Lettuce leaves

Dissolve gelatin in boiling water. Add grapefruit juice, vinegar, and mayonnaise; mix until well blended. Refrigerate until partially set; beat until fluffy. Fold in grapefruit sections and celery.

Spoon into a 4-cup mold; chill until firm. Serve on lettuce leaves. Yield: 4 servings.

SUMMER PEACH PIE

1 envelope (1 tablespoon) plus 1 teaspoon
    unflavored gelatin
½ cup plus 2 tablespoons cold water,
    divided
¼ cup sugar
1 (12-ounce) can peach nectar
1 tablespoon lemon juice
4 large fresh peaches, peeled and sliced
1 baked 9-inch pastry shell
2 cups whipped cream

Dissolve gelatin in ½ cup cold water; bring to a boil, stirring constantly. Remove from heat; stir in sugar and peach nectar. Chill until thickened.

Combine lemon juice and remaining 2 tablespoons water; stir in peaches until well coated with liquid. Drain peach slices; arrange in pastry shell. Cover with gelatin mixture; chill until firm.

Just before serving, top with whipped cream and garnish with additional peach slices. Yield: one 9-inch pie.

Sprinkle freshly cut avocados, bananas, apples, and peaches with lemon juice to prevent darkening.

Use shiny cookie sheets and cakepans for baking rather than darkened ones. Dark pans absorb more heat and can cause baked products to overbrown.

Always use standard fractional measuring cups and spoons. One of the newest items on the market is the glass measuring cup that gives the familiar measure as well as the metric measure.

The reason some hard-cooked eggs have discolored yolks is that the eggs have been cooked at too high a temperature, or they have not been cooled rapidly following cooking. The greenish color comes from sulfur and iron compounds in the eggs. These compounds form at the surface of the yolks when they have been overcooked. This does not interfere with the taste or nutritional value of the eggs, however.

Gourmet Chicken with Rice
(Dinner for Six to Eight)

Chicken Eugene
Gourmet Rice
Cheese-Topped Green Beans
Millionaire Salad
Cottage Cheese Rolls
Brownie Pecan Pie or Unusual Blueberry Pie

CHICKEN EUGENE

3 to 4 chicken breasts, halved, boned, and skinned
Salt to taste
Paprika
6 to 8 thin slices cooked ham
½ cup melted butter or margarine
1 (10¾-ounce) can cream of mushroom soup, undiluted
½ cup sherry
1 (8-ounce) carton commercial sour cream
1 (4-ounce) can sliced mushrooms, drained

Sprinkle chicken with salt and paprika. Place ham slices in a shallow baking dish; top with chicken. Combine remaining ingredients, blending well; pour over chicken. Bake at 350° for 1 to 1½ hours or until done. Yield: 6 to 8 servings.

GOURMET RICE
(see Index)

CHEESE-TOPPED GREEN BEANS

1 pound fresh green beans, cut into 1-inch pieces
¼ cup dry onion soup mix
1 cup water
3 tablespoons melted butter or margarine
⅓ cup toasted slivered almonds
3 tablespoons grated Parmesan cheese
½ teaspoon paprika

Combine green beans, onion soup mix, and water; cook over low heat until beans are tender. Drain; spoon into serving dish. Stir in butter, almonds, and cheese. Sprinkle with paprika. Yield: 6 to 8 servings.

MILLIONAIRE SALAD

1 (3-ounce) package cream cheese, softened
2 tablespoons whipping cream or half-and-half
⅓ cup salad dressing or mayonnaise
2 tablespoons lemon juice
⅛ teaspoon salt
2 tablespoons sugar
1 cup diced pineapple
1 cup orange sections
½ cup halved maraschino cherries
½ cup quartered light sweet cherries
½ cup chopped pecans
1 cup miniature marshmallows
1 cup whipping cream, whipped

Combine cream cheese and 2 tablespoons whipping cream; add salad dressing, lemon juice, salt, and sugar. Combine cheese mixture with fruit, pecans, and marshmallows. Fold in whipped cream. Freeze in individual molds or an 8-inch square pan. Yield: 8 to 10 servings.

COTTAGE CHEESE ROLLS
(see Index)

BROWNIE PECAN PIE

⅔ cup sugar
⅛ teaspoon salt
1 cup light corn syrup
1 (4-ounce) package sweet cooking chocolate, broken into pieces
3 tablespoons butter or margarine
3 eggs, slightly beaten
1 teaspoon vanilla extract
1 cup coarsely chopped pecans
1 unbaked 9-inch pastry shell
Whipped cream

Combine sugar, salt, and corn syrup in a small saucepan. Bring to a boil over medium heat, stirring until sugar is dissolved; boil 2 minutes. Remove from heat; add chocolate and butter, stirring until chocolate is melted and mixture is smooth. Cool.

Gradually pour chocolate mixture over eggs, stirring constantly. Add vanilla and pecans; mix well. Pour into pastry shell. Bake at 350° for 50 minutes; cool. Top with whipped cream. Yield: one 9-inch pie.

UNUSUAL BLUEBERRY PIE

1 (2-ounce) package whipped topping mix
¾ cup cold milk
1 teaspoon vanilla extract
1 cup sugar
1 (8-ounce) package cream cheese, softened
1 large banana, sliced
1 baked 10-inch pastry shell
1 (22-ounce) can blueberry pie filling

Combine whipped topping mix, milk, and vanilla; blend well. Add sugar and cream cheese; beat until stiff.

Arrange banana slices in bottom of pastry shell; spread cream cheese mixture over banana slices. Spread blueberry pie filling over cream cheese mixture. Chill at least 4 hours or overnight. Yield: one 10-inch pie.

Serve Steak-in-the-Round

(Dinner for Six)

Round Steak with Mushroom Stuffing
Italian Rice
Sweet-and-Sour Carrots
Green Salad Continental
Braided Lightbread
Apricot Cream or Cherry Dessert
Iced Tea   Coffee

ROUND STEAK WITH MUSHROOM STUFFING

    1 medium onion, finely chopped
    1 (9-ounce) can sliced mushrooms,
      drained
    2 tablespoons melted butter or margarine
    1 cup breadcrumbs
    ¼ teaspoon thyme
    ¼ teaspoon sage
    1 (1½-pound) round steak
      Salt and pepper to taste
      All-purpose flour
      Salad oil
    ¼ cup water

Sauté onion and mushrooms in butter; add breadcrumbs, thyme, and sage, stirring well.

Season steak with salt and pepper; spread with breadcrumb mixture. Roll up steak and fasten with skewers; dredge in flour. Brown in hot oil; add water.

Cover and bake at 325° for 45 minutes or until meat is tender. Yield: 6 servings.

ITALIAN RICE

    1 cup uncooked regular rice
    2 tablespoons melted butter or margarine
    2½ cups boiling water
    1 (0.6-ounce) envelope Italian salad
      dressing mix
    1 (10¾-ounce) can condensed cream of
      chicken soup, undiluted

Sauté rice in butter until golden brown. Add water, salad dressing mix, and soup; mix well. Bring to a boil; cover and simmer 25 to 30 minutes or until rice is tender. Yield: 6 servings.

SWEET-AND-SOUR CARROTS

3 tablespoons butter or margarine
2 tablespoons cornstarch
½ teaspoon salt
  Dash of pepper
2 tablespoons firmly packed brown sugar
2 tablespoons vinegar
1 cup hot water
4 cups sliced, cooked carrots

Brown butter; blend in cornstarch and continue browning, stirring constantly. Add salt and pepper.

Combine sugar, vinegar, and water, stirring until sugar is dissolved. Gradually stir into butter mixture; cook slowly, stirring constantly, until smooth and thickened. Pour over hot carrots. Yield: 6 servings.

GREEN SALAD CONTINENTAL

6 cups torn mixed salad greens
2 medium oranges, peeled and sectioned
1 small white onion, sliced and separated
    into rings
3 tablespoons crumbled blue cheese
¼ cup salad oil
2 tablespoons lemon juice
1 teaspoon sugar
¼ teaspoon pepper
  Few drops pepper sauce

Place salad greens in a large salad bowl; top with orange sections and onion rings, and sprinkle with blue cheese. Combine remaining ingredients in a jar with a tight-fitting lid; shake well to mix. Drizzle over salad mixture; toss to coat well. Yield: 6 to 8 servings.

BRAIDED LIGHTBREAD

3 cups very warm water, divided (105° to 115°)
2 packages dry yeast
4 teaspoons sugar
10 cups all-purpose flour, divided
4 teaspoons salt
2 eggs, slightly beaten
3 tablespoons salad oil
1 beaten egg yolk
1 teaspoon water
  Sesame or poppy seeds (optional)

Combine 2 cups water, yeast, and sugar in a small bowl; set aside. Combine 9 cups flour, salt, eggs, and oil in a large mixing bowl. Add yeast mixture and 1 cup water; mix well.

Sprinkle 1 cup flour on pastry cloth or board. Turn out dough and knead until smooth and elastic, about 8 to 10 minutes. Place in a greased bowl, turning to grease top. Cover and let rise in a warm place until doubled in bulk, about 1 hour.

Turn out on floured surface. Punch down and divide in half. Divide each half into 3 equal parts, and form into 15-inch lengths. Place 3 lengths on a greased baking sheet and braid. Repeat with remaining 3 lengths. Press ends of each braid together, and turn under firmly. Cover and let rise until doubled in bulk, about 45 minutes.

Combine egg yolk and water; brush top of braids. Sprinkle with sesame or poppy seeds, if desired. Bake at 350° for 45 minutes. Cool on wire racks. Yield: 2 loaves.

APRICOT CREAM

1 (17-ounce) can apricot halves, drained
1 envelope (1 tablespoon) unflavored
   gelatin
3 tablespoons cold water
2 tablespoons lemon juice
⅓ cup sugar
1½ cups whipping cream, whipped

Puree apricot halves in electric blender, or force through a sieve. Soften gelatin in cold water. Combine apricot puree, gelatin, lemon juice, and sugar; heat until gelatin and sugar are dissolved. Refrigerate 30 minutes.

Fold whipped cream into gelatin mixture; pour into a 4-cup mold. Refrigerate until firm. Yield: 6 servings.

CHERRY DESSERT

1 (8-ounce) package cream cheese,
   softened
1 (3-ounce) package cream cheese,
   softened
2 tablespoons milk
1 cup powdered sugar
1 (9-inch) graham cracker crust
½ cup chopped pecans
1 (1¾-ounce) package whipped topping
   mix
1 teaspoon almond extract
1 (21-ounce) can cherry pie filling

Combine cream cheese, milk, and powdered sugar; beat until smooth. Spoon into pie shell, spreading evenly. Sprinkle with nuts.

Prepare whipped topping mix according to package directions; spread over nuts. Combine almond extract and cherry pie filling, mixing well; spoon over whipped topping. Chill. Yield: one 9-inch pie.

When canning non-acid vegetables, such as turnip greens and mustard greens, remember that they should be processed in a pressure cooker. Some bacteria do not begin to grow until air is excluded, and it takes a temperature higher than boiling to kill them. Ten pounds' pressure in a pressure cooker puts the temperature at 240 degrees. There are some handy family-size pressure cookers on the market, which make home canning more convenient.

To make good yeast breads, it is essential to learn the "feel" of the dough. This takes experience. You will note that most recipes state "about" followed by the number of cups of flour. Some flours absorb more liquid than others, and it is difficult to give an exact measurement. Too much flour results in a heavy loaf, crumbliness, and dryness with an off-flavor. Keep the dough on the soft side, but still easy to handle.

Slow Cooking Roast Dinner

(Dinner for Six to Eight)

Savory Pot Roast   Rice
Stuffed Mushrooms
Tomato-Corn Bake
Gold Mold Salad or Cool Bean Salad
Potato Rolls
Strawberry Snow

SAVORY POT ROAST

  1 (3-pound) boneless chuck roast, cut into
     bite-size pieces
  Salt
  Hot cooking oil
¼ cup catsup
¼ cup wine vinegar
  2 tablespoons Worcestershire sauce
½ teaspoon garlic powder
¼ cup red wine
  2 tablespoons soy sauce
  1 teaspoon dried rosemary
½ teaspoon dry mustard
  Hot cooked rice

Season roast with salt to taste; brown in hot oil in a skillet. Place meat in electric slow cooker. Combine remaining ingredients except rice; pour over meat. Cover and cook on low setting 8 to 10 hours. Serve over rice. Yield: 6 to 8 servings.

STUFFED MUSHROOMS

 12 to 16 fresh mushrooms
½ cup melted butter or margarine,
    divided
  3 tablespoons chopped green pepper
  3 tablespoons finely chopped onion
1½ cups fresh bread cubes
½ teaspoon salt
  Dash of black pepper
  Dash of cayenne

Clean mushrooms with a damp cloth; remove stems, leaving caps intact. Chop stems. Sauté caps in 3 tablespoons butter; set aside.

Sauté stems, green pepper, and onion in remaining butter about 5 minutes. Add bread cubes and seasonings; mix well.

Stuff each mushroom cap with bread cube mixture. Place in a greased baking dish; bake at 350° for 10 minutes. Yield: 6 to 8 servings.

TOMATO-CORN BAKE

4 small tomatoes
 Salt
1 (8¾-ounce) can whole kernel corn,
 drained
½ cup shredded Swiss cheese
1 tablespoon sliced green onion

Cut tomatoes in half crosswise; scoop out pulp, leaving shells intact. Sprinkle inside of tomato shells lightly with salt; invert to drain.

Combine corn, cheese, and onion. Spoon into tomato shells, and place in a shallow baking dish. Bake at 350° for 20 to 25 minutes. Yield: 8 servings.

Note: Tomato pulp may be used in salads, soups, and sauces.

GOLD MOLD SALAD

1½ cups fresh orange juice
1 envelope (1 tablespoon) unflavored
 gelatin
¼ cup pineapple juice
¼ cup lemon juice
¼ teaspoon salt
¼ cup sugar
1 cup coarsely grated carrot
1 (8-ounce) can crushed pineapple,
 drained
½ cup chopped pecans
 Lettuce
 Mayonnaise (optional)

Heat orange juice. Soften gelatin in pineapple juice; add to orange juice along with lemon juice, salt, and sugar. Stir until gelatin is dissolved. Chill until consistency of unbeaten egg white.

Stir carrot, pineapple, and pecans into thickened gelatin. Pour into a lightly greased 1-quart mold; chill until firm. Unmold on lettuce; serve with mayonnaise, if desired. Yield: 6 to 8 servings.

COOL BEAN SALAD

2 (16-ounce) cans French-style green
 beans, drained
12 pitted ripe olives, sliced
½ cup sliced water chestnuts
1 (6-ounce) can sliced mushrooms,
 drained
½ onion, thinly sliced into rings
¼ teaspoon pepper
¼ teaspoon garlic powder
2 tablespoons grated Parmesan cheese
 Commercial Italian salad dressing

Combine all ingredients except salad dressing; toss until well mixed. Add enough salad dressing to almost cover vegetables. Cover and refrigerate at least 2 hours, stirring frequently. Drain off excess dressing before serving. Yield: 6 to 8 servings.

POTATO ROLLS

2 medium potatoes, peeled and quartered
3 cups water
½ cup sugar
1½ teaspoons salt
2 packages dry yeast
2 eggs, beaten
⅔ cup shortening
 About 6½ cups all-purpose flour

Boil potatoes in water until done; drain, reserving 1½ cups water. Cool water to lukewarm. Add sugar, salt, and yeast to potato water, stirring until yeast is dissolved.

Mash potatoes; add 1 cup mashed potatoes, eggs, and shortening to yeast mixture, mixing well. Gradually add about half of flour; beat until smooth. Gradually add remaining flour to make a soft dough.

Turn dough out onto a lightly floured board; knead until smooth and elastic, about 7 minutes. Place in a greased bowl, turning to grease all sides. Cover and let rise in a warm place free from drafts until doubled in bulk, about 1 hour.

Punch dough down, and turn out onto a lightly floured board; knead lightly. Roll dough into 1½-inch balls, and place in 3 greased 9-inch round pans. Cover; let rise in a warm place until doubled in bulk, about 1 hour. Bake at 400° for 15 minutes. Yield: about 3 dozen rolls.

STRAWBERRY SNOW

2 cups strawberries
⅓ to ½ cup sugar
3 egg whites
½ pint whipping cream, whipped

Puree strawberries in electric blender; add sugar, blending well. Beat egg whites until stiff; fold in strawberry puree and whipped cream. Spoon mixture into parfait glasses. Chill about 4 hours before serving. Yield: 6 to 8 servings.

Chocolate must be treated delicately. It should always be stored at a temperature under 75 degrees. If a gray color develops, this is a sign that the cocoa butter has risen to the surface. Flavor and quality will not be lessened, and the gray color will disappear when the chocolate is melted. Temperature, time, and stirring are important when melting chocolate. Chocolate will scorch at too high a temperature; heating too long and stirring too much will cause chocolate to separate into particles that will not melt and blend together.

If baked foods consistently undercook or overcook at the temperatures and cooking times specified in recipes, have the thermostat of your oven checked. Home service advisors of the gas or electric company will usually do this for you. However, you can check it yourself with a dependable oven thermometer. Place the thermometer in the center of the oven, and set the oven on the desired temperature. Allow enough time for the oven to heat, and compare the thermometer reading with the oven setting.

Springtime Sunday Special
(Dinner for Eight)

Luau Pork Roast
Parsleyed New Potatoes
Spinach Milano
Deluxe Perfection Salad or Fresh Vegetable Salad
Refrigerator Rolls
Sour Cream Cheesecake
Iced Tea   Coffee

LUAU PORK ROAST

1 (5-pound) pork loin roast
4 (4¾-ounce) jars strained apricot baby
    food, divided
⅓ cup honey
½ cup lemon juice
½ cup soy sauce
½ clove garlic, minced
1 small onion, finely chopped
1 cup ginger ale
⅛ teaspoon pepper
1 tablespoon coarsely grated lemon rind
1 (17-ounce) can whole apricots, drained
    Watercress

Have the butcher saw across the rib bones at the base of the backbone, separating ribs from backbone.

Combine 2 jars strained apricots, honey, lemon juice, soy sauce, garlic, onion, ginger ale, and pepper. Pour over roast; marinate overnight or at least 4 to 5 hours, turning occasionally.

Place roast in broiler pan. Bake at 350° about 3½ hours, basting frequently with marinade.

Spread 1 jar strained apricots on top of roast during last 5 minutes of baking.

Combine remaining jar of strained apricots and lemon rind in a saucepan. Heat well; serve as sauce with roast.

For easy carving, remove backbone and allow roast to stand 15 to 20 minutes. Place roast on a serving platter; garnish with whole apricots and watercress. Yield: about 8 servings.

PARSLEYED NEW POTATOES

3 pounds small new potatoes
5 cups water
    Salt to taste
¾ cup melted butter or margarine
6 tablespoons minced parsley

Cook scraped potatoes in boiling salted water 25 to 30 minutes or until tender. Combine butter and parsley; serve over hot, drained potatoes. Yield: 8 servings.

SPINACH MILANO

2 (10-ounce) packages frozen chopped
spinach
¼ cup all-purpose flour
¼ cup melted butter or margarine
3 eggs, beaten
4 slices pasteurized process American
cheese, cut into cubes
4 slices natural brick cheese, cut into cubes
1 (12-ounce) carton cottage cheese
Salt and pepper to taste

Cook spinach according to package directions;
drain. Gradually add flour to butter, blending
until smooth; add to spinach along with remaining ingredients, mixing well.

Spoon mixture into a lightly greased 1½-quart
casserole. Bake at 350° for 1 hour. Yield: 8
servings.

DELUXE PERFECTION SALAD

2 envelopes (2 tablespoons) unflavored
gelatin
6½ cups water, divided
2 (6-ounce) packages lemon-flavored
gelatin
1 cup sugar
2 teaspoons salt
½ cup lemon juice
2 cups chopped cabbage
2 cups shredded carrot
2 cups chopped celery
½ cup chopped green pepper
¼ cup chopped pimiento
Mayonnaise
Paprika

Sprinkle unflavored gelatin in 3¼ cups water;
heat slowly until gelatin is dissolved. Stir in
lemon gelatin, sugar, and salt. Add remaining
water and lemon juice; chill until consistency of
unbeaten egg white.

Stir cabbage, carrot, celery, pepper, and
pimiento into thickened gelatin mixture; pour
into a 6-cup mold. Chill until firm. Serve with
mayonnaise sprinkled with paprika. Yield: 8 to
10 servings.

FRESH VEGETABLE SALAD

½ cup chopped green pepper
1 cup chopped onion
1 cup chopped celery
4 cups chopped fresh tomatoes
¼ cup sugar
1 tablespoon salt
1 cup vinegar
2 teaspoons poppy seeds
½ cup salad oil

Combine green pepper, onion, celery, and tomatoes; set aside. Combine remaining ingredients,
mixing well; pour over vegetable mixture. Yield:
8 servings.

REFRIGERATOR ROLLS

¾ cup hot water
½ cup sugar
1 tablespoon salt
3 tablespoons margarine
2 packages dry yeast
1 cup very warm water (105° to 115°)
1 egg, beaten
About 5¼ cups all-purpose flour,
divided
Melted butter

Combine hot water, sugar, salt, and margarine; cool to lukewarm.

Soften yeast in very warm water. Add sugar mixture, egg, and half of flour; beat until smooth. Add enough remaining flour to make a soft dough.

Turn dough out on a lightly floured board; knead about 10 minutes or until smooth and elastic. Place in a greased bowl, turning to grease top. Cover tightly with waxed paper or aluminum foil. Store in refrigerator until doubled in bulk or until needed. (Dough may be kept 4 to 5 days.)

To use, punch dough down, and turn out on a lightly floured board. Shape into crescent, Parker House, cloverleaf, fan tan, or pan rolls.

Cover; let rise until doubled in bulk. Brush with melted butter. Bake at 400° about 10 to 15 minutes. Yield: 2½ to 4 dozen, depending on shape.

SOUR CREAM CHEESECAKE

    2 eggs
    ½ cup sugar
    2 teaspoons vanilla extract
1½ cups commercial sour cream
    2 (8-ounce) packages cream cheese,
        softened and cut into pieces
    2 tablespoons butter, melted
        Crumb Crust
    1 (21-ounce) can cherry pie filling
        (optional)

Blend eggs, sugar, vanilla, and sour cream for 15 seconds in blender. Continue blending and gradually add cream cheese. Add butter; blend well. Pour cheese mixture into 9-inch Crumb Crust. Bake at 325° for 35 minutes or until set in center. Filling will be very soft but will firm up as cake cools. Top with cherry pie filling, if desired; chill thoroughly before serving. Yield: one 9-inch cheese cake.

Crumb Crust:

15 graham cracker squares, crushed
½ cup sugar
½ teaspoon ground cinnamon
¼ cup butter, melted

Combine all ingredients. Press into buttered 9-inch piepan. Bake at 400° for 6 minutes. Cool before filling. Yield: one 9-inch pie shell.

Sour cream keeps best if stored in the tightly covered container in which it is purchased. If stored upside down in the refrigerator, maximum retention of texture and flavor is assured.

To make shredding of very soft cheese easier, put in the freezer for 15 minutes.

Southern Sunday Dinner

(Dinner for Four)

Dixie Fried Chicken
Cream Gravy
Fluffy Potatoes or Rice
Fresh Green Beans
Yellow Squash Casserole or Sliced Tomatoes
Country Biscuits
Lemon Chess Pie or Peanut Pie
Iced Tea   Coffee

DIXIE FRIED CHICKEN

  1 (2- to 3-pound) broiler-fryer chicken,
     cut up
   Salt and pepper
  2 cups all-purpose flour
  1 teaspoon red pepper
  1 egg, slightly beaten
 ½ cup milk
   Hot oil

Season chicken with salt and pepper. Combine flour and red pepper; set aside. Combine egg and milk; dip chicken in egg mixture; then dredge in flour mixture, coating well.

Heat 1 inch of oil in a skillet; place chicken in skillet. Cover and cook over medium heat about 30 minutes or until golden brown; turn occasionally. Drain on paper towels. Yield: 4 servings.

CREAM GRAVY

  4 tablespoons drippings
  4 tablespoons all-purpose flour
2½ to 3 cups hot milk
   Salt and pepper

Pour off all except 4 tablespoons drippings in which chicken was fried; place skillet over medium heat; add flour and stir until browned. Gradually add hot milk; cook, stirring constantly, until thickened. Add salt and pepper to taste. Serve hot. Yield: about 2 cups.

Dixie Fried Chicken served with green beans, biscuits, and cream gravy is a typical Sunday dinner. This delicious menu is above.

FLUFFY POTATOES

2 pounds potatoes
3 to 4 cups water
Salt
⅓ to ½ cup milk
¼ cup butter or margarine, softened
Dash of pepper
Paprika (optional)
Parsley (optional)

Peel potatoes and cut into large pieces. Cook in boiling salted water 15 to 20 minutes or until tender. Drain.

Mash potatoes until no lumps remain. Add milk in small amounts, beating after each addition. (Amount of milk needed to make potatoes fluffy depends on kind of potatoes.) Add butter, ½ teaspoon salt, and pepper; beat vigorously until potatoes are light and fluffy. Sprinkle with paprika or snipped parsley, if desired. Yield: 4 to 6 servings.

FRESH GREEN BEANS

1 pound fresh green beans
4 cups water
¼ pound diced salt pork or ham hock
Salt to taste
Dash of sugar

String the beans, cut into 1½-inch pieces, and wash. Put water in a 2-quart saucepan and add diced salt pork. Cover and cook about 5 minutes. Add beans, salt, and sugar. Cover and cook over medium heat 25 to 35 minutes or until tender. Yield: 4 servings.

Luau Pork Roast (page 55) combines the delicate flavor of pork with the tangy sweetness of apricots.

YELLOW SQUASH CASSEROLE

4 medium-size yellow squash, sliced
⅓ cup chopped onion
⅓ cup melted margarine
2 hard-cooked eggs, chopped
½ cup shredded Cheddar cheese
1 cup buttered cracker crumbs

Cook squash in small amount of boiling salted water 10 to 15 minutes or until tender; drain. Sauté onion in margarine until tender.

Combine all ingredients except cracker crumbs in a lightly greased 1-quart casserole; sprinkle with cracker crumbs. Bake at 350° for 15 to 20 minutes. Yield: 4 to 6 servings.

COUNTRY BISCUITS

2 cups all-purpose flour
4 teaspoons baking powder
½ teaspoon salt
2 tablespoons shortening
¾ cup milk

Combine flour, baking powder, and salt; cut in shortening until mixture resembles coarse crumbs. Add milk, and stir until blended.

Turn dough out onto floured surface, and knead 3 or 4 times. Pat out to ½-inch thickness, and cut with biscuit cutter. Place on a greased baking sheet, and bake at 400° for 15 to 20 minutes or until golden brown. Yield: about 1 dozen biscuits.

LEMON CHESS PIE

2 cups sugar
1 tablespoon all-purpose flour
1 tablespoon cornmeal
¼ teaspoon salt
¼ cup melted butter or margarine
¼ cup lemon juice
    Grated rind of 2 lemons
¼ cup milk
4 eggs
1 unbaked 9-inch pastry shell

Combine sugar, flour, cornmeal, and salt. Add butter, lemon juice, lemon rind, and milk; mix well. Add eggs, one at a time, beating well after each addition. Pour into pastry shell. Bake at 350° for 50 minutes. Yield: one 9-inch pie.

PEANUT PIE

20 round buttery crackers
¾ cup finely chopped roasted peanuts
    (skins removed)
1 cup sugar, divided
3 egg whites
½ teaspoon cream of tartar
1 teaspoon vanilla extract
1 cup whipping cream, whipped
    Bittersweet chocolate, shredded

Process crackers in an electric blender, or roll them into fine crumbs. Combine crumbs, peanuts, and ½ cup sugar.

Beat egg whites until frothy; add cream of tartar, continuing to beat. Gradually add remaining sugar and vanilla, beating until whites stand in stiff peaks; fold in peanut mixture.

Spoon filling into a lightly greased 9-inch pie-plate. Bake at 350° for 25 minutes. Chill 3 hours. Garnish with whipped cream and chocolate before serving. Yield: one 9-inch pie.

To help a pastry shell keep its shape while baking, line it with fitted waxed paper and fill with dried peas or rice. Bake about 5 minutes or until shell sets; remove paper and dried peas or rice.

Keep butter, margarine, and fat drippings tightly covered in the refrigerator. Vegetable shortening can be kept covered at room temperature. Homemade salad dressings should be kept in the refrigerator; mayonnaise and commercial salad dressings should be refrigerated after opening. Foods mixed with mayonnaise, such as potato salad or egg salad, should be refrigerated and used within two days.

QUICK OR EASY SUPPERS

An Autumn Favorite

Easy Oven Meal

Late Night Supper

Make-Ahead Meal

Cold Weather Special

Quick Gourmet Fare

Make It a Gourmet Occasion

After-the-Theatre Dinner

Sensational Sandwich Supper

Jiffy Fish Bake

Make It in a Microwave

If you're one of those busy homemakers who work outside the home and manage a family, too, you'll find this section especially helpful. We've included five easy menus that can be made ahead in a jiffy, and six quick menus for those last-minute meals. There are quickie (but sensational) sandwiches, freezer casseroles, easy oven meals, and one-pot slow-cooker dishes; there's even a microwave menu planned with your time and energy in mind so that you can spend more time doing things you want to do.

An Autumn Favorite

(Dinner for Four)

Creole Pork Chops
Cabbage Wedges with Butter
Candied Apples
Relish Tray
Quick Rolls
Macaroon Pie or Mint Brownies
Tea   Coffee

CREOLE PORK CHOPS

  4 center-cut loin chops
    Salt and pepper to taste
  1 cup uncooked rice
  2 medium-size green peppers, chopped
  2 medium onions, chopped
  3 cups boiling water
  ¼ cup catsup

Season chops with salt and pepper, and place in a large skillet. Cover with rice, green pepper, and onion; season with salt and pepper.

Combine boiling water and catsup; pour over chops, and bring to a boil. Lower heat; cover and simmer 1 hour or until rice is tender. Yield: 4 servings.

CABBAGE WEDGES WITH BUTTER

  ½ medium head cabbage
  ½ teaspoon salt
  2 tablespoons melted butter or margarine
    Pepper to taste

Remove outer leaves from cabbage; wash cabbage, and cut into 4 wedges. Add water to a medium skillet to a depth of ½ inch; bring to a boil. Add cabbage wedges and salt; simmer, covered, 8 minutes. Carefully turn cabbage wedges, and simmer 7 to 8 minutes longer or until tender.

Pour off any remaining water, and return to low heat until moisture has evaporated. Add butter, being sure cabbage is thoroughly coated. Sprinkle with pepper. Yield: 4 servings.

CANDIED APPLES

4 apples
4 cups sugar
Juice of 2 oranges

Cut each apple into 8 wedges, removing core. Combine apples and sugar in a large saucepan, mixing well. Add orange juice. Cover and bring to a boil over low heat; remove cover, and cook over medium heat until juice thickens (about 30 to 45 minutes). Yield: about 4 to 6 servings.

RELISH TRAY
(see Index)

QUICK ROLLS
(see Index)

MACAROON PIE

12 saltine crackers, finely crushed
12 dates, finely chopped
¼ cup chopped walnuts
1 cup sugar
½ teaspoon baking powder
3 egg whites
1 teaspoon vanilla extract
Whipped cream

Combine cracker crumbs, dates, walnuts, sugar, and baking powder.

Beat egg whites until stiff but not dry; add vanilla. Fold into dry ingredients and pour into a buttered 9-inch piepan. Bake at 350° for 30 minutes. Cool. Serve with whipped cream. Yield: one 9-inch pie.

MINT BROWNIES

1 (23-ounce) package double-fudge
    brownie mix
12 chocolate-covered mints

Prepare brownies according to directions on package. Spoon batter into a 13- x 9- x 2-inch pan. Bake at 350° for 25 to 30 minutes. While brownies are still hot, place mints on top. Return brownies to oven long enough for mints to melt. Swirl topping with a knife; cool. Cut into 1-inch squares. Yield: about 4 dozen squares.

It's easier to cut raw meat into thin slices if it is slightly frozen. Even 30 minutes in the freezer will make slicing easier.

Using kitchen shears for cutting many foods saves time and gives a neat-looking cut. When cutting sticky foods like marshmallows or dates, dip the shears in hot water.

Easy Oven Meal
(Dinner for Four)

Cream of Cauliflower Soup
Ham Slices Baked with Apples
Sweet Potato Bake
Creamy Spinach
Crusty Rolls   Butter
Makes-Its-Own-Crust Custard Pie
Iced Tea   Coffee

CREAM OF CAULIFLOWER SOUP

  1 (10-ounce) package frozen cauliflower
  1 (10¾-ounce) can cream of potato soup,
     undiluted
  2 cups milk
  1 teaspoon dry mustard
  3 tablespoons melted butter or margarine
  1 tablespoon chopped chives
    Salt and pepper to taste

Cook cauliflower according to package directions; drain.

   Combine all ingredients except chives in blender; blend until smooth. Add chives; heat well, and season. Yield: 4 to 6 servings.

HAM SLICES BAKED WITH APPLES

  2 (½-inch-thick) ham slices
  2 cups thinly sliced tart apples
  1 cup seedless raisins
  3 tablespoons firmly packed brown sugar
  ⅔ cup apple cider

Place 1 slice of ham in a shallow baking dish; cover with apple slices, raisins, and brown sugar. Top with remaining ham slice. Pour cider over ham, and bake at 350° for 40 to 50 minutes. Yield: 4 servings.

SWEET POTATO BAKE

  1 (16-ounce) can whole sweet potatoes,
     drained
    Salt
  ½ cup firmly packed brown sugar
  1 tablespoon cornstarch
  ¼ teaspoon salt
  1 cup orange juice
  2 tablespoons sherry or rum
  ½ cup walnut halves
  ½ teaspoon grated orange peel

Arrange potatoes in a shallow 1-quart baking dish. Sprinkle lightly with salt.

Combine brown sugar, cornstarch, ¼ teaspoon salt, and orange juice in a saucepan; blend well. Cook over high heat, stirring constantly, until mixture boils. Add sherry and blend well. Pour over potatoes and sprinkle with walnuts and orange peel. Bake, uncovered, at 350° for 25 minutes. Yield: 4 servings.

CREAMY SPINACH

2½ cups chopped, cooked spinach
1 (8-ounce) package cream cheese, softened
½ cup melted butter or margarine, divided
    Salt and pepper to taste
1 cup breadcrumbs

Combine spinach, cream cheese, ¼ cup butter, salt, and pepper; mix well. Spoon into a lightly greased 1-quart casserole.

Combine remaining butter and breadcrumbs; sprinkle over spinach mixture. Bake at 350° for 20 to 25 minutes. Yield: 6 servings.

MAKES-ITS-OWN-CRUST CUSTARD PIE

3 eggs
1 (13-ounce) can evaporated milk
1 cup sugar
3 tablespoons all-purpose flour
3 tablespoons melted margarine
    Ground nutmeg to taste

Grease and flour a 9-inch glass piepan. Be sure all areas are well covered.

Combine all ingredients in a blender; blend 30 seconds. Pour into piepan, and bake at 350° for 40 to 45 minutes or until a knife inserted in center comes out clean.

Pie will rise but will settle as it cools and form a light crust. Yield: one 9-inch pie.

Stains or discolorations on aluminum utensils can be removed by boiling a solution of 2 to 3 tablespoons cream of tartar, lemon juice, or vinegar to each quart of water in the utensil for 5 to 10 minutes.

Lightly oil the cup or spoon used to measure honey or molasses. No-stick cooking spray works well for this.

Late Night Supper
(Dinner for Four)

Tomato-Celery Soup
Quiche Unique or Welsh Rarebit
Spinach Salad
Cantaloupe Compote
Wine

TOMATO-CELERY SOUP

1 small onion, chopped
2 tablespoons melted butter or margarine
1 (10½-ounce) can tomato soup,
    undiluted
1 soup can water
1 teaspoon minced parsley
½ cup finely chopped celery
1 tablespoon lemon juice
1 teaspoon sugar
¼ teaspoon salt
⅛ teaspoon pepper

Sauté onion in butter until tender; add remaining ingredients, and simmer 5 minutes. Serve hot. Yield: 4 servings.

QUICHE UNIQUE

¾ cup shredded Swiss cheese
¾ cup shredded mozzarella cheese
½ cup chopped pepperoni
1 tablespoon chopped green onion
1 unbaked 9-inch pastry shell
3 eggs, beaten
1 cup half-and-half
½ teaspoon salt
¼ teaspoon oregano
    Parsley

Combine cheese, pepperoni, and onion; sprinkle in pastry shell. Combine eggs, half-and-half, salt, and oregano; mix well, and pour into pastry shell. Bake at 325° for 45 minutes. Allow to stand 10 minutes or more before cutting. Garnish with parsley. Yield: 4 servings.

WELSH RAREBIT

1 tablespoon butter or margarine
1 pound sharp Cheddar cheese, cut into
   ½-inch cubes
¾ to 1 cup milk or beer
1 teaspoon Worcestershire sauce
½ teaspoon salt
½ teaspoon paprika
½ teaspoon dry mustard
   Dash of red pepper
1 egg, beaten
6 tomato slices
6 slices bread, toasted
6 slices bacon, cooked and halved

Combine butter and cheese in top of a double boiler; stir until cheese is melted. Gradually stir in milk; add Worcestershire sauce, salt, paprika, mustard, and pepper. Stir in egg. Cook until slightly thickened, stirring constantly.

To serve, pour cheese sauce into a chafing dish. Place a tomato slice on each slice of bread; top each tomato with 2 bacon halves. Spoon cheese sauce over bacon, and serve immediately. Yield: 4 to 6 servings.

SPINACH SALAD

4 slices bacon
4 cups torn spinach leaves
1 (8¼-ounce) can pineapple tidbits,
   chilled and drained
½ cup sliced onion
   Piquant Salad Dressing

Cook bacon until crisp; drain and crumble. Place spinach in large salad bowl. Top with pineapple tidbits and onion slices. Sprinkle crumbled bacon over top. Just before serving, add Dressing and toss lightly. Yield: 4 servings.

Piquant Salad Dressing:

1 cup salad oil
3 tablespoons lemon juice
1 teaspoon sugar
1 teaspoon salt
2 teaspoons paprika
1 small onion, chopped
1 teaspoon dry mustard
1 clove garlic

Combine all ingredients in blender; cover and blend well. Chill thoroughly; stir before serving. Yield: 1⅓ cups.

CANTALOUPE COMPOTE

½ cup sugar
¼ cup water
¼ cup Cointreau
5 cups cantaloupe balls, chilled
   Mint leaves

Combine sugar and water; bring to a boil. Remove from heat, and add Cointreau; chill. Place cantaloupe balls in sherbet glasses; pour Cointreau mixture over fruit. Garnish with mint. Yield: 4 to 6 servings.

Make-Ahead Meal
(Dinner for Six to Eight)

Chile Chicken
Broiled Tomatoes
Tossed Salad   Delicious Avocado Dressing
Coffee Ice Cream Pie
Iced Tea   Coffee

CHILE CHICKEN

  4 chicken breasts, cooked, boned, and
     chopped
 ¼ cup chopped green chiles
 ½ pound Cheddar cheese, shredded
  1 (10¾-ounce) can cream of mushroom
     soup, undiluted
  1 cup milk
 12 corn tortillas
  1 cup crushed potato chips

Combine all ingredients except tortillas and
potato chips. Place 4 tortillas in bottom of a
greased 9-inch square pan. Spread about one-
third of chicken mixture on top. Repeat until
all tortillas are used, ending with chicken mixture; top with crushed potato chips. Bake at 350°
about 30 minutes. Seal securely and freeze. Yield:
6 to 8 servings.
  Note: If frozen, thaw at room temperature
several hours; bake at 350° about 30 minutes
or until bubbly.

BROILED TOMATOES

 12 thick slices tomato
     About ⅓ cup breadcrumbs, divided
     Pinch basil
     Olive oil

Top each tomato slice with about 1½ teaspoons
breadcrumbs and a pinch of basil; drizzle with
oil. Broil until golden brown. Yield: 6 to 8 servings.

DELICIOUS AVOCADO DRESSING

4 avocados, peeled and chopped
2 tablespoons lemon juice
   Salt and pepper to taste
3 cloves garlic
½ to ⅔ cup commercial Italian dressing

Combine all ingredients in blender; cover and blend well. Chill thoroughly before serving. Yield: about 2 cups.

COFFEE ICE CREAM PIE

1 quart coffee-flavored ice cream, softened
1 (9-inch) graham cracker crust
1 (16.5-ounce) can ready-to-spread fudge frosting
½ cup pecan halves

Spread ice cream in crust, and freeze until firm. Spread frosting over ice cream, and garnish with pecan halves. Freeze until firm. Thaw slightly to serve. Yield: one 9-inch pie.

Fresh meat, poultry, and fish should be loosely wrapped and refrigerated; use in a few days. Loosely wrap fresh ground meat, liver, and kidneys; use in one or two days. Wieners, bacon, and sliced sandwich meats can be stored in original wrapping in refrigerator. Store all meat in the coldest part of the refrigerator.

Use the water-displacement method for measuring shortening if the water that clings to the shortening will not affect the product. Do not use this method for measuring shortening for frying. To measure ¼ cup shortening using this method, put ¾ cup water in a measuring cup; add shortening until the water reaches the 1-cup level. Be sure that the shortening is completely covered with water. Drain off the water before using shortening.

Cold Weather Special
(Supper for Eight)

Easy Chili or
Beef Ragout
Mexican Salad Bowl
Buttermilk Cornbread
Caramel Cookies
Tea

EASY CHILI

2 pounds ground beef
2 to 3 (15½-ounce) cans kidney beans,
    drained
1 (32-ounce) can tomato juice
1 (1⅜-ounce) package dry onion soup mix
3 tablespoons chili powder
2 cloves garlic, minced
    Salt and pepper to taste

Cook beef until lightly browned; drain. Combine all ingredients in an electric slow cooker. Cover and cook on low setting 10 to 12 hours or on high 5 to 6 hours. Yield: 8 servings.

BEEF RAGOUT

3 pounds lean stew meat, cut into 1-inch
    cubes
3 teaspoons salt, divided
½ teaspoon pepper
¼ cup melted shortening
1 onion, chopped
2 stalks celery, chopped
2 cloves garlic, minced
2 cups water, divided
¾ cup all-purpose flour
1 cup red wine
1 cup canned or fresh chopped tomatoes
2 bay leaves
1 tablespoon chopped parsley
¼ teaspoon ground thyme
12 small onions
6 carrots, halved
12 small potatoes

Sprinkle meat with 2 teaspoons salt and the pepper; brown on all sides in shortening in a skillet. Add chopped onion, celery, and garlic; cook until onion is lightly browned.

Gradually add 1 cup water to flour, stirring until well blended and smooth. Add to meat mixture, stirring constantly until smooth. Spoon mixture into a 4½-quart electric slow cooker.

Stir in 1 teaspoon salt, 1 cup water, and remaining ingredients. Cover and cook on high setting 5 to 6 hours or on low setting 10 to 12 hours. Yield: 8 to 10 servings.

MEXICAN SALAD BOWL

    4 cups torn salad greens
    2 medium tomatoes, cut into wedges
    ¼ cup chopped green onion
    ¼ cup sliced pitted ripe olives
    ¼ cup shredded Cheddar cheese
    1 cup coarsely crushed corn chips
       (optional)
    Avocado Salad Dressing

Combine salad greens, tomatoes, green onion, olives, and cheese in a large salad bowl. Toss lightly, and sprinkle with corn chips, if desired. Serve with Avocado Salad Dressing. Yield: 8 servings.

Avocado Salad Dressing:

    1 large ripe avocado, peeled and cubed
    ½ cup commercial sour cream
    ⅓ cup salad oil
    2 tablespoons lemon juice
    1 teaspoon seasoned salt
    ½ teaspoon chili powder
    ½ teaspoon sugar

Combine all ingredients in blender; process until smooth. Cover and refrigerate until chilled. Yield: about 1½ cups.

BUTTERMILK CORNBREAD

    1 cup cornmeal
    ⅓ cup all-purpose flour
    ¼ teaspoon soda
    1 teaspoon baking powder
    1 teaspoon salt
    1 egg, beaten
    1 cup buttermilk

Combine dry ingredients; add egg and buttermilk, mixing well. Pour into a greased 8- or 9-inch iron skillet. Bake at 400° for 20 minutes or until lightly browned. Yield: 8 servings.

CARAMEL COOKIES

    ½ cup melted margarine
    ½ cup melted butter
    1 cup firmly packed brown sugar
    1 cup chopped pecans
    18 (5-inch-long) graham crackers, halved

Combine margarine, butter, sugar, and pecans in a saucepan. Bring to a rolling boil over low heat; boil 3 minutes, stirring constantly.

Place graham crackers in a 15- x 10- x 1-inch pan; spoon butter mixture over crackers. Bake at 350° for 10 to 12 minutes. Cut into squares. Yield: 3 dozen cookies.

Quick Gourmet Fare

(Dinner for Four to Six)

Oysters on the Half Shell
Chicken Livers Burgundy
Rice
Celery Amandine
Red Apple Salad
Quick Rolls
Incredible Coconut Pie
Wine   Coffee

OYSTERS ON THE HALF SHELL

Allow 3 to 4 oysters per person. Shuck oysters (or allow each person to shuck his own). Arrange half-shell oysters on a bed of crushed ice. Place a bowl of Cocktail Sauce in the center. Garnish with lemon wedges and parsley.

Cocktail Sauce:

1 cup catsup
1 tablespoon grated horseradish
1 tablespoon grated onion
  Few drops of hot sauce
2 tablespoons vinegar
1 tablespoon minced celery
½ teaspoon salt
1 teaspoon Worcestershire sauce

Blend all ingredients. Pour into a jar, cover, and chill. Yield: 1¼ cups.

CHICKEN LIVERS BURGUNDY

2 (16-ounce) packages chicken livers
¼ cup melted butter
2 (15½-ounce) jars meatless spaghetti
    sauce with mushrooms
⅓ cup red wine
  Hot cooked rice

Sauté livers in butter until tender. Combine spaghetti sauce and wine; heat well, and pour over livers. Simmer about 5 minutes. Serve over rice. Yield: 4 to 6 servings.

CELERY AMANDINE

4 cups diagonally sliced celery
½ cup melted butter or margarine,
    divided
    Salt and pepper to taste
2 tablespoons finely chopped chives
2 tablespoons grated onion
1 clove garlic, crushed
2 tablespoons dry white wine
½ to 1 cup slivered almonds

Sauté celery in ¼ cup butter, stirring occasionally; add salt, pepper, chives, onion, garlic, and wine. Cover and cook over low heat about 10 minutes or until celery is tender.

Sauté almonds in remaining butter; add to celery, and cook 1 additional minute. Yield: 4 to 6 servings.

RED APPLE SALAD

1½ cups sugar
¼ teaspoon salt
½ cup red cinnamon candies
3 cups water
4 to 6 small firm tart apples, peeled and
    cored
1 (3-ounce) package cream cheese,
    softened, or ½ cup cottage cheese
¼ cup chopped green pepper or celery
    Lettuce

Combine sugar, salt, candies, and water; heat until candies are dissolved. Add apples; cover and cook slowly over low heat 15 to 20 minutes or until tender, turning occasionally to color evenly. Drain and chill.

Combine cream cheese and pepper; spoon into apples. Serve on lettuce. Yield: 4 to 6 servings.

QUICK ROLLS

2 cups self-rising flour
¼ cup mayonnaise
1 cup milk
1 teaspoon sugar

Combine all ingredients, mixing well. Spoon into lightly greased 2-inch muffin pans; bake at 450° for 10 minutes or until golden brown. Yield: 1 dozen rolls.

INCREDIBLE COCONUT PIE

½ cup self-rising flour
1⅓ cups sugar
4 eggs, beaten
2 cups milk
¼ cup melted margarine
1 teaspoon vanilla extract
1 (7-ounce) can flaked coconut

Combine flour and sugar. Add eggs, milk, margarine, and vanilla; mix well, and stir in coconut. Pour into a deep dish 9-inch pieplate. Bake at 375° for 30 to 35 minutes. Yield: one 9-inch pie.

Make It a Gourmet Occasion

(Dinner for Four)

Lemon Soup
Chinese Pepper Steak
Savory Fresh Mushrooms
Tossed Salad   Mill Salad Dressing
Commercial Crusty Rolls   Butter
Cherries Jubilee
Wine   Coffee

LEMON SOUP

1 (10½-ounce) can chicken with rice
    soup, undiluted
1⅓ cups water
1 egg, beaten
2 teaspoons lemon juice
    Butter or margarine
    Ground nutmeg

Combine soup and water in a saucepan, blending well; heat thoroughly. Combine egg and lemon juice; blend well. Add a little hot soup to egg mixture, stirring constantly. Remove soup from heat; slowly stir in egg mixture.

    Spoon into soup bowls immediately; add a small amount of butter to each serving, and sprinkle with nutmeg. Yield: 2½ cups.

CHINESE PEPPER STEAK

1 (1½-pound) round steak, cut into thin
    strips
2 tablespoons salad oil
    Salt to taste
1 green pepper, cut into strips
1 onion, chopped
1 tablespoon soy sauce
1 tablespoon sherry
⅛ teaspoon garlic powder
¼ teaspoon ground ginger
2 tablespoons cornstarch
3 tablespoons water
1 tomato, cut into wedges
    Hot cooked rice

Quickly brown meat in hot oil; add salt, green pepper, onion, soy sauce, sherry, garlic powder, and ginger. Cover and cook over low heat 10 minutes.

Combine cornstarch and water; stir until cornstarch is dissolved. Add to meat mixture; cook, stirring constantly, over low heat until slightly thickened.

Add tomato; cover and simmer about 10 minutes. Additional water may be added, if needed. Serve over rice. Yield: 4 servings.

SAVORY FRESH MUSHROOMS

1 pound fresh mushrooms, sliced
2 tablespoons sherry
2 tablespoons butter or margarine
¼ teaspoon paprika
1 teaspoon seasoned salt
⅛ teaspoon pepper
¼ cup chopped parsley

Combine all ingredients except parsley in a skillet. Cover and cook over medium heat 10 minutes, stirring occasionally. Sprinkle with parsley before serving. Yield: 4 to 6 servings.

MILL SALAD DRESSING

1 cup vinegar
¾ cup sugar
¼ cup prepared mustard
½ cup salad oil
½ cup water
½ teaspoon salt
½ teaspoon garlic juice
Juice of ½ lemon

Combine all ingredients in blender; cover and blend well. Yield: about 3 cups.

CHERRIES JUBILEE

1 (16-ounce) can dark pitted cherries
½ cup sugar
Dash of salt
1 tablespoon cornstarch
2 to 4 tablespoons brandy
Vanilla ice cream

Drain cherries; reserve juice, and set cherries aside. Add enough water to juice to make 1 cup liquid.

Combine juice, sugar, salt, and cornstarch in a saucepan; cook over medium heat, blending until smooth. Add cherries; cook, stirring constantly, until slightly thickened. Heat brandy over medium heat. Do not boil. Ignite and pour over sauce. Spoon over ice cream. Yield: 4 to 6 servings.

Use baking soda on a damp cloth to shine up your kitchen appliances.

Do not wash eggs before storing; washing removes the coating that prevents the entrance of bacteria. Wash just before using, if desired.

After-the-Theatre Dinner

(Dinner for Six)

Shrimp Newburg
Orange-Glazed Carrots
Fresh Asparagus Spears
Sherry Wine Cake
Wine   Coffee

SHRIMP NEWBURG

  6 frozen patty shells
  1 (10¾-ounce) can cream of shrimp soup,
     undiluted
¼ cup milk
  1 cup shrimp, peeled and deveined
  1 (8-ounce) can green peas, drained
  2 tablespoons cooking sherry
  2 ounces shredded sharp Cheddar cheese,
     divided

Bake patty shells according to package directions. Heat soup and milk in a saucepan; stir in shrimp and peas. Continue to heat to simmering, stirring constantly. Cook slowly about 5 minutes. Stir in cooking sherry and half of the cheese.

Sprinkle remaining cheese in baked patty shells; fill shells with shrimp mixture. Yield: 6 servings.

ORANGE-GLAZED CARROTS

¼ cup melted butter or margarine
  1 teaspoon sugar
  1 cup orange juice
  1 pound carrots, peeled and sliced

Combine all ingredients in a saucepan. Cover and simmer 15 to 20 minutes or until carrots are tender. Uncover and cook until liquid is absorbed. Yield: 6 servings.

FRESH ASPARAGUS SPEARS
(see Index)

SHERRY WINE CAKE

  1 (18½-ounce) package yellow cake mix
  1 (3¾-ounce) package vanilla instant
     pudding and pie filling
  4 eggs
½ cup salad oil
  1 teaspoon ground nutmeg
¾ cup cream sherry
   Powdered sugar

Combine all ingredients except powdered sugar in a large mixing bowl. Beat 2 to 4 minutes at medium speed of electric mixer.

Spoon batter into a lightly greased and floured 10-inch Bundt pan. Bake at 350° for 35 to 40 minutes. Allow cake to cool in pan for 30 minutes before turning out. Sprinkle with powdered sugar. Yield: one 10-inch cake.

Sensational Sandwich Supper

(Supper for Four or Five)

Avocado-Bacon Dip   Chips
Saucy Franks or Beany Beefburgers
Cottage Cheese Coleslaw
Peanut Butter Sauce   Ice Cream
Soft Drinks   Beer

AVOCADO-BACON DIP

2 ripe avocados, peeled and chopped
1 tablespoon grated onion
1 cup chopped celery
¾ teaspoon seasoned salt
1 tablespoon lemon juice
  Dash of hot sauce
  Dash of Worcestershire sauce
1 tablespoon bacon bits
  Chips

Beat avocado with an electric mixer until smooth; add remaining ingredients, mixing well. Serve with chips. Yield: about 2 cups.

SAUCY FRANKS

1 pound frankfurters
2 tablespoons melted butter or margarine
1 (10¾-ounce) can condensed tomato soup, undiluted
¼ cup firmly packed brown sugar
¼ cup water
3 tablespoons vinegar
1 tablespoon Worcestershire sauce
1 tablespoon lemon juice
1 small onion, thinly sliced
¼ cup chopped green pepper
  Frankfurter buns

Score frankfurters in corkscrew fashion; lightly brown in butter. Stir in next 7 ingredients. Cover and simmer about 10 minutes. Add green pepper; cover and simmer 5 minutes. Serve in buns. Yield: 4 to 5 servings.

BEANY BEEFBURGERS

2 pounds ground beef
2 teaspoons salt
¼ teaspoon pepper
½ cup catsup
1 teaspoon chili powder
1 (16-ounce) can red beans or pinto
    beans, drained
2 tablespoons finely chopped onion
2 tablespoons finely chopped green
    pepper
6 hamburger buns, split

Combine ground beef, salt, and pepper; shape into 6 patties ½ inch thick. Place in a small skillet, and cook on both sides until done; remove from heat, and set aside.

Combine catsup, chili powder, beans, onion, and green pepper in a small saucepan; simmer 5 to 10 minutes, stirring occasionally. Remove from heat.

Place a beef patty on bottom half of each hamburger bun; top each patty with 3 to 4 table-spoons hot bean sauce. Cover with bun tops. Yield: 6 servings.

COTTAGE CHEESE COLESLAW

½ medium head cabbage, shredded
¼ to ½ cup mayonnaise
½ medium onion, chopped
 1 cup small-curd cottage cheese
¼ teaspoon salt
⅛ teaspoon pepper

Combine all ingredients, stirring well. Refrigerate until ready to serve. Yield: 4 to 5 servings.

PEANUT BUTTER SAUCE

1½ cups light corn syrup
⅛ teaspoon salt
⅔ cup crunchy-style peanut butter
 1 egg white, stiffly beaten
    Ice cream

Combine corn syrup and salt in a small saucepan; bring to a boil. Remove from heat; add peanut butter, stirring until melted. Pour syrup in a fine stream over beaten egg white, beating constantly. Serve warm or cold over ice cream. Yield: 2½ cups.

Freshen wilted vegetables by letting them stand about 10 minutes in cold water to which a few drops of lemon juice have been added; drain well, and store in a plastic bag in the refrigerator.

Packaged meat should be rewrapped before freezing. Remove the plastic wrap and tray from meat; rewrap with freezer paper or heavy-duty aluminum foil. Seal the package securely; label and freeze at once. To ensure easy separation of individual servings of frozen meat, separate the pieces of meat with two pieces of freezer paper before overwrapping.

Jiffy Fish Bake

(Dinner for Four)

Gourmet Fish Fillets
Fresh Broccoli with Hollandaise
Bloody Mary Salad
Lazy Man's Hush Puppies
Quick Apple Dessert
Iced Tea

GOURMET FISH FILLETS

1 (1½-pound) package frozen turbot or
    flounder, thawed
1 teaspoon melted margarine
½ cup mayonnaise
¼ cup Dijon-style mustard
2 tablespoons frozen chives

Place fish in baking dish. Combine remaining
ingredients; spoon over fish. Bake at 350° about
15 minutes or until fish flakes easily when tested
with a fork. Yield: 4 servings.

FRESH BROCCOLI WITH HOLLANDAISE

1 bunch broccoli
5 egg yolks
    Juice of 1 lemon
    Dash of hot sauce
    Salt to taste
½ cup melted butter

Trim off large leaves of broccoli. Remove tough
ends of lower stalks, and wash broccoli

thoroughly. If stalks are more than 1 inch in
diameter, make lengthwise slits in stalks. Cook
broccoli, covered, in a small amount of boiling
salted water for 12 to 15 minutes or until crisp-
tender.

Combine egg yolks, lemon juice, hot sauce,
and salt in blender; process on high speed until
well blended. Gradually add melted butter and
continue to blend. Drain broccoli. Serve with
sauce. Yield: 4 servings.

BLOODY MARY SALAD

1 envelope (1 tablespoon) unflavored
    gelatin
½ cup water
1 cup Bloody Mary cocktail mix
¼ cup chopped onion
¼ cup chopped celery

Sprinkle gelatin in water; heat slowly until gelatin
is dissolved. Stir in cocktail mix; chill until consistency of unbeaten egg white. Stir in onion and
celery; pour into a 2-cup mold or 4 individual
molds. Chill until firm. Yield: 4 servings.

LAZY MAN'S HUSH PUPPIES

1 (6-ounce) package cornbread mix
1 (0.8-ounce) package instant grits
½ teaspoon salt
1 tablespoon sugar
   Onion flakes to taste
¼ cup milk or water
1 egg
   Hot salad oil

Combine cornbread mix, grits, salt, sugar, and onion flakes. Stir in milk and egg, mixing until well blended.

Shape batter into walnut-size balls; drop into hot oil. Fry until golden brown, turning once. Drain on absorbent paper. Serve hot. Yield: 1½ dozen hush puppies.

To combine egg yolks with a hot mixture and have a smooth product, follow this procedure: Beat the egg yolks; then add a small amount of the hot liquid to the yolks, beating briskly. When enough of the hot liquid has been added to raise the temperature of the yolks, add to the hot mixture and continue stirring and cooking until mixture is of consistency desired. The mixture will curdle if beaten yolks are added directly to the hot mixture.

QUICK APPLE DESSERT

3 cups sliced apples
1 (3-ounce) package raspberry or
   strawberry-flavored gelatin
1 cup all-purpose flour
1 cup sugar
½ cup butter or margarine, softened

Place apples in a buttered 10- x 6- x 1¾-inch baking dish. Sprinkle gelatin over apples. Combine flour and sugar in a small bowl; cut in butter until mixture is crumbly. Sprinkle over apples. Bake at 350° for 30 minutes. Yield: 4 to 6 servings.

To test cake for doneness, touch lightly in center. Cake will spring back if it has baked long enough. It should also pull away from sides of pan.

Make It in a Microwave
(Dinner for Six)

Chipper Fillets
Broccoli and Carrots au Gratin
Tossed Green Salad   Roquefort Salad Dressing
Fudge Pie

CHIPPER FILLETS

2 pounds frozen fish fillets, thawed
½ cup commercial Caesar salad dressing
1 cup crushed potato chips
½ cup shredded Cheddar cheese

Cut fillets into 6 portions. Dip into salad dressing. Place in a single layer in a 13- x 9- x 2-inch glass baking dish, placing thicker parts of fillets toward the outside of the dish.

Combine potato chips and cheese. Sprinkle over fillets. Place in microwave oven and cook 4 to 5 minutes; give dish a half turn. Cook 4 to 5 additional minutes or until fish flakes easily. Yield: 6 servings.

BROCCOLI AND CARROTS AU GRATIN

1 (10-ounce) package frozen chopped broccoli, partially thawed
1 (10-ounce) package frozen carrots with brown sugar glaze, partially thawed
½ cup non-dairy coffee creamer
3 tablespoons all-purpose flour
¼ cup grated Parmesan cheese
½ teaspoon salt
Dash of pepper
1 chicken bouillon cube
¾ cup boiling water

Combine broccoli and carrots; spoon into a 1½-quart glass baking dish. Combine coffee creamer, flour, cheese, salt, and pepper; sprinkle over vegetables. Dissolve bouillon cube in boiling water; pour over vegetables. Place in microwave oven; cover and cook 4 minutes; stir through mixture. Cook 4 additional minutes. Stir mixture. Cover and let stand 5 minutes. Yield: 6 servings.

ROQUEFORT SALAD DRESSING

8 ounces Roquefort or blue cheese
2 cups mayonnaise
1 cup buttermilk
1 small onion, grated
1 teaspoon Worcestershire sauce
1 clove garlic, finely chopped

Combine all ingredients, mixing until well blended. Refrigerate several hours before using. Yield: about 1 quart.

FUDGE PIE

½ cup butter or margarine
1 cup sugar
2 eggs
½ cup all-purpose flour
1 square (1 ounce) unsweetened chocolate
1 teaspoon vanilla extract
½ cup chopped pecans
Vanilla ice cream (optional)

Put butter in a glass mixing bowl. Place in microwave oven and cook 30 to 45 seconds or until melted. Add sugar to melted butter; beat well. Add eggs; beat well. Stir in flour.

Put chocolate in a glass bowl. Place in microwave oven and cook 2 to 3 minutes or until melted; stir into sugar mixture. Stir in vanilla and pecans. Pour into a 9-inch pieplate. Cook in microwave 6 minutes. Top with vanilla ice cream, if desired. Yield: one 9-inch pie.

Buy quantities you can store and use. Large quantities are usually bargains, but they may not be bargains for small families if they spoil before being used or if leftovers have to be thrown out. Staples (flour, sugar, etc.) generally cost less per pound if purchased in large quantities.

This is a handy method for freezing casseroles: Line a casserole dish with heavy-duty aluminum foil, put the food in it, seal, and freeze. When the casserole is frozen, lift out the package, and mold foil to surface of food; seal securely with freezer tape, label, and return to the freezer.

HOLIDAY DINNERS

Welcome in the New Year

A Feast for the Holidays

An Easter Tradition

Celebrate the Fourth Outdoors

Turkey with All the Trimmings

For a Festive Thanksgiving

Christmas Dinner for a Crowd

Ring in the New Year! Happy Easter! Merry Christmas! On these very special holidays when the whole family gets together, very special menus are in order, for it is dinners such as these that start traditions. So that you can spend more time with your loved ones on these festive occasions, we've planned complete holiday menus for you. We have included all the traditional classics such as ham and turkey, as well as some new ideas. Whatever you choose to serve, let it begin a tradition, for traditions make lasting memories.

Welcome in the New Year
(Dinner for Eight to Ten)

Pork Loin Roast
Candied Sweet Potatoes
Hopping John or Delicious Black-Eyed Peas
Turnip Greens
Congealed Ambrosia Salad
Southern Cornbread
Chocolate Chess Pie
Tea   Coffee

PORK LOIN ROAST

4- to 6-pound pork loin roast
  Salt
  Pepper
  Parsley
  Canned mandarin orange sections,
    drained

Have the butcher saw across the rib bones at base of the backbone, separating ribs from backbone. Place roast, fat side up, on a rack in an open roasting pan. Season with salt and pepper.

Insert meat thermometer so the bulb is centered in the thickest part. Be sure that the bulb does not rest on bone or in fat; do not add water and do not cover.

Roast at 325° until meat thermometer registers 170°. Allow 30 to 40 minutes per pound for roasting; total roasting time should be 2¾ to 3½ hours. Slice, and serve hot. Garnish with parsley and mandarin orange sections. Yield: 8 to 10 servings.

CANDIED SWEET POTATOES

8 medium or 6 large sweet potatoes
1 cup melted butter or margarine
2 cups sugar
½ cup water

Peel potatoes, and cut into 2-inch slices. Combine butter, sugar, and water in an electric skillet; add sweet potatoes. Cover and simmer at 250° for 1 hour or until done, turning frequently. Yield: 8 to 10 servings.

HOPPING JOHN

2 cups dried black-eyed peas
½ pound salt pork, diced
2 medium-size green peppers, chopped
2 medium onions, chopped
2 cups uncooked regular rice
2 tablespoons butter or margarine
  Pinch of cayenne pepper
  Salt and pepper to taste

Pick over peas; wash thoroughly. Place in a heavy saucepan; cover with water. Soak overnight; drain. Return peas to saucepan; add salt pork, green pepper, and onion. Cover with water and simmer 2 hours or until peas are tender.

Cook rice according to package directions. When peas are done and water has cooked very low, add remaining ingredients. Cover and cook over low heat until all liquid is absorbed. Serve hot. Yield: 8 to 10 servings.

DELICIOUS BLACK-EYED PEAS

1 pound dried black-eyed peas
1 tablespoon salt
1 clove garlic, cut in half
½ cup bacon drippings or salad oil
3 cloves garlic, crushed
3 medium-size green peppers, chopped
3 medium onions, chopped
2 bay leaves, pulverized
3 tablespoons vinegar
1 teaspoon salt
Black pepper to taste

Pick over peas; wash thoroughly. Place in a heavy saucepan and cover with water; soak overnight.

Drain peas, and return to saucepan; cover with fresh boiling water. Add 1 tablespoon salt and garlic halves; cover and simmer 3 hours, adding boiling water as needed.

Just before serving, heat bacon drippings in skillet; add crushed garlic, green pepper, onion, and bay leaves. Cook until vegetables are soft. Stir in vinegar, 1 teaspoon salt, and black pepper. Spoon into cooked peas; mix well. Yield: 8 to 10 servings.

TURNIP GREENS

1 large bunch turnip greens (about 2 to 2½ pounds)
Salt
¼ pound salt pork, diced
½ cup boiling salted water
Vinegar or pepper sauce

Check leaves of greens carefully; remove pulpy stems and discolored spots on leaves. Wash thoroughly in several changes of warm water; add a little salt to the last rinse. Put greens in colander to drain.

Cook salt pork, covered, about 10 minutes in ½ cup boiling salted water. Add greens, a few at a time; cover and cook slowly until greens are tender. Do not overcook. Serve with vinegar. Yield: 8 to 10 servings.

Note: An alternate method is to wash greens carefully and put them into a large cooker with only the water that clings to leaves. Add salt and bacon drippings after the greens have cooked tender.

CONGEALED AMBROSIA SALAD

1 (3-ounce) package orange-flavored gelatin
½ cup sugar
1 cup boiling water
3 oranges, peeled and cut into 1-inch pieces
1 (8¼-ounce) can crushed pineapple, undrained
1 cup flaked coconut
1 cup chopped pecans
1 (8-ounce) carton commercial sour cream

Dissolve gelatin and sugar in boiling water; chill until mixture starts to thicken. Fold in remaining ingredients, and blend well. Pour into a 13- x 9- x 2-inch pan; chill until firm. Yield: 10 to 12 servings.

SOUTHERN CORNBREAD

2 cups cornmeal
1 teaspoon soda
1 teaspoon salt
2 eggs, beaten
2 cups buttermilk
¼ cup bacon drippings

Combine cornmeal, soda, and salt; stir in eggs and buttermilk. Heat bacon drippings in an iron skillet until very hot; add drippings to batter, mixing well.

Pour batter into hot skillet, and bake at 450° about 25 minutes or until bread is golden brown. Yield: 8 to 10 servings.

CHOCOLATE CHESS PIE

1¾ cups sugar
⅓ cup cocoa
1¼ cups melted margarine
4 eggs, beaten
¼ cup evaporated milk
1 teaspoon vanilla extract
2 unbaked 9-inch pastry shells
Whipped cream or ice cream (optional)

Combine sugar, cocoa, and margarine, mixing well. Add eggs, milk, and vanilla; mix thoroughly. Pour into pastry shells, and bake at 350° for 35 to 40 minutes. Serve with whipped cream, if desired. Yield: two 9-inch pies.

When buying meats, consider the cost per serving rather than the cost per pound. Don't ignore the cheaper or less-tender cuts of meat; learn to serve them. Think twice about bypassing boneless meat because of its higher price. Even though a boneless roast is more expensive per pound than a bone-in roast, it has no excess fat and no bones, thus yielding more servings.

Packaged meat should always be rewrapped before it's put in the freezer. Remove the plastic or cardboard tray from meat; rewrap with heavy-duty aluminum foil or freezer wrapping paper, or put in a heavy plastic bag. Seal the package securely; label and freeze at once.

A Feast for the Holidays

(Dinner for Twelve)

Wassail Cup
Oysters Rockefeller
Maryland Stuffed Ham or Tennessee Spiced Round
Holiday Potatoes and Peas   Glazed Acorn Rings
Perfection Salad
Watermelon Rind Pickles   Squash Pickles
Light and Tender Rolls
Honey-Glaze Pecan Cake
Lemon-Vanilla White Fruitcake
Wine   Coffee

WASSAIL CUP

1½ cups sugar
2 cups water
6 whole cloves
1 stick cinnamon
½ to 1 teaspoon whole allspice
1 tablespoon chopped preserved ginger
1 tablespoon grated lemon rind
1 tablespoon grated orange rind
2 cups unsweetened apple cider
1½ cups orange juice
¾ cup lemon juice
Bourbon to taste (optional)

Combine sugar and water; boil 5 minutes. Tie spices, lemon rind, and orange rind in a cheesecloth bag; add to hot mixture. Cover and let stand 2 hours; remove spice bag.

Stir in apple cider, orange juice, and lemon juice; bring to a boil. Remove from heat; add bourbon, if desired. Serve hot. Yield: 7½ cups.

OYSTERS ROCKEFELLER

Rock salt
¼ pound chopped bacon
¼ cup melted butter
½ cup all-purpose flour
½ cup finely chopped green onions
2 cloves garlic, minced
2 cups finely chopped cooked spinach, undrained
½ cup finely chopped parsley
⅛ teaspoon cayenne pepper
½ cup oyster liquid
Salt to taste
¼ cup Pernod
3 dozen oysters on the half shell, drained

Put a ½-inch layer of rock salt in 6 piepans; place in a 375° oven for 10 minutes to preheat salt.

Cook bacon until browned; drain. Add butter and flour to bacon; cook, stirring constantly, until golden brown. Add onion, garlic, spinach, parsley, cayenne, oyster liquid, and salt; simmer 20 minutes. Add Pernod, mixing well.

Arrange 6 oyster shells on salt in each piepan; place an oyster in each shell, and top with sauce. Place under broiler about 6 inches from source of heat until thoroughly heated or lightly browned. Garnish as desired. Yield: 12 appetizer servings.

MARYLAND STUFFED HAM

1 (12- to 14-pound) country-cured ham
2 pounds kale, finely chopped
2 pounds cabbage, finely chopped
2 pounds watercress or field cress, finely chopped (cabbage, kale, or spinach may be substituted)
1 bunch celery, finely chopped
1 bunch green onions, finely chopped
4 medium onions, finely chopped
2 tablespoons chopped parsley
1 tablespoon monosodium glutamate
3 tablespoons salt
1 tablespoon cracked peppercorns
1 tablespoon ground red pepper
1 tablespoon mustard seeds
2 tablespoons celery seeds
1 teaspoon sage
1 teaspoon thyme
2 tablespoons dry mustard
½ to 1 teaspoon hot sauce
½ to 1 cup white wine or reserved ham liquor
 Parsley
 Canned spiced peaches

Choose a lean ham with a short hock. Parboil ham for 20 minutes in water to cover. Remove skin while ham is warm; trim off excess fat, and return ham to cooking water until cool. When ham is cool, remove from pot liquor, reserving liquor; pat ham dry.

Starting at butt end of ham, make a row of 3 lengthwise slits, 2 inches long, all the way through to the bone. Make a second row of slits about 1 inch from the first row, making sure slits in second row are not parallel with slits in the first row.

Repeat rows over entire top of ham, making sure slits do not cut into other slits; there should be a total of 10 to 12 slits.

Combine kale, cabbage, watercress, celery, onions, and parsley; blanch by pouring lightly salted boiling water over vegetables; rinse immediately in cold water, and drain well. Combine seasonings, and add to chopped vegetables; mix well. Add enough wine or ham liquor to moisten stuffing.

Using fingers, pack stuffing mixture tightly into slits in ham; place any excess stuffing on top of ham.

Wrap ham securely in an old pillow case, doubled cheesecloth, or linen; fasten by sewing or pinning. Place wrapped ham back in reserved liquor in which it was parboiled, adding more water if necessary to cover ham.

Bring water to a boil; reduce heat and simmer 20 minutes per pound, adding more boiling water as needed to keep ham completely immersed. Ham is done when the hock bone is loose or when an internal temperature of 160° is reached.

Remove pot from heat, and allow ham to cool in pot liquor, about 2 hours. Remove ham from liquor, and place on a wire rack to drain. After draining well, refrigerate ham at least 12 hours.

To serve, remove cloth and place excess stuffing in a serving bowl (it is served cold). Place ham on a platter and garnish with parsley and canned spiced peaches. Ham should be sliced very thin, about ⅛ inch thick, and diagonally, so as to include some stuffing in each slice.

Maryland Stuffed Ham is always served cold, never hot. Yield: 20 to 30 servings.

TENNESSEE SPICED ROUND

1 (10- to 12-pound) round of beef, 3 to 4
    inches thick
1 tablespoon ground cinnamon
1 tablespoon ground cloves
2 tablespoons ground allspice
2 tablespoons black pepper
    Strips of pork fat or slab bacon
    (about 2 pounds)
1 cup firmly packed brown sugar
1 ounce saltpeter (available at most
    drugstores)
2 gallons water
6 cups sugar
1 tablespoon ground allspice
1 tablespoon ground cinnamon
1 tablespoon ground cloves
    Cold water
1 cup sugar
    Canned spiced apple rings

With a stick or steel (used for sharpening knives), make dime-size vertical holes about 1 inch apart all the way through the beef round. Combine 1 tablespoon cinnamon, 1 tablespoon cloves, 2 tablespoons allspice, and pepper; roll pork fat strips in spice mixture, and push strips into holes in beef.

Combine brown sugar and saltpeter; rub into beef round. If necessary, tie beef with string or fasten with small skewers. Wrap beef in cheesecloth to hold fat in place.

Combine 2 gallons water, 6 cups sugar, 1 tablespoon allspice, 1 tablespoon cinnamon, and 1 tablespoon cloves to make a brine. Bring brine to a boil; then cool completely.

Place beef in brine and let stand for 3 to 4 weeks in refrigerator or other cool place; do not allow to freeze.

To cook spiced round, remove from brine, and soak 1 hour in enough cold water to cover beef; drain and rinse. Place beef in a large container, and cover with water again; add 1 cup

sugar, and simmer 15 minutes per pound. Add water as needed to keep meat completely covered. When beef is done, remove from heat and cool in broth; drain meat and refrigerate.

To serve, cut spiced round into 4 pie-shaped wedges; turn wedges sideways and slice in very thin slices across the fat-stuffed holes so that slices are dotted with fat, not striped with long streaks. Garnish with canned spiced apple rings. Yield: 20 to 24 servings.

Note: After spiced round is cooked, it can be kept moist by wrapping tightly in cheesecloth that has been dipped in a solution of 1 part vinegar and 2 parts water; redampen cloth every 4 to 5 days.

HOLIDAY POTATOES AND PEAS

½ cup butter or margarine
½ cup all-purpose flour
 2 teaspoons salt
¼ teaspoon pepper
4½ cups milk
 2 cups shredded sharp Cheddar cheese
 2 (10-ounce) packages frozen green peas
 6 cups sliced cooked potatoes
 1 (4-ounce) jar chopped pimiento
   Buttered breadcrumbs

Melt butter in a saucepan over low heat; blend in flour, salt, and pepper. Gradually stir in milk, and cook until smooth and thickened, about 5 minutes. Remove from heat; add cheese, stirring until smooth.

Cook peas in lightly salted boiling water until tender but still crisp; drain and combine with potatoes and pimiento in a lightly greased 3-quart casserole. Pour cheese sauce over top, and sprinkle with breadcrumbs. Bake at 325° for 50 to 60 minutes. Yield: 12 servings.

GLAZED ACORN RINGS

2 large acorn squash
⅔ cup orange juice
1 cup firmly packed brown sugar
½ cup light corn syrup
½ cup melted butter or margarine
4 teaspoons grated lemon rind
¼ teaspoon salt

Trim ends from squash, and cut into crosswise slices ¾ inch thick. Remove seeds and membrane. Place slices in a large shallow casserole or baking dish; add orange juice. Cover and bake at 350° for 30 minutes.

Combine remaining ingredients in a saucepan, and simmer 5 minutes; pour over squash rings. Bake, uncovered, an additional 15 to 20 minutes, basting occasionally. Yield: 12 servings.

PERFECTION SALAD

2 envelopes (2 tablespoons) unflavored gelatin
¼ cup cold water
1½ cups boiling water
⅓ cup sugar
½ cup cider vinegar
2 teaspoons salt
1 teaspoon curry powder
Dash of cayenne pepper
2 green onions, finely chopped
1½ cups finely shredded cabbage
1¼ cups finely chopped celery
½ cup grated carrot
½ cup chopped green pepper
¼ cup sliced radishes
Mayonnaise

Sprinkle gelatin in cold water; add boiling water, stirring until gelatin dissolves. Add sugar, vinegar, salt, curry, and pepper; chill mixture until slightly thickened.

Stir vegetables into thickened gelatin mixture; pour into an 8-cup mold, and chill until firm. Serve with mayonnaise. Yield: 12 servings.

WATERMELON RIND PICKLES

1 watermelon
1 gallon water
1 cup slaked lime
1 quart vinegar
8 cups sugar
1 teaspoon pickling spices

Select a melon that has a thick rind. Remove outer green skin and pink flesh; use only the greenish-white parts of the rind. Cut rind into 1-inch cubes.

Combine water and lime (slaked lime can be purchased at a hardware store); add cubed rind, and soak overnight in refrigerator in a glass, enamel, or stainless steel bowl.

Drain and rinse cubes in cold water several times. Then cover with cold water, and boil 30 minutes. Drain.

Combine vinegar, sugar, and pickling spices; cover cubes with this mixture. Boil slowly until cubes look clear (about 1 hour or longer), being sure cubes are covered with syrup throughout cooking. Add water if syrup cooks down.

Pack pickles in hot, sterilized jars; cover with syrup, and seal. Process pints for 5 minutes in boiling-water bath. Yield: about 7 pints.

Add an extra measure of elegance to your holiday table by serving one of these meats: Tennessee Spiced Round (page 91), Maryland Stuffed Ham (page 90), or Holiday Roast Goose (page 109).

SQUASH PICKLES

8 cups sliced squash
2 cups sliced onion
1 tablespoon salt (not iodized)
1 cup diced green pepper
2 cups cider vinegar
3½ cups sugar
1 teaspoon celery seeds
1 teaspoon mustard seeds

Combine squash and onion; sprinkle with salt, and let stand 1 hour. Combine green pepper, vinegar, sugar, celery seeds, and mustard seeds; bring to a boil.

Pack squash and onion into hot, sterilized jars; cover with vinegar mixture and seal. Process pints for 5 minutes in boiling-water bath. Yield: about 4 pints.

LIGHT AND TENDER ROLLS

1½ cups scalded milk
2 tablespoons sugar
1½ teaspoons salt
⅓ cup shortening
2 packages dry yeast
⅓ cup very warm water (105° to 115°)
1 egg, well beaten
4½ to 5 cups all-purpose flour
Melted margarine

Combine milk, sugar, salt, and shortening; let stand until lukewarm.

Dissolve yeast in very warm water; add to milk mixture. Stir in egg. Gradually add enough flour to make a soft dough that leaves sides of bowl.

Cover with a towel, and let rise in a warm place until doubled in bulk.

Punch dough down, and turn out on a lightly floured board or pastry cloth; knead lightly. Shape into crescent, Parker House, cloverleaf, fan tan, or pan rolls. Brush with melted margarine. Let rise until doubled in bulk (about 45 minutes). Bake at 425° for 10 to 15 minutes. Yield: about 3 dozen rolls, depending on shape.

Note: To freeze rolls and brown later, bake rolls at 250° about 25 minutes. Do not brown. Cool; then wrap in moistureproof wrapping, and freeze.

To serve, remove from freezer, and let stand about 10 minutes; bake at 425° until brown (5 to 10 minutes).

Old-Fashioned Roast Turkey and all the trimmings are featured at this elegant Thanksgiving table. You'll find this holiday menu on page 103.

HONEY-GLAZE PECAN CAKE

1 tablespoon vinegar
About 1 cup milk
1 cup salad oil
1½ cups sugar
3 eggs
1 teaspoon vanilla extract
2 cups all-purpose flour
1 tablespoon baking powder
½ teaspoon soda
1 teaspoon ground cinnamon
¼ teaspoon ground cloves
½ cup chopped pecans
¼ cup honey
1 tablespoon lemon juice
1 tablespoon water

Combine vinegar and enough milk to make 1 cup liquid (the vinegar will sour the milk). Stir well, and set aside.

Combine salad oil, sugar, eggs, and vanilla; beat 1 minute at medium speed of electric mixer. Combine flour, baking powder, soda, cinnamon, and cloves; add to creamed mixture alternately with sour milk; beat 1 minute. Stir in pecans.

Pour batter into a greased and floured 10-inch Bundt pan. Bake at 350° for 40 minutes. Let stand 10 minutes; remove from pan, and prick holes in cake. Combine honey, lemon juice, and water; drizzle over cake. Yield: one 10-inch cake.

LEMON-VANILLA WHITE FRUITCAKE

1 pound candied cherries, chopped
1 pound candied pineapple, chopped
2 tablespoons lemon extract
2 tablespoons vanilla extract
4 cups chopped pecans or walnuts
2 cups all-purpose flour, divided
1 cup butter or margarine, softened
1 cup sugar
4 eggs
½ teaspoon baking powder

Combine cherries and pineapple; pour lemon and vanilla extract over fruit, and mix well. Cover and let stand overnight at room temperature. Place nuts in separate bowl; add ½ cup flour to fruit and ½ cup to nuts; stir each to coat well.

Cream butter until smooth; add sugar, and continue creaming until mixture is light and fluffy. Add eggs, one at a time, beating well after each addition. Combine 1 cup flour and baking powder; stir into creamed mixture. Combine fruit and nuts; add batter, mixing thoroughly (may require mixing with hands).

Grease three 9- x 5- x 3-inch loaf pans; line with greased brown paper. Spoon batter into pans, and cover with greased brown paper. Bake at 250° for 2 to 2½ hours or until cakes test done. Yield: 3 loaf cakes.

Place fresh cranberries in the refrigerator unwashed; they can be kept in the refrigerator for one to four weeks. Wash before using.

Small amounts of jelly left in jars may be combined, melted, and used to glaze a ham.

An Easter Tradition

(Dinner for Eight to Ten)

Minted Grapefruit
Smoked Ham with Apple Glaze
Raisin Sauce
Sweet Potato Delight
Swiss Asparagus
Roquefort-Stuffed Celery
Creamy Raspberry Salad
Rich Dinner Rolls
Easy Cheesecake
Coffee

MINTED GRAPEFRUIT

   3 (16-ounce) cans grapefruit sections or
      6 cups fresh grapefruit sections,
      drained
½ cup crème de menthe
   Mint sprigs

Combine grapefruit sections and crème de menthe, stirring to coat well. Refrigerate several hours. Spoon into sherbet glasses, and garnish with mint. Yield: 8 to 10 servings.

SMOKED HAM WITH APPLE GLAZE

   1 (8- to 10-pound) uncooked smoked ham
      Whole cloves
   1 cup apple jelly
½ cup firmly packed dark brown sugar
   1 teaspoon dry mustard
¼ teaspoon ground ginger
½ teaspoon ground cloves
¼ cup pineapple juice
      Grapes (optional)
      Watercress (optional)

Place ham, fat side up, on rack in a shallow roasting pan. Score ham in a diamond pattern, making cuts ¼ inch deep in ham fat.

   Insert a meat thermometer into center of thickest part of meat, making sure the point does not rest in fat or on bone. Bake at 325° for 2½ to 3 hours (about 18 to 20 minutes per pound) or until thermometer registers 160°.

Remove ham from oven about 30 minutes before it is done. Stud with whole cloves. Heat apple jelly over medium heat until melted; add brown sugar, spices, and pineapple juice, stirring until well blended. Spoon half of glaze over ham.

Return ham to oven; baste with remaining glaze during last 30 minutes of baking time. Lift ham onto a platter. Garnish with grapes and watercress, if desired. Yield: 16 to 20 servings.

RAISIN SAUCE

⅓ cup raisins
½ cup water
⅓ cup currant jelly
½ teaspoon grated orange peel
½ cup orange juice
2 tablespoons firmly packed brown sugar
1 tablespoon cornstarch
Dash of salt
Dash of ground allspice

Combine raisins, water, jelly, orange peel, and orange juice in saucepan; bring to a boil. Combine remaining ingredients; stir into orange mixture. Cook over medium heat, stirring constantly, until thick and clear. Serve warm over ham. Yield: about 1¾ cups.

SWEET POTATO DELIGHT

4 pounds sweet potatoes, cooked and mashed
½ cup melted butter or margarine
¼ cup bourbon
⅓ cup orange juice
⅓ cup firmly packed brown sugar
¾ teaspoon salt
½ teaspoon apple pie spice
½ to ¾ cup pecan halves

Combine all ingredients except pecans in a large mixing bowl, mixing well. Pour into a greased 2½-quart casserole; arrange nuts around edge of dish. Bake at 350° for 45 minutes. Yield: 8 to 10 servings.

SWISS ASPARAGUS

5 tablespoons melted butter or margarine, divided
½ teaspoon salt
¼ teaspoon paprika
¼ cup all-purpose flour
1 cup milk
1 (10¾-ounce) can cream of mushroom soup, undiluted
1 (8-ounce) package pasteurized process cheese, cubed
2 tablespoons chopped celery
1 tablespoon chopped onion
1 tablespoon chopped pimiento
2 hard-cooked eggs, chopped
3 (14½-ounce) cans chopped asparagus, drained
⅔ cup breadcrumbs or croutons

Combine 4 tablespoons butter, salt, paprika, and flour in a small saucepan; place over low heat, and blend until smooth. Add milk gradually; cook, stirring constantly, until smooth and thickened. Add soup and cheese, stirring until cheese is melted.

Sauté celery and onion in 1 tablespoon butter. Add to soup mixture along with pimiento and egg.

Alternate layers of asparagus and sauce in a lightly greased 2-quart casserole; top with breadcrumbs. Bake at 350° for 30 minutes or until bubbly. Yield: 8 to 10 servings.

ROQUEFORT-STUFFED CELERY

6 stalks celery
¼ cup crumbled Roquefort cheese
1 (3-ounce) package cream cheese, softened
Dash of cayenne pepper
Paprika

Wash celery, and cut into 3-inch pieces. Combine Roquefort cheese, cream cheese, and cayenne pepper; blend well. Spread on celery, and sprinkle with paprika. Yield: about 1½ dozen pieces.

CREAMY RASPBERRY SALAD

    1 envelope (1 tablespoon) unflavored
        gelatin
    ¼ cup cold water
    2 (3-ounce) packages raspberry-flavored
        gelatin
    ¾ cup boiling water
    1 pint raspberry sherbet, softened
    1 (9-ounce) container frozen whipped
        topping, thawed
    1 (10-ounce) package frozen raspberries,
        thawed and drained

Soften unflavored gelatin in cold water. Dissolve raspberry gelatin in boiling water. Add unflavored gelatin to hot liquid, stirring until dissolved. Add sherbet, and stir until melted. Blend in whipped topping and raspberries. Pour mixture into a 6-cup mold; chill until firm. Yield: 8 to 10 servings.

RICH DINNER ROLLS

    1 cup milk
    ¼ cup sugar
    1 teaspoon salt
    ¼ cup margarine
    2 packages dry yeast
    ½ cup very warm water (105° to 115°)
    2 eggs, beaten
        About 5¼ cups all-purpose flour
        Melted butter

Scald milk; stir in sugar, salt, and margarine. Cool to lukewarm.

Soften yeast in very warm water. Add milk mixture, eggs, and 2 cups flour; beat until smooth. Add enough remaining flour to make a soft dough.

Turn dough out on a lightly floured board; knead about 8 to 10 minutes or until smooth and elastic. Place in a greased bowl, turning to grease top. Cover and let rise in a warm place until doubled in bulk (about 30 minutes). Punch down.

Turn dough out on a lightly floured board. Shape into crescent, Parker House, cloverleaf, fan tan, or pan rolls.

Cover; let rise in a warm place until doubled in bulk (about 30 minutes). Brush with melted butter. Bake at 400° about 10 to 15 minutes. Yield: 2½ to 4 dozen rolls, depending on shape.

EASY CHEESECAKE

    3 (8-ounce) packages cream cheese,
        softened
    1 cup plus 3 tablespoons sugar, divided
    4 eggs
    2 teaspoons vanilla extract
        Graham Cracker Crust
    1 (8-ounce) carton commercial sour
        cream
        Fresh strawberries

Combine cream cheese and 1 cup sugar; beat until smooth and creamy. Add eggs and vanilla; blend well.

Pour filling into a 10-inch springform pan lined with Graham Cracker Crust. Bake at 350° for 1 hour or until slightly firm around edges.

Combine sour cream and 3 tablespoons sugar; spread over cheesecake, and bake 10 minutes. Let cool completely. Remove cake from pan; chill. Garnish with strawberries. Yield: 10 to 12 servings.

Graham Cracker Crust:

1½ cups graham cracker crumbs
    ½ cup sugar
    ½ teaspoon ground cinnamon
    ½ cup melted butter or margarine

Combine all ingredients, and press into bottom of a 10-inch springform pan. Yield: one 10-inch crust.

Celebrate the Fourth Outdoors
(Cookout for Six)

Barbecued Chicken Deluxe
Herbed Barbecued Spareribs
Grilled Corn-on-the-Cob
Marinated Tomatoes
Three Bean Salad
Cheese Bread
Fresh Peach Ice Cream or Buttermilk Ice Cream
Minted Lemonade

BARBECUED CHICKEN DELUXE

½ cup dry white wine
½ cup salad oil
1 teaspoon chopped chives
2 tablespoons chopped parsley
3 (2-pound) chickens, cut-up
Tomato Wine Sauce

Combine wine, salad oil, chives, and parsley; marinate chicken at room temperature for 1 hour in this mixture. Turn chicken in the marinade several times. Broil or grill for 30 minutes or until done, turning frequently and basting with Tomato Wine Sauce. Yield: 8 servings.

Tomato Wine Sauce:

1 cup canned tomatoes
1 cup dry white wine
1 cup thinly sliced okra
1½ cups beef bouillon
½ cup finely chopped celery
1 tablespoon lemon juice
¼ teaspoon hot sauce
2 cloves garlic, minced
1 teaspoon salt
1 teaspoon chili powder
¼ cup Worcestershire sauce
½ cup salad oil
1 tablespoon sugar
1 bay leaf, crumbled
½ teaspoon oregano
½ teaspoon basil
½ cup finely chopped onion
Freshly ground black pepper

Combine all ingredients and bring to a boil. Reduce heat and simmer for 45 minutes. Strain or put through blender. Serve with Barbecued Chicken Deluxe. This sauce is also excellent with ham, pork, or lamb. Yield: about 6 cups.

HERBED BARBECUED SPARERIBS

    6 pounds spareribs
      Boiling water
    1 medium onion
10 to 12 cloves
    1 teaspoon rosemary
    1 teaspoon thyme
    1 teaspoon marjoram
    1 teaspoon oregano
    1 cup dry red wine
  1/3 cup catsup
    1 tablespoon soy sauce
  1/4 teaspoon ginger
    2 tablespoons honey
    1 teaspoon minced garlic

Cut ribs into serving-size pieces, and place in a large pot. Cover with boiling water. Peel onion and stud with cloves; add onion and herbs to ribs. Bring to a boil, reduce heat, and simmer until tender (about 50 minutes). Drain; place meat in a shallow baking pan.

Blend remaining ingredients, and pour over meat. Let marinate in refrigerator at least 2 hours. Drain well, reserving marinade.

Grill ribs over hot coals, or bake at 350° for 30 minutes. Baste with marinade frequently during cooking. Yield: 6 servings.

GRILLED CORN-ON-THE-COB

    6 ears fresh corn
      Melted butter
      Salt and pepper

Husk corn right before cooking. Brush with melted butter, and sprinkle with salt and pepper. Wrap each ear tightly in aluminum foil. Roast on grill 10 to 20 minutes, turning frequently. Yield: 6 servings.

MARINATED TOMATOES

    1 (0.7-ounce) package cheese-garlic salad
      dressing mix
    4 to 6 firm, ripe tomatoes
      Lettuce
      Parsley

Prepare salad dressing according to directions on package. Slice tomatoes; place in a deep bowl. Pour dressing over tomatoes, and chill several hours. Place tomatoes on a lettuce-lined platter; garnish with parsley. Yield: 6 servings.

THREE BEAN SALAD

    1 (16-ounce) can cut green beans,
      drained
    1 (16-ounce) can cut yellow wax beans,
      drained
    1 (16 ounce) can red kidney beans,
      drained
  1/4 cup chopped green pepper
    1 medium onion, thinly sliced
  1/2 cup cider vinegar
  1/3 cup salad oil
  1/2 cup sugar
    1 teaspoon salt
    1 teaspoon pepper

Rinse beans well; drain. Combine beans, green pepper, and onion. Combine remaining ingredients; add to bean mixture. Toss well, and chill overnight. Store leftovers in refrigerator. Yield: 10 to 12 servings.

CHEESE BREAD

½ cup milk
1 egg, beaten
1½ cups biscuit mix
2 tablespoons chopped parsley
1 tablespoon minced onion
1 cup shredded Cheddar cheese, divided
¼ cup melted butter or margarine

Combine milk and egg. Add biscuit mix, parsley, onion, and ½ cup cheese; pour into a greased 8- or 9-inch round pan. Sprinkle remaining ½ cup cheese on batter; pour melted butter over top. Bake at 350° for 25 minutes or until golden brown. Yield: 6 servings.

FRESH PEACH ICE CREAM

5 eggs
2½ cups sugar, divided
1 (14-ounce) can sweetened condensed milk
1 (13-ounce) can evaporated milk
1 tablespoon vanilla extract
Milk
2 cups mashed peaches

Beat eggs until frothy; add 2 cups sugar, and beat well. Add condensed milk, evaporated milk, and vanilla; continue to beat until well blended. Pour mixture into a 1-gallon freezer container.

Add milk to fill freezer container 4 inches from top; freeze about 5 minutes or until custard is thick.

Combine peaches and ½ cup sugar; remove dasher, and add peaches to custard. Return dasher, and freeze until firm according to freezer instructions. Let ripen about 1 hour. Yield: 1 gallon.

BUTTERMILK ICE CREAM

2 quarts buttermilk
1 quart whipping cream
2 cups sugar
1½ tablespoons vanilla extract

Combine all ingredients, and pour into freezer can of a 1-gallon hand-turned or electric freezer. Freeze according to manufacturer's directions. Yield: 1 gallon.

MINTED LEMONADE

1½ cups sugar
2½ cups water
1 cup fresh mint leaves
Juice of 2 oranges
Juice of 6 lemons
Grated rind of 1 orange
Orange or lemon slices
Sprigs of mint

Combine sugar and water in a small saucepan; bring to a boil, and boil 5 minutes. Remove from heat, and cool slightly.

Put mint leaves in a small bowl; add sugar syrup, orange juice, lemon juice, and grated orange rind. Cover and let steep 1 hour. Strain into a 1-quart glass container. Cover and refrigerate.

To serve, mix 1 part mint-citrus mixture with 2 parts water. Serve over ice. Garnish with orange slices and mint sprigs. Yield: about 3 quarts.

Turkey with All the Trimmings

(Dinner for Eight)

Oyster Stew
Old-Fashioned Roast Turkey
Southwest Cornbread Dressing
Giblet Gravy
Parsleyed New Potatoes
Green Bean Casserole
Cran-Apple Relish
Apricot Dream Salad
Commercial Crescent Rolls
Relish Tray
Holiday Nut Cake
Wine   Coffee

OYSTER STEW

2 green onions, chopped
2 tablespoons melted butter or margarine
1 pint oysters, undrained
1 quart half-and-half or milk
Salt to taste
Cayenne pepper to taste
Crackers

Sauté onions in butter; add oysters and their liquid and cook over low heat 3 to 4 minutes or until edges of oysters curl. Add milk, salt, and pepper; heat thoroughly. Serve with crackers. Yield: 8 servings.

OLD-FASHIONED ROAST TURKEY

1 (14- to 16-pound) turkey
Melted butter or margarine
1 tablespoon salt
½ teaspoon pepper
2 teaspoons seasoned salt
1 teaspoon poultry seasoning
1 teaspoon garlic powder
½ teaspoon ground ginger
1 teaspoon paprika
¼ teaspoon cayenne pepper
¼ teaspoon basil
1 cup water

Rinse turkey quickly and pat dry; reserve neck and giblets for gravy. Brush turkey with melted butter. Combine seasonings, and rub on skin and in cavity.

Truss and tie securely; place breast side up in roaster, and insert meat thermometer in thickest part of thigh. Add water; cover and bake at 350° about 3 to 4 hours. If turkey is not evenly browned, remove cover for last 30 minutes and lower temperature to 300°.

Turkey is done when meat thermometer registers 185°. The breast meat should feel soft when pressed with the fingers, and drumsticks and thigh joints should move easily.

Lift turkey onto a platter. Cover with foil, and allow to stand 30 minutes. This will let the juices be absorbed into the meat, making carving easier. Yield: 20 servings.

SOUTHWEST CORNBREAD DRESSING

2 (6-ounce) packages cornbread mix
1 cup chopped celery
1 cup chopped green onion
½ cup chopped green pepper
1 clove garlic, minced
½ cup butter or margarine
  Turkey giblets
2 slices bread
1 (10¾-ounce) can chicken broth
3 eggs, slightly beaten
6 tamales, mashed
½ teaspoon salt
  Crushed red pepper to taste

Prepare cornbread mix according to package directions; cool. Crumble into a large bowl; set aside. Sauté celery, onion, green pepper, and garlic in butter until soft. Stir into cornbread; set aside.

Put giblets in a saucepan; cover with water. Bring to a boil; reduce heat, cover, and simmer until tender. Chop liver; add to cornbread mixture along with ⅓ cup stock. Reserve remaining giblets for Giblet Gravy.

Soak bread in chicken broth. Stir bread and broth into cornbread mixture. Add remaining ingredients; mix thoroughly. Spoon into a greased 2-quart casserole. Bake at 350° for 30 to 35 minutes. Yield: 8 servings.

GIBLET GRAVY

  Giblets from 1 turkey
  Turkey neck
2 cups chicken broth
1 medium onion, chopped
1 cup chopped celery
½ teaspoon poultry seasoning
½ cup cornbread dressing
  Salt and pepper to taste
2 hard-cooked eggs, sliced

Simmer giblets and turkey neck in chicken broth until tender, about 2 hours. Chop giblets into broth; discard neck. Add onion, celery, poultry seasoning, and dressing; cook until vegetables are tender. Add salt and pepper to taste and egg slices. If thicker gravy is desired, add more dressing. Yield: about 2 cups.

Note: Flour may be used instead of dressing to thicken gravy. Dissolve 2 tablespoons flour in a small amount of water and stir into broth.

PARSLEYED NEW POTATOES
(see Index)

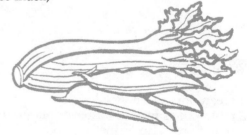

GREEN BEAN CASSEROLE

2 (16-ounce) cans French-cut green
  beans, drained
2 (10¾-ounce) cans cream of mushroom
  soup, undiluted
1 cup diced celery
1 cup diced green pepper
1 cup diced onion
5 to 6 ripe olives, sliced
1 cup crushed potato chips
¼ cup slivered almonds
5 to 6 pimiento-stuffed olives, sliced

Combine beans, soup, celery, green pepper, and onion. Spoon into a buttered 2-quart casserole. Top with a layer of ripe olives, potato chips, almonds, and stuffed olives. Bake at 325° for 35 to 40 minutes. Yield: 8 servings.

CRAN-APPLE RELISH

1 (1-pound) bag fresh cranberries
1 orange, unpeeled
5 to 6 red apples, unpeeled
2 cups sugar
1 (20-ounce) can crushed pineapple, well drained
½ cup chopped pecans

Wash cranberries thoroughly and drain. Quarter and seed orange and apples. Grind cranberries, orange, and apples coarsely in a food grinder or blender. Add sugar, pineapple, and pecans; mix well. Refrigerate overnight. Yield: 2 quarts.

APRICOT DREAM SALAD

2 (6-ounce) packages dried apricots
¾ cup water
½ cup sugar
3 (3-ounce) packages lemon-flavored gelatin
5 cups boiling water
1 (20-ounce) can crushed pineapple, drained
1 cup slivered almonds
Deluxe Dressing

Combine apricots and ¾ cup water in saucepan; simmer until tender. Remove from heat; stir in sugar. Mash with a fork until smooth; reserve ½ cup for Deluxe Dressing.

Dissolve gelatin in boiling water. Stir in remaining apricots, pineapple, and almonds. Pour into a 13- x 9- x 2-inch pan. Chill until firm. Spread Deluxe Dressing over top before serving. Cut into squares. Yield: about 15 servings.

Deluxe Dressing:

1 (8-ounce) package cream cheese, softened
½ cup reserved mashed apricots
2 tablespoons sherry
½ pint whipping cream, divided
¼ cup powdered sugar
½ teaspoon vanilla extract
½ teaspoon almond extract

Combine cream cheese, apricots, sherry, and 4 tablespoons cream; beat until smooth. Combine remaining cream, sugar, vanilla and almond extracts; whip until stiff. Fold into cheese mixture. Yield: about 2½ cups.

RELISH TRAY
(see Index)

HOLIDAY NUT CAKE

1 cup butter, softened
2 cups sugar
6 eggs, separated
4 cups all-purpose flour, divided
2 teaspoons baking powder
Dash of ground nutmeg
1 cup whiskey
4 cups pecan halves
1 (8-ounce) package chopped dates
½ pound chopped candied cherries

Cream butter and sugar thoroughly. Add egg yolks, one at a time, beating well after each addition. Combine 3¾ cups flour, baking powder, and nutmeg; add alternately with whiskey, mixing well. Combine remaining ¼ cup flour, pecans, dates, and cherries. Stir into flour mixture. Beat egg whites until stiff; fold into cake batter. Spoon into a greased and floured 10-inch tube pan. Bake at 350° for 1 hour and 40 minutes. Cover top of cake with foil if needed to prevent over-browning. Yield: one 10-inch cake.

For a Festive Thanksgiving
(Dinner for Four)

Hot Spiced Cranberry Delight
Smoked Duck with Gourmet Rice
Asparagus Soufflé
Cucumber Mousse
Beets with Orange Sauce
Cranberry-Orange Relish
Rich Dinner Rolls
Pecan Tarts or Pumpkin Cheese Pie
Wine   Coffee

HOT SPICED CRANBERRY DELIGHT

3 cups boiling water
½ cup sweetened lemon-flavored ice tea
    mix
3 cups cranberry juice cocktail
    Lemon slices
    Whole cloves
    Cinnamon sticks

Combine water, tea mix, and cranberry juice; heat thoroughly. Serve hot in mugs or cups with a lemon slice decorated with cloves. Stir with a cinnamon stick. Yield: 6 cups.

SMOKED DUCK WITH GOURMET RICE

½ cup lemon juice
½ cup soy sauce
½ teaspoon salt
¼ teaspoon coarsely ground black pepper
¼ teaspoon paprika
⅛ teaspoon garlic salt
1 (4- to 5-pound) duck
8 cloves
2 onions
    Gourmet Rice
    Parsley

Combine lemon juice, soy sauce, salt, pepper, paprika, and garlic salt; pour over duck, and marinate in refrigerator several hours. Stick 4 cloves in each onion, and place in duck cavity. Place duck on rack in smoker. (Use smoker with water pan.)

Cook about 5 hours in smoker. Do not raise lid; allow duck to cook slowly without being disturbed until very crisp.

If you do not have a smoker, duck can be cooked in the oven at 325° for 2 hours. Serve duck on bed of Gourmet Rice. Garnish with parsley. Yield: 4 servings.

Gourmet Rice:

4 cloves
1 onion
1 duck heart, liver, kidney, and neck
1 carrot
2 stalks celery with leaves
  Salt to taste
1 teaspoon peppercorns
1 bay leaf
1 clove garlic
  About ¼ teaspoon red pepper seeds
  About 4 sprigs parsley
1 cup uncooked regular rice
½ cup diced celery
¼ cup chopped scallions
½ cup sliced mushrooms
2 tablespoons melted butter

Stick cloves in onion; combine with next 9 ingredients. Cover with water, and cook about 1 hour over medium heat or until meat is tender. Remove meat and vegetables from broth; discard vegetables, and chop meat. Strain broth, reserving 2 cups.

Cook rice in reserved broth over low heat about 25 minutes or until tender. Sauté diced celery, scallions, and mushrooms in butter; add to rice along with chopped meat, tossing lightly to mix. Yield: 4 servings.

ASPARAGUS SOUFFLÉ

4 eggs
1 (15½-ounce) can asparagus spears,
  drained
1 cup shredded Cheddar cheese
1 cup mayonnaise
1 (10¾-ounce) can cream of mushroom
  soup, undiluted
1 teaspoon salt

Beat eggs with electric mixer or in blender. Add remaining ingredients, one at a time, blending well after each addition. Pour into a lightly greased 1½-quart casserole. Place casserole in pan of water; bake at 350° for 55 to 60 minutes or until knife inserted in center comes out clean. Yield: 4 servings.

CUCUMBER MOUSSE

2 cucumbers
1 envelope (1 tablespoon) unflavored
  gelatin
½ cup cold water
1 (3-ounce) package lime-flavored gelatin
1¼ cups boiling water
½ cup lemon juice
2 teaspoons onion juice
¾ teaspoon salt
⅛ teaspoon cayenne pepper
½ cup chopped celery
¼ cup chopped parsley
½ pint whipping cream, whipped

Peel cucumbers; remove and discard seeds. Coarsely grate cucumbers.

Soften unflavored gelatin in cold water. Dissolve lime-flavored gelatin in boiling water; stir in unflavored gelatin, lemon juice, onion juice, salt, and cayenne pepper. Chill until consistency of unbeaten egg white.

Fold cucumber, celery, parsley, and whipped cream into thickened gelatin. Pour into a 4-cup mold, and chill until firm. Yield: 4 to 6 servings.

BEETS WITH ORANGE SAUCE

½ cup sugar
2 teaspoons cornstarch
½ cup boiling water
1 teaspoon grated orange rind
1 teaspoon lemon juice
¼ cup orange juice
1 tablespoon butter or margarine
1 (16-ounce) can whole beets, undrained

Combine sugar and cornstarch; add water, stirring until smooth. Cook over low heat 15 minutes; stir in orange rind, lemon juice, orange juice, and butter.

Place beets in a saucepan, and heat thoroughly; drain off juice. Pour sauce over beets, and serve. Yield: 4 servings.

CRANBERRY-ORANGE RELISH

2 oranges
1 pound fresh cranberries, rinsed and
    drained
2 cups sugar
½ teaspoon ground nutmeg
½ teaspoon ground cardamom

Juice oranges; mince rind in food chopper. Combine orange juice, rind, and remaining ingredients in a saucepan over medium heat. Bring mixture to a boil; reduce heat and simmer 10 minutes or until berries are tender, stirring occasionally. Store in refrigerator. Yield: about 4 cups.

RICH DINNER ROLLS
(see Index)

PECAN TARTS

1 cup sugar
½ cup dark corn syrup
¼ cup light corn syrup
1 tablespoon lemon juice
1 teaspoon vanilla extract
6 tablespoons melted butter or margarine
3 eggs, beaten
10 unbaked 3-inch tart shells
1 cup pecan halves

Combine first 7 ingredients, mixing well. Spoon into tart shells, filling two-thirds full; cover with pecan halves. Bake at 325° for 30 minutes. Yield: 10 tarts.

Note: Tart shells can be made by shaping pastry circles around the back of muffin tins or custard cups.

PUMPKIN CHEESE PIE

1 (8-ounce) package cream cheese,
    softened
¼ cup sugar
½ teaspoon vanilla extract
1 egg
1 unbaked 9-inch pastry shell
1¼ cups canned or cooked pumpkin
½ cup sugar
    Dash of salt
1 teaspoon ground cinnamon
¼ teaspoon ground ginger
¼ teaspoon ground nutmeg
2 eggs, slightly beaten
1 cup evaporated milk

Combine cream cheese, sugar, and vanilla, beating until light and fluffy. Add 1 egg, mixing well. Spread mixture in pastry shell.

Combine pumpkin, sugar, salt, and spices, mixing well. Blend in eggs and milk. Carefully pour pumpkin mixture over cream cheese layer. Bake at 350° for 65 to 70 minutes or until done. Cool. Yield: one 9-inch pie.

Christmas Dinner for a Crowd
(Dinner for Fifteen)

Holiday Nog
Holiday Roast Goose
Shrimp-Crabmeat Casserole
Marinated Broccoli Supreme
Stewed Pears
Cranberry Fruit Salad
Relish Tray
Cottage Cheese Rolls
Peach Brandy Pound Cake
Coconut-Sour Cream Layer Cake
Wine   Coffee

HOLIDAY NOG

```
 8 eggs, separated
2½ cups sugar
 1 pint bourbon
 5 cups whipping cream, whipped
 2 cups milk
 2 ounces rum
   Ground nutmeg
```

Combine egg yolks and sugar; beat until smooth. Add bourbon very slowly, beating constantly.

Add 1 cup whipped cream to egg yolk mixture, and beat until smooth; add milk, beating well. Add remaining whipped cream, and beat until smooth; stir in rum. Fold in stiffly beaten egg whites. Chill thoroughly. Sprinkle with nutmeg before serving. Yield: about 16 cups.

HOLIDAY ROAST GOOSE

```
 3 cups chopped apple
¾ cup melted butter or margarine
 6 cups toasted breadcrumbs
1½ cups chopped onion
 1 tablespoon salt
 1 tablespoon celery seeds
 1 tablespoon pepper
¾ cup apple cider
 1 (10-pound) dressed goose
   Salt and pepper
   Green grapes
```

Cook apples in butter until transparent; add breadcrumbs, onion, and seasonings; toss lightly. Add cider, and mix well.

Lightly rub goose with salt and pepper inside and out. Stuff the body and neck cavity loosely with apple stuffing; truss goose. Prick breast, legs, and wings of goose to allow fat to run out; place breast side up on rack in shallow roasting pan.

Roast, uncovered, at 325° for 4 to 5 hours or until an internal temperature of 180° to 185° is reached. Do not baste. Spoon off drippings every half hour.

Goose is done when drumsticks and thighs move easily or when juices run clear instead of pink if thigh is pricked with a fork. Serve on a platter garnished with grapes. Yield: 15 servings.

SHRIMP-CRABMEAT CASSEROLE

2 cups chopped onion
2 cups chopped celery
2 medium-size green peppers, chopped
¼ cup melted butter or margarine
1 cup wild rice, cooked
1 cup regular rice, cooked
2 pounds shrimp, peeled, deveined, and cooked
2 (6-ounce) packages frozen crabmeat, thawed and drained
3 (10¾-ounce) cans cream of mushroom soup, undiluted
½ cup water
2 (4-ounce) cans sliced mushrooms, drained
½ cup slivered almonds
1 (2-ounce) jar sliced pimiento, drained
1 cup breadcrumbs, divided

Sauté onion, celery, and green pepper in butter until tender but not brown. Add remaining ingredients except breadcrumbs; stir well. Spoon mixture into 2 lightly greased 2-quart casseroles; sprinkle each with ½ cup breadcrumbs. Bake at 350° for 1 hour or until bubbly. Yield: 15 to 20 servings.

MARINATED BROCCOLI SUPREME

2 teaspoons onion salt
2 teaspoons oregano
1 teaspoon thyme
2 teaspoons garlic salt
1 teaspoon pepper
1 teaspoon dry mustard
6 tablespoons white vinegar
1⅓ cups salad oil
2 bunches fresh broccoli or 4 (10-ounce) packages frozen broccoli spears, cooked and drained
4 hard-cooked eggs, chopped
  Lemon slices
  Parsley

Combine first 8 ingredients in a mixing bowl; beat 1 minute at medium speed of electric mixer. Place broccoli in a 13- x 9- x 2-inch dish; add marinade. Cover and refrigerate overnight.

Before serving, drain off marinade. Place broccoli in serving dish, and sprinkle with chopped eggs. Garnish with lemon slices and parsley. Yield: 15 servings.

STEWED PEARS

8 fresh pears
¼ cup butter
1 cup sugar
1 cup water
1 cup white wine
4 small pieces lemon rind
1 tablespoon plus 1 teaspoon lemon juice

Peel and core pears; cut into ½-inch slices. Sauté pear slices in butter 3 minutes; sprinkle with sugar. Add remaining ingredients. Cover, and simmer until pears are tender (about 15 minutes). Yield: 16 servings.

CRANBERRY FRUIT SALAD

1 (8¼-ounce) can pineapple tidbits
2 (3-ounce) packages black raspberry-flavored gelatin
2 cups boiling water
1 cup cold water
2 tablespoons lemon juice
Dash of salt
2 cups fresh cranberries
½ unpeeled orange, seeded
¾ cup sugar
1 (11-ounce) can mandarin orange sections, drained

Drain pineapple, reserving juice. Dissolve gelatin in boiling water; add cold water, reserved pineapple juice, lemon juice, and salt. Chill until partially set.

Put cranberries and orange through a food chopper or food mill. Add sugar, pineapple, and mandarin oranges to cranberry mixture; stir into gelatin. Pour into a 6-cup ring mold. Chill until firm. Yield: 15 servings.

RELISH TRAY
(see Index)

COTTAGE CHEESE ROLLS

2 packages dry yeast
½ cup very warm water (105° to 115°)
2 cups cottage cheese
¼ cup sugar
2 teaspoons salt
½ teaspoon soda
2 eggs, beaten
About 5 cups all-purpose flour

Dissolve yeast in very warm water. Heat cottage cheese in small saucepan over low heat until warm, but not hot; remove from heat. Combine cottage cheese, yeast, sugar, salt, soda, eggs, and 1 cup flour in large bowl; beat at medium speed of electric mixer 2 minutes. Gradually add enough flour to form a soft dough.

Place dough in a greased bowl, turning to grease all sides. Cover and let rise in a warm place free from drafts until doubled in bulk, about 1½ hours.

Turn dough out onto a floured board; divide dough into 24 equal pieces, and shape each into a ball. Place balls in 2 greased 9-inch round baking pans. Cover; let rise in warm place until doubled in bulk, about 30 minutes. Bake at 350° for 20 minutes. Yield: 2 dozen rolls.

PEACH BRANDY POUND CAKE

    3 cups sugar
    1 cup butter or margarine, softened
    6 eggs
    3 cups all-purpose flour
    ¼ teaspoon soda
      Pinch of salt
    1 cup commercial sour cream
    2 teaspoons rum
    1 teaspoon orange extract
    ¼ teaspoon almond extract
    ½ teaspoon lemon extract
    1 teaspoon vanilla extract
    ½ cup peach brandy

Combine sugar and butter; cream until light and fluffy. Add eggs, one at a time, mixing well after each addition.

Combine dry ingredients; add to creamed mixture alternately with sour cream, beating well after each addition. Stir in remaining ingredients.

Pour batter into a well-greased and floured 10-inch Bundt pan or tube pan. Bake at 325° for 1 hour and 20 minutes or until cake tests done. Yield: one 10-inch cake.

COCONUT-SOUR CREAM LAYER CAKE

    1 (18½-ounce) package butter-flavored
      cake mix
    2 cups sugar
    1 (16-ounce) carton commercial sour
      cream
    1 (12-ounce) package frozen coconut,
      thawed
    1½ cups frozen whipped topping, thawed

Prepare cake mix according to package directions, making two 8-inch layers; when completely cool, split both layers.

Combine sugar, sour cream, and coconut, blending well; chill. Reserve 1 cup sour cream mixture for frosting; spread remainder between layers of cake.

Combine reserved sour cream mixture with whipped topping; blend until smooth. Spread on top and sides of cake. Seal cake in an airtight container, and refrigerate for 3 days before serving. Yield: one 8-inch layer cake.

Make croutons from stale bread. Cut bread into cubes and toast at 250° until golden; then toss lightly in melted butter.

Freshen dry, crusty rolls or French bread by sprinkling with a few drops of water, wrapping in aluminum foil, and reheating at 350° about 10 minutes.

DINNER PARTIES

A Chicken Classic

Ham with All the Trimmings

Chicken for a Gourmet Occasion

Country Captain Buffet

Elegant Cornish Hen Dinner

Veal with a French Accent

A Simple but Sensational
Dinner Party

Special Sirloin Dinner

Stuffed Flounder Feast

A Pork Chop Flambé

A Gourmet Debut

Party Lamb Dinner

Flank Steak from the Grill

Seafood in a Chafing Dish

The Ultimate in Dining—
Beef Wellington

A dinner party in your home is a delightful way to dispense Southern hospitality. It is a way to relax and enjoy an evening with your guests. But a successful party doesn't just happen; it's the result of careful planning and preparation.

We offer a wide variety of dinner parties from which to choose—from small to crowd-size, from seated dinners to buffet service, from casual to elegant.

Our classic seated dinners are an opportunity to serve an elegantly garnished roast and a spectacular dessert. If your party plans call for a large crowd, our buffets offer elegant dining with easy serving. Enjoy the parties just as we planned them or alter the menus to suit your taste or needs.

A Chicken Classic
(Dinner for Eight)

Chicken Kiev
Gourmet Rice
Broccoli Topped with Hollandaise
Summer Fruit Bowl
Commercial French Rolls   Butter
Frosty Apricot Delight or Brandy Soufflé
Wine   Coffee

CHICKEN KIEV

 1 cup butter, softened
 2 tablespoons chopped parsley
 1 teaspoon rosemary
 ¾ teaspoon salt
 ⅛ teaspoon pepper
 6 whole chicken breasts, split, boned,
    and skinned
 ¾ cup all-purpose flour
 3 eggs, well beaten
 1½ to 2 cups breadcrumbs
    Salad oil

Combine butter and seasonings in a small bowl; blend thoroughly. Shape butter mixture into 2 sticks; cover and put in freezer about 45 minutes or until firm.

Place each half of chicken breast on a sheet of waxed paper; flatten to ¼-inch thickness, using a meat mallet or rolling pin.

Cut each stick of butter mixture into 6 pats; place a pat in center of each half of chicken breast. Fold long sides of chicken over butter; fold ends over and secure with toothpick. Dredge each piece of chicken in flour, dip in egg, and coat with breadcrumbs. Cover and refrigerate about 1 hour.

Fry chicken in salad oil heated to 350°. Cook 5 minutes on each side or until browned, turning with tongs. Place in warm oven until all chicken is fried. Yield: 12 servings.

GOURMET RICE

 2 cups uncooked regular rice
 4 chicken bouillon cubes
 3 cups boiling water
    Garlic powder to taste
    Seasoned pepper to taste
 1 (4-ounce) can sliced mushrooms,
    undrained
 ½ cup melted butter or margarine
 1 (1⅜-ounce) package onion soup mix
 1 (10½-ounce) can consommé

Combine all ingredients in a large Dutch oven; mix well. Bring mixture to a boil; reduce heat to simmer. Cover; simmer 30 minutes or until rice is tender. Yield: 8 to 10 servings.

BROCCOLI TOPPED WITH HOLLANDAISE

2 bunches broccoli
7 egg yolks
  Juice of 2 lemons
  Dash of hot sauce
  Salt to taste
1 cup melted butter

Trim off large leaves of broccoli. Remove tough ends of lower stalks, and wash broccoli thoroughly. If stalks are more than 1 inch in diameter, make lengthwise slits in stalks. Cook broccoli, covered, in a small amount of boiling salted water for 12 to 15 minutes or until crisp-tender.

Combine egg yolks, lemon juice, hot sauce, and salt in blender; process on high speed until well blended. Gradually add melted butter and continue to blend. Drain broccoli; serve with sauce. Yield: 8 servings.

SUMMER FRUIT BOWL

2 cups grapefruit sections
2 cups orange sections
1 cup sliced peaches
  Salad greens
1 cup halved strawberries
  Poppy Seed Dressing

Combine grapefruit, oranges, and peaches; chill. Line individual salad bowls with salad greens. Arrange chilled fruit on greens, and garnish with strawberries. Serve with Poppy Seed Dressing. Yield: 8 servings.

Poppy Seed Dressing:

⅓ cup frozen lemonade concentrate,
  thawed and undiluted
5 tablespoons honey
⅓ cup salad oil
2 tablespoons lemon juice
1 teaspoon poppy seeds

Combine all ingredients; beat until smooth. Yield: about 1 cup.

FROSTY APRICOT DELIGHT

¼ cup chopped toasted almonds
1⅓ cups crushed vanilla wafers
2 tablespoons melted margarine
1 teaspoon almond extract
½ gallon vanilla ice cream, softened
1 (12-ounce) jar apricot preserves

Combine almonds, vanilla wafer crumbs, margarine, and almond extract; mix well, and set aside ¼ cup.

Put half of remaining crumb mixture in the bottom of a 9-inch pan; add half of ice cream and half of preserves. Repeat layers. Sprinkle reserved crumbs on top. Freeze until firm. Yield: 9 to 12 servings.

BRANDY SOUFFLÉ

5 eggs, separated
¾ cup sugar
¼ cup brandy
¼ cup sherry
¼ cup Benedictine
2 tablespoons lemon juice
3 envelopes (3 tablespoons) unflavored
  gelatin
½ cup water
2 cups whipping cream, whipped

Wrap a collar of greased aluminum foil around the top of a lightly greased and sugared 1½-quart soufflé dish.

Beat egg yolks until light and lemon colored. Gradually add sugar, brandy, sherry, Benedictine, and lemon juice; beat until well blended.

Soften gelatin in water; place over low heat, stirring until dissolved. Add to egg mixture. Beat egg whites until stiff but not dry; fold into gelatin mixture along with whipped cream.

Pour mixture into soufflé dish; chill overnight or until firm. Remove foil collar before serving. Yield: 8 to 10 servings.

Ham with All the Trimmings
(Buffet Dinner for Twelve)

Golden Glazed Ham
Tangy Raisin Sauce or Mustard Sauce
Rum-Sweet Potato Bake
Broccoli-Cheese Casserole
Cardinal Salad
Commercial Crescent Rolls   Butter
Coconut Cake or Strawberry Refrigerator Cake
Coffee   Tea

GOLDEN GLAZED HAM

  1 (6- to 7-pound) uncooked ham
  1 (6-ounce) can frozen orange juice
     concentrate, thawed and undiluted
1¼ cups firmly packed brown sugar
  ½ cup steak sauce
     Pineapple slices (optional)

Place ham, fat side up, on a large piece of aluminum foil in a shallow roasting pan. Combine remaining ingredients except pineapple slices. Pour half of glaze mixture over ham. Wrap foil loosely around ham. Bake at 325° for 3 to 3½ hours (about 30 minutes per pound).

Remove ham from oven about 30 minutes before cooking time is up. Score ham in a diamond pattern, making cuts ¼ inch deep in ham fat. Spoon remaining glaze mixture over ham, and return ham to oven. Bake, uncovered, at 400° for 30 minutes, basting frequently. Garnish with pineapple slices, if desired. Yield: 12 to 14 servings.

TANGY RAISIN SAUCE

  1 cup sugar
  ½ cup water
  1 cup raisins
  2 tablespoons butter or margarine
  2 tablespoons vinegar
     Dash of Worcestershire sauce
  ½ teaspoon salt
  ¼ teaspoon ground cloves
  2 teaspoons cornstarch

Combine all ingredients except cornstarch; bring to a boil. Cook until raisins are plump. Dissolve cornstarch in a small amount of cold water; gradually add to hot mixture. Cook until clear, stirring constantly. Yield: about 2 cups.

MUSTARD SAUCE

2 hard-cooked egg yolks
1 uncooked egg yolk
¼ cup salad oil
1 tablespoon sugar
¼ teaspoon salt
Dash of pepper
1½ tablespoons lemon juice
Pulp from ½ lemon
1 tablespoon prepared brown mustard
1 tablespoon whipping cream

Press hard-cooked egg yolks through a fine sieve; blend in uncooked yolk to make a smooth paste. Add oil, a few drops at a time, beating well after each addition. Add remaining ingredients in order listed, beating thoroughly after each addition. Yield: about 1 cup.

RUM-SWEET POTATO BAKE

4 pounds sweet potatoes, cooked and peeled
½ cup melted butter or margarine
¾ cup brown sugar
6 tablespoons dark rum
1 teaspoon salt
Chopped pecans

Combine potatoes, butter, sugar, rum, and salt; beat until smooth. Spoon into a lightly greased 3-quart casserole; sprinkle with pecans. Bake at 350° for 30 minutes. Yield: 12 servings.

BROCCOLI-CHEESE CASSEROLE

2 medium onions, chopped
1 cup melted butter or margarine, divided
2 (10¾-ounce) cans cream of mushroom soup, undiluted
2 (4-ounce) cans chopped mushrooms, drained
2 (6-ounce) rolls pasteurized process cheese food with garlic, chopped
2 teaspoons chopped parsley
Salt and pepper to taste
½ cup slivered almonds
4 (10-ounce) packages frozen chopped broccoli, partially cooked and drained
4 cups herb-seasoned stuffing mix

Sauté onion in ½ cup butter until tender. Combine onion, soup, mushrooms, cheese, parsley, salt, pepper, almonds, and broccoli; mix well. Spoon into two lightly greased 2-quart casseroles.

Combine stuffing mix and ½ cup butter; spoon over broccoli mixture. Bake at 350° for 20 to 30 minutes. Yield: 12 to 14 servings.

CARDINAL SALAD

2 (3-ounce) packages lemon-flavored gelatin
2 cups boiling water
1½ cups beet juice
6 tablespoons vinegar
1 teaspoon salt
4 teaspoons grated onion
2 tablespoons horseradish
1½ cups chopped celery
2 cups cooked, chopped beets
Mayonnaise

Dissolve gelatin in boiling water. Add beet juice, vinegar, salt, onion, and horseradish; chill until consistency of unbeaten egg white.

Fold in remaining ingredients except mayonnaise. Spoon into an 8-cup mold or individual molds; chill until firm. Serve with mayonnaise. Yield: 12 to 14 servings.

COCONUT CAKE

½ cup shortening
1 cup sugar
2 eggs
1¼ cups self-rising flour
½ cup milk
1½ teaspoons vanilla extract
   Marshmallow-Coconut Frosting
   Flaked coconut

Cream shortening and sugar until light and fluffy; add eggs, beating well. Add flour to creamed mixture alternately with milk, ending with milk; beat well after each addition. Stir in vanilla.

Pour batter into 2 greased and lightly floured 8-inch cakepans. Bake at 375° about 20 minutes or until cake tests done. Turn out on rack to cool. Spread Marshmallow-Coconut Frosting between layers and on top and sides of cake. Sprinkle with coconut. Yield: one 8-inch layer cake.

Marshmallow-Coconut Frosting:

2 egg whites
1½ cups sugar
5 tablespoons water
1½ teaspoons vanilla extract
6 large marshmallows

Combine egg whites, sugar, water, and vanilla in top of a double boiler. Place over boiling water; cook, beating constantly with electric mixer or rotary beater; scrape bottom and sides of pan frequently. When mixture stands in peaks, remove from heat and add marshmallows.

Continue beating until frosting is thick enough to spread. Yield: enough for one 8-inch layer cake.

STRAWBERRY REFRIGERATOR CAKE

1 (6-ounce) package strawberry-flavored
   gelatin
2 cups boiling water
1½ cups crushed strawberries
1 tablespoon lemon juice
½ cup sugar
⅛ teaspoon salt
1 pint whipping cream, whipped
7 or 8 whole ladyfingers
   Additional whipped cream (optional)
   Whole strawberries (optional)

Dissolve gelatin in boiling water. Combine crushed strawberries, lemon juice, sugar, and salt; add to gelatin. Chill until consistency of unbeaten egg white. Fold whipped cream into thickened gelatin.

Line sides of an 8- or 9-inch springform pan with waxed paper. Split ladyfingers; cut tip from one end of each ladyfinger. Arrange ladyfingers, rounded end up, around edge of pan.

Carefully spoon strawberry mixture into pan, and chill 6 hours or until firm. Remove sides from pan. Garnish with additional whipped cream and whole strawberries, if desired. Yield: 12 servings.

When making coffee for a crowd, allow 1 pound of coffee plus 2 gallons water for 40 servings.

How many ice cubes?—Make ice cubes ahead of time and store them in plastic bags in the freezer. Count on 350 cubes for 50 people, or seven cubes per person.

Chicken for a Gourmet Occasion
(Dinner for Six)

Avocado Cocktail
Chicken Imperial or Chicken Marengo
Gourmet Stuffed Potatoes
Harlequin Spinach
Cranberry Ice Cream Salad
Commercial Hard Rolls   Butter
Bourbon Pie
Wine   Coffee

AVOCADO COCKTAIL

1 cup chili sauce
¼ cup sherry
2 teaspoons horseradish
1 teaspoon Worcestershire sauce
2 tablespoons lemon juice
2 tablespoons mayonnaise
1 teaspoon salt
3 to 4 avocados, chilled
    Lettuce

Combine all ingredients except avocados and lettuce; stir until smooth. Chill.

Peel and slice avocados; arrange on lettuce in sherbet glasses, and top with sauce. Yield: 6 servings.

CHICKEN IMPERIAL

6 chicken breasts
1 cup sherry
1 cup breadcrumbs
1 teaspoon salt
¼ teaspoon freshly ground pepper
1 cup grated Parmesan cheese
2 tablespoons parsley
1 clove garlic, crushed
1 cup chopped or slivered almonds,
    divided
¾ cup melted butter or margarine

Marinate chicken in sherry 2 to 3 hours. Pat dry with paper towel. Combine breadcrumbs, salt, pepper, Parmesan cheese, parsley, garlic, and ¾ cup almonds.

Dip chicken in butter; roll in breadcrumb mixture. Arrange in a 13- x 9- x 2-inch pan, and sprinkle with remaining almonds. Bake at 350° for 1 hour. Yield: 6 servings.

CHICKEN MARENGO

1 cup sliced fresh mushrooms
2 tablespoons butter or margarine
3 pounds chicken thighs, legs, and
    breasts or 1 (3-pound) broiler-fryer,
    cut in serving-size pieces
  Salt and pepper to taste
2 to 3 tablespoons olive oil or salad oil
4 green onions with tops removed, sliced
1 clove garlic, minced
½ cup dry white wine or consommé
2 tomatoes, cut in wedges and seeded
¼ teaspoon thyme
1 tablespoon minced parsley
  Parsley sprigs

Sauté mushrooms in butter 2 minutes; set aside.

Sprinkle chicken with salt and pepper; sauté in hot oil until brown. Remove chicken from skillet, and set aside; reserve drippings. Sauté onion and garlic in drippings until onion is soft. Stir in wine, tomatoes, thyme, salt, and pepper, scraping bottom of skillet well.

Add chicken to skillet; cover and simmer 30 minutes or until chicken is tender. Add sautéed mushrooms; sprinkle with minced parsley, and garnish with sprigs of parsley. Yield: 6 servings.

GOURMET STUFFED POTATOES

6 baking potatoes
1 (8-ounce) package cream cheese,
    softened
1 (4-ounce) can deviled ham
1 teaspoon onion flakes
3 to 4 tablespoons mayonnaise
  Paprika

Wrap each potato in aluminum foil; bake at 400° for 1 hour and 15 minutes. Combine cream cheese, deviled ham, onion flakes, and mayonnaise; set aside.

Unwrap potatoes; allow to cool to touch. Slice skin away from top of each potato. Carefully scoop out pulp, leaving shells intact.

Combine potato pulp and cream cheese mixture; whip until smooth. Stuff shells with potato mixture; sprinkle with paprika. Bake at 350° for 15 to 20 minutes. Yield: 6 servings.

HARLEQUIN SPINACH

2 (10-ounce) packages frozen chopped
    spinach
½ cup chopped onion
2 tablespoons melted butter or margarine
⅔ cup catsup
1 tablespoon lemon juice
½ teaspoon chili powder
¼ cup shredded Cheddar cheese

Cook spinach according to package directions; drain. Sauté onion in butter. Combine all ingredients except cheese.

Spoon mixture into a 1-quart casserole; sprinkle with cheese. Bake at 350° for 20 minutes or until bubbly. Yield: 6 servings.

CRANBERRY ICE CREAM SALAD

1 (16-ounce) can whole berry cranberry
    sauce
1 tablespoon lemon juice
1 (6-ounce) package orange-flavored
    gelatin
1 pint vanilla ice cream
2 teaspoons grated orange rind
2 large oranges, peeled and diced

Place cranberry sauce in a small saucepan over low heat; drain, reserving liquid. Combine cranberry liquid and lemon juice; add just enough water to measure 1 cup. Heat liquid to boiling and pour over gelatin, stirring until dissolved. Add ice cream, mixing until well blended.

Chill until partially set; fold in cranberry sauce, orange rind, and oranges. Pour into a 4-cup mold; chill until set. Yield: 6 to 8 servings.

BOURBON PIE

1 envelope (1 tablespoon) unflavored
    gelatin
½ cup cold water
1½ cups milk
¾ cup sugar
3 tablespoons cornstarch
3 eggs, well beaten
1 tablespoon butter
¼ cup bourbon
½ teaspoon vanilla extract
½ pint whipping cream, whipped
1 baked 10-inch pastry shell
    Ground nutmeg

Soften gelatin in cold water; set aside.

Scald milk in top of double boiler; combine sugar and cornstarch and add to milk. Cook, stirring constantly, until thick. Cook an additional 15 minutes, stirring often.

Add a small amount of custard to eggs, and mix well. Add egg mixture to custard, and cook 1 minute longer. Add butter and gelatin. Chill 30 minutes in refrigerator, but do not let mixture get hard.

Add bourbon and vanilla; blend well. Fold in whipped cream; pour into pastry shell. Sprinkle with nutmeg. Chill 4 to 6 hours before serving. Yield: one 10-inch pie.

To make sucessful white sauce, follow this procedure: Melt butter in a saucepan; then remove from heat to blend in flour and add liquid. Use cold milk; add it gradually, stirring constantly. Return to heat; cook, stirring constantly, until mixture thickens and bubbles. Add seasonings; cook at least 5 minutes, stirring occasionally.

Stocking the bar—When buying liquor, remember that there are seventeen 1½-ounce drinks in a fifth of liquor (about 200 drinks to a case). For easy calculation, plan three drinks per guest. Although some guests will have only one drink, it's better to have too much than not enough. Provide a large pitcher of chilled fruit juice and an assortment of carbonated drinks for nondrinkers. Have a tray or table handy for used glasses.

Country Captain Buffet
(Buffet Dinner for Eight to Ten)

Country Captain
Acorn Squash Wedges with Creamed Onions
Citrus-Avocado Salad
Commercial Hard Rolls   Butter
Chocolate Pastry Torte or Party Pumpkin Cake
Coffee   Tea

COUNTRY CAPTAIN

3½ to 4 pounds chicken thighs, legs, and
    boned breasts
    All-purpose flour
    Salt and pepper to taste
1 cup shortening
2 onions, finely chopped
2 green peppers, chopped
1 small clove garlic, minced
1½ teaspoons salt
 ½ teaspoon white pepper
3 teaspoons curry powder
2 (16-ounce) cans tomato wedges,
    undrained
 ½ teaspoon chopped parsley
 ½ teaspoon ground thyme
3 heaping tablespoons currants
    Hot cooked rice
¼ pound slivered almonds, toasted
    Parsley for garnish

Remove skin from chicken. Combine flour and
salt and pepper to taste. Dredge chicken in flour
mixture, and brown in hot shortening. Remove

chicken from skillet, but keep it hot (this step
is important for the success of the dish).

Pour off all but ¼ cup drippings from skillet.
Add onion, green pepper, and garlic; cook very
slowly, stirring constantly, until vegetables are
tender. Season with 1½ teaspoons salt, ½ teaspoon white pepper, and curry powder (amount
of curry powder may be varied according to
taste). Add tomatoes, ½ teaspoon parsley, thyme,
and currants; stir gently to mix.

Put chicken in a roaster or large casserole; add
sauce. If sauce does not cover chicken, add water.
Cover tightly and bake at 350° about 45 minutes
or until the chicken is tender.

Place chicken in center of a large platter and
pile rice around it. Spoon sauce over rice; sprinkle
almonds on top. Garnish with parsley. Yield: 8
to 10 servings.

ACORN SQUASH WEDGES WITH CREAMED ONIONS

3 acorn squash
Salt and pepper to taste
1 tablespoon melted butter or margarine
1 tablespoon all-purpose flour
¾ cup milk
1 (16-ounce) can small whole onions, drained
2 tablespoons chopped pimiento

Wash squash, and cut into quarters; remove seeds and membrane. Place in a lightly greased 2-quart shallow casserole, and sprinkle with salt and pepper. Cover and bake at 350° for 40 to 50 minutes or until squash is tender.

Combine butter and flour in a saucepan, blending until smooth. Gradually add milk; cook over low heat, stirring constantly, until smooth and thickened. Stir in salt, onions, and pimiento; spoon over squash. Return to oven, and bake 10 additional minutes. Yield: 8 to 10 servings.

CITRUS-AVOCADO SALAD

2 (32-ounce) jars grapefruit and orange sections, drained
1 avocado, peeled and sliced
1 green pepper, cut into rings (optional)
⅓ cup chopped walnuts
Lettuce
Orange French Dressing

Combine first 4 ingredients; toss gently to mix. Serve on lettuce and top with Orange French Dressing. Yield: 8 to 10 servings.

Orange French Dressing:

1 (6-ounce) can frozen orange juice concentrate, thawed and undiluted
½ cup salad oil
¼ cup cider vinegar
3 to 4 tablespoons sugar
½ teaspoon dry mustard
¼ teaspoon salt

Combine all ingredients, mixing well. Chill thoroughly before serving. Yield: 1½ cups.

CHOCOLATE PASTRY TORTE

2 (4-ounce) packages sweet cooking chocolate
½ cup sugar
½ cup water
1½ teaspoons instant coffee powder
2 teaspoons vanilla extract
1 (11-ounce) package piecrust sticks
2 cups whipping cream
Chopped nuts or chocolate curls

Combine chocolate, sugar, water, and coffee in a saucepan. Cook over low heat, stirring constantly until smooth. Blend in vanilla; allow to cool to room temperature.

Prepare piecrust according to package directions, but omit water. Blend ¾ cup of the chocolate sauce into piecrust mix. Divide pastry into 6 equal parts. Press each part onto the bottom of an inverted 8-inch round pan to within ½ inch of edge. Bake at 425° for 5 to 8 minutes.

While layers are still warm, trim to even edges, if desired. Let cool; then run the tip of a knife under edges to loosen. Lift carefully, and transfer to cake rack.

Whip cream to soft peak stage; fold in remaining chocolate sauce. Spread chocolate cream between layers and over top. Chill overnight or at least 8 hours. Top with chopped nuts or chocolate curls. Yield: 9 to 12 servings.

PARTY PUMPKIN CAKE

2 cups sugar
1 cup salad oil
4 eggs
2 cups all-purpose flour
2 teaspoons soda
2 teaspoons ground cinnamon
1 teaspoon baking powder
½ teaspoon salt
2 cups cooked, mashed pumpkin or
    1 (16-ounce) can pumpkin
  Cream Cheese Frosting
½ cup chopped nuts

Combine sugar, salad oil, and eggs in a large mixing bowl; mix well. Combine dry ingredients; add to oil mixture, beating well. Stir in pumpkin.

Pour batter into 2 greased and floured 9-inch cakepans. Bake at 350° for 35 to 40 minutes. Turn out on racks to cool. Frost with Cream Cheese Frosting; sprinkle nuts over top. Yield: one 9-inch layer cake.

Cream Cheese Frosting:

¼ cup butter or margarine, softened
1 (8-ounce) package cream cheese,
    softened
1 (1-pound) package powdered sugar
2 teaspoons vanilla extract

Combine all ingredients, mixing until smooth. Yield: enough for one 9-inch layer cake.

Make two schedules—Regardless of the informality of your party, make two time schedules. The first schedule includes any preparation that can be done ahead—preparing some food, checking that linens are in order, polishing silver, or ordering flowers or items that must be rented. The second schedule stipulates timing for all preparation to be done the day of the party. Allow time to relax and get yourself ready at a leisurely pace in time enough to greet early arrivals.

Organize your grocery list—After deciding on the menu for your party, make the grocery list in two parts: Things that can be bought and prepared ahead of time or stored, and the perishables that have to be purchased the day of the party.

Elegant Cornish Hen Dinner
(Buffet Dinner for Six)

Cornish Hens with Orange Rice
Mint Glazed Carrots
Chinese Peas and Water Chestnuts
Asparagus Salad
Parmesan French Bread
Strawberry Shortcake
Coffee   Tea

CORNISH HENS WITH ORANGE RICE

6 Cornish hens
1 cup melted butter or margarine
1 cup apple jelly
¼ cup cornstarch
1⅓ cups Sauterne
½ cup orange juice
  Salt to taste
2 cups white seedless grapes
  Orange Rice

Brown hens in butter; remove from skillet, and place in a baking dish. Melt apple jelly over low heat; set aside. Add cornstarch to drippings in skillet, blending well; stir in apple jelly, Sauterne, orange juice, and salt. Cook, stirring constantly, until smooth and thickened.

Pour sauce over hens; bake, uncovered, at 350° for 1 hour. Add grapes, and bake about 10 additional minutes or until grapes are warm.

Arrange hens and Orange Rice on plattter; garnish with grapes. Serve sauce with hens. Yield: 6 servings.

Orange Rice:

2 cups diced celery and leaves
6 tablespoons chopped onion
½ cup melted butter or margarine
2 cups uncooked regular rice
1 teaspoon salt
2½ cups boiling water
1½ cups orange juice
¼ cup grated orange rind

Sauté celery and onion in butter until tender. Stir rice and salt into boiling water; cover and simmer 15 to 17 minutes. Add orange juice, orange rind, and sautéed vegetables. Cover; cook 5 minutes or until tender. Yield: 6 servings.

MINT GLAZED CARROTS

2 (1-pound) packages carrots, peeled and
   halved
  Salt to taste
¼ cup melted butter or margarine
¼ cup sugar
1 teaspoon vinegar
1 tablespoon chopped fresh mint

Simmer carrots, covered, in unsalted water just
until tender; drain. Sprinkle with salt. Combine
remaining ingredients in a skillet. Add carrots;
cook over medium heat, stirring often until
lightly glazed. Yield: 6 to 8 servings.

CHINESE PEAS AND WATER CHESTNUTS

6 tablespoons salad oil
3 tablespoons chopped green onions
2 cloves garlic, finely minced
½ teaspoon salt
½ teaspoon monosodium glutamate
3 (6-ounce) packages frozen Chinese pea
   pods, thawed
1 (5-ounce) can water chestnuts, drained
   and sliced
3 tablespoons soy sauce
¾ cup chicken broth
1 tablespoon cornstarch
1 tablespoon water

Heat oil in a wok or skillet. Add onion and garlic;
stir-fry 2 minutes. Sprinkle with salt and monosodium glutamate. Add pea pods, water chestnuts,
and soy sauce; stir-fry 1 minute. Add chicken
broth; cover and cook 2 minutes.

Combine cornstarch and water; add to vegetables. Cook until thickened, stirring constantly.
Yield: 6 to 8 servings.

ASPARAGUS SALAD

2 (14½-ounce) cans chopped asparagus
2 cups sugar
1 cup vinegar
1 teaspoon salt
4 envelopes (4 tablespoons) unflavored
   gelatin
1 cup cold water
2 cups chopped celery
1 cup chopped pecans
1 (4-ounce) jar chopped pimiento,
   drained
2 small onions, grated
  Juice of 1 lemon
  Lettuce

Drain asparagus, reserving juice. Add enough
water to juice to make 2 cups. Combine juice
mixture, sugar, vinegar, and salt; bring to a boil.
Soften gelatin in cold water; add to hot mixture,
stirring until dissolved. Chill until consistency
of unbeaten egg white.

Add remaining ingredients except lettuce to
thickened gelatin; mix well. Pour into an 8-cup
mold, and chill until firm. To serve, unmold
on a bed of lettuce. Yield: 6 to 8 servings.

*Roasted golden brown and garnished with green grapes, Cor-
nish Hens with Orange Rice is glazed with a wine sauce.*

PARMESAN FRENCH BREAD

    1 tablespoon chopped chives
    ⅛ teaspoon garlic salt
    ¼ cup grated Parmesan cheese
    ½ cup butter or margarine, softened
    1 (1-pound) loaf French bread, sliced

Combine chives, garlic salt, cheese, and butter;
spread on bread slices. Reassemble into a loaf,
and wrap in aluminum foil; bake at 350° for
20 minutes. For crisper bread, leave foil open.
Yield: 6 to 8 servings.

STRAWBERRY SHORTCAKE

    2 pints fresh strawberries, sliced
    8 tablespoons sugar, divided
    2 cups all-purpose flour
    3 teaspoons baking powder
    1 teaspoon salt
    ¼ teaspoon soda
    ⅓ cup shortening
    1 (8-ounce) carton commercial sour
        cream
    ⅓ cup milk
    1 (9-ounce) carton frozen whipped
        topping, thawed

Combine strawberries and 6 tablespoons sugar;
chill.

Combine remaining 2 tablespoons sugar, flour,
baking powder, salt, and soda; cut in shortening
with a pastry blender until mixture resembles
coarse cornmeal. Add sour cream and milk, stirring just until blended. Spoon batter into 2
greased 8-inch cakepans. Bake at 450° for 15 to
20 minutes; cool slightly.

Spoon half of strawberries on bottom layer
of shortcake; top with half of whipped topping.
Add top layer; spoon on remaining strawberries
and whipped topping. Cut into wedges to serve.
Yield: 8 to 10 servings.

*Fresh blueberries enhance the flavor and add a crowning
touch to Blueberry Cheesecake (page 141).*

Veal with a French Accent

(Buffet Dinner for Six)

Oysters Bienville
Blanquette of Veal
Gourmet Green Rice
Ginger Carrots
Fresh Spinach Salad
Onion Rolls
Strawberries and Grapes or Orange Bavarian Cream
Wine   Coffee

OYSTERS BIENVILLE

Rock salt
¼ cup finely chopped green onions
3 tablespoons melted butter
¼ cup all-purpose flour
¾ cup fish stock
3 tablespoons white wine
¼ teaspoon salt
Dash of cayenne pepper
1 egg yolk, beaten
½ cup cooked, peeled, and deveined
   shrimp, finely chopped
½ cup mushrooms, finely chopped
2 truffles, minced
1 teaspoon Worcestershire sauce
2 teaspoons chopped parsley
1 dozen oysters on the half shell, drained
Paprika

Put a ½-inch layer of rock salt in 2 piepans; place in a 400° oven to preheat salt.

Sauté onion in butter over medium heat. Blend in flour; cook, stirring constantly, about 5 minutes. Do not brown. Remove from heat, and stir in fish stock, wine, salt, and cayenne; mix well.

Blend a small amount of hot mixture into egg yolk; stir into remaining hot mixture. Add shrimp, mushrooms, truffles, Worcestershire sauce, and parsley; cook over low heat about 15 minutes.

Arrange 6 oyster shells on salt in each piepan; place an oyster in each shell. Spoon sauce over each oyster, and sprinkle with paprika. Bake at 350° for 10 to 15 minutes or until edges of oysters begin to curl. Garnish as desired. Yield: 12 appetizer servings.

BLANQUETTE OF VEAL

2½ pounds veal, cut into 1-inch cubes
   Salt and pepper
   All-purpose flour
6 tablespoons melted butter or margarine
3½ tablespoons all-purpose flour
5 cups chicken broth
2 tablespoons dried parsley flakes
¼ cup wine vinegar
1 teaspoon salt
¼ teaspoon pepper
¼ teaspoon thyme
¼ teaspoon rosemary
⅛ teaspoon ground cloves
2 (16-ounce) cans small white onions,
   drained

Sprinkle veal with salt and pepper; coat lightly with flour. Brown meat in butter in a heavy skillet; using a slotted spoon, transfer to a Dutch oven.

Blend 3½ tablespoons flour into butter remaining in skillet; stir constantly over low heat until smooth. Gradually add broth; cook, stirring constantly, until smooth.

Pour broth mixture over veal; add remaining ingredients except onions. Cover and simmer 2 hours. Add onions just before serving; heat thoroughly. Yield: 6 servings.

Note: If a thicker gravy is desired, make a paste of 2 to 3 tablespoons additional flour and a small amount of cooking liquid. Gradually stir into veal; cook over low heat, stirring constantly, until smooth and thickened.

GOURMET GREEN RICE

4 or 5 green onions, finely chopped
½ green pepper, finely chopped
¼ cup melted butter or margarine
⅓ cup minced fresh parsley
3 cups chicken broth
1½ cups uncooked regular rice
¼ teaspoon salt
⅛ teaspoon pepper

Sauté onion and green pepper in butter for 5 to 10 minutes or until tender. Stir in remaining ingredients; bring to a boil. Reduce heat; cover and simmer about 20 minutes or until done. Yield: 6 servings.

GINGER CARROTS

3 to 4 cups diagonally sliced carrots
1 cup orange juice
½ cup chicken broth
3 whole cloves
¾ teaspoon ground ginger
1½ teaspoons grated lemon rind
3 tablespoons sugar

Combine all ingredients except sugar in a saucepan; bring to a boil. Stir in sugar; cover and simmer about 30 minutes or until carrots are tender. Yield: 6 servings.

FRESH SPINACH SALAD

¾ cup corn oil
¼ cup garlic-flavored wine vinegar
2 tablespoons white wine
2 tablespoons soy sauce
1 teaspoon sugar
1 teaspoon dry mustard
½ teaspoon curry powder
½ teaspoon salt
½ teaspoon seasoned pepper
1 bunch fresh spinach
   Onion slices (optional)
5 or 6 bacon slices, cooked and crumbled
2 hard-cooked eggs, chopped

Combine first 9 ingredients; mix well.

Wash and drain spinach; tear into bite-size pieces, and place in a large salad bowl. Garnish with onion slices, if desired. Pour dressing over spinach. Sprinkle bacon and egg over salad. Yield: 6 to 8 servings.

ONION ROLLS
(see Index)

STRAWBERRIES AND GRAPES

    2 quarts fresh strawberries
1½ pounds white grapes
    1 (8-ounce) carton commercial sour
       cream
       Sifted powdered sugar

Wash strawberries, and remove hulls. Wash
grapes; combine with strawberries, and chill.
Serve fruits topped with sour cream and powdered sugar. Yield: 6 servings.

ORANGE BAVARIAN CREAM

    2 envelopes (2 tablespoons) unflavored
       gelatin
½ cup cold water
1½ cups orange juice
¼ cup lemon juice
    1 teaspoon grated orange rind
⅔ cup sugar, divided
½ teaspoon salt
    2 egg whites
½ pint whipping cream, whipped
       Orange slices (optional)
       Lemon slices (optional)
       Mint leaves (optional)

Soften gelatin in cold water. Combine juices,
orange rind, and 6 tablespoons sugar; bring to
a boil. Add softened gelatin, stirring well; chill
until consistency of unbeaten egg white.
    Add salt to egg whites, and beat until stiff;
slowly add remaining sugar, beating until glossy.
    Fold egg whites and whipped cream into gela-
tin mixture; pour into a 6-cup mold. Chill until
firm. Garnish with orange and lemon slices and
mint leaves, if desired. Yield: 8 servings.

Your guest list—When making a guest list for
your next party, include people who have something in common, those you think will be com-
patible even though they may not know each
other well.

Use of candles—Candles should be used only
after sundown or on a dark, gloomy day. If
candles are on the table, always light them.

A Simple but Sensational Dinner Party

(Buffet Dinner for Six)

Zesty Shrimp Dip   Raw Vegetables
Italian Beef Tips
Corn Curry or Pineapple Carrots
Stuffed Peppers
Cauliflower-Radish Salad
Spoonbread
Applesauce Sherbet
Wine   Coffee

ZESTY SHRIMP DIP

  1 (5-ounce) can shrimp, drained
  1 (8-ounce) carton cottage cheese
  3 tablespoons chili sauce
½ teaspoon onion juice
½ teaspoon lemon juice
¼ teaspoon Worcestershire sauce
    About 4 tablespoons milk

Combine all ingredients in blender. Blend until smooth. Chill. Serve with raw vegetables. Yield: about 2 cups.

ITALIAN BEEF TIPS

  3 pounds lean stew meat, boneless chuck,
    or rump roast
    Salt
¼ teaspoon pepper
  2 tablespoons salad oil

1½ cups water
  2 (6-ounce) cans tomato paste
  2 tablespoons lemon juice
½ teaspoon sugar
  1 teaspoon oregano
  1 small carrot, thinly sliced
  1 clove garlic, minced
    Hot cooked rice
¼ cup grated Parmesan cheese

Cut beef into 1½- to 2-inch cubes, and sprinkle with 1 teaspoon salt and pepper. Brown meat in oil in a large skillet.

Combine water, tomato paste, lemon juice, sugar, oregano, carrot, and garlic; pour over meat. Cover and simmer 1½ to 2 hours or until meat is tender. Add more water if sauce becomes too thick. Season to taste with salt. Serve over rice, and sprinkle with Parmesan cheese. Garnish as desired. Yield: 6 servings.

CORN CURRY

¼ cup melted margarine
3 cups frozen or canned whole kernel corn
2 tablespoons chopped green pepper
3 tablespoons chopped pimiento
3 tablespoons chopped onion
½ teaspoon curry powder
¾ cup commercial sour cream
½ teaspoon salt
Freshly ground pepper

Combine margarine, vegetables, and curry powder in a skillet; cook over low heat 8 to 10 minutes or until vegetables are tender. Stir in sour cream, salt, and pepper. Heat thoroughly, stirring often; do not allow to boil. Yield: 6 servings.

PINEAPPLE CARROTS

2 (1-pound) packages carrots, sliced
1 teaspoon salt
2 cups boiling water
½ cup sugar
4 teaspoons cornstarch
1 (6-ounce) can pineapple juice
2 tablespoons butter or margarine
2 tablespoons chopped fresh mint leaves

Combine carrots, salt, and water in a saucepan. Cover and simmer 25 minutes; drain. Combine sugar, cornstarch, and pineapple juice; cook, stirring constantly over medium heat, until sauce thickens and boils 3 minutes. Add butter; stir until melted. Stir in carrots and mint. Yield: 6 to 8 servings.

STUFFED PEPPERS

6 medium-size green peppers
1 clove garlic, crushed
1 to 2 medium tomatoes, chopped
1 large eggplant, peeled and cubed
⅓ cup olive oil
1 cup dry breadcrumbs
Salt to taste
¼ cup grated Parmesan cheese
2 tablespoons chopped parsley

Cut off top of each green pepper; remove seeds. Cook peppers about 5 minutes in enough boiling water to cover; drain.

Sauté garlic, tomatoes, and eggplant in oil until tender. Combine eggplant mixture, breadcrumbs, salt, Parmesan, and parsley; mix well. Stuff peppers with eggplant mixture; place in a baking pan. Bake at 325° for 40 minutes or until thoroughly heated. Yield: 6 servings.

CAULIFLOWER-RADISH SALAD

1 (6-ounce) package lemon-flavored gelatin
1 teaspoon salt
2 cups boiling water
1½ cups cold water
2 cups diced radishes
1½ cups chopped uncooked cauliflower
2½ tablespoons vinegar
1 teaspoon grated onion

Dissolve gelatin and salt in boiling water; add cold water. Chill until slightly thickened.

Combine remaining ingredients, and marinate in refrigerator 20 minutes; fold into gelatin. Pour into a 6-cup mold, and refrigerate until firm. Yield: 6 servings.

SPOONBREAD

1 cup cornmeal
3 cups milk, divided
1 teaspoon salt
1 teaspoon baking powder
2 tablespoons salad oil
3 eggs, separated

Combine cornmeal and 2 cups milk in a saucepan; cook over medium heat, stirring constantly, until consistency of mush. Remove from heat; add salt, baking powder, oil, and 1 cup milk.

Beat egg yolks, and stir into cornmeal mixture; fold in stiffly beaten egg whites. Pour into a 1½-quart casserole. Bake at 325° for 1 hour. Yield: 6 servings.

APPLESAUCE SHERBET

2 cups buttermilk
1 (16-ounce) can applesauce
1 cup sugar
2 tablespoons lemon juice
1 tablespoon lime juice
  Grated lemon or lime rind

Combine all ingredients except lemon rind, blending well. Pour into a 9-inch square pan, and freeze until firm. Sprinkle with lemon rind before serving. Yield: 6 servings.

Cut raw turnips into strips and serve as a snack or hors d'oeuvre. They're good served with a dip.

Assistance from a friend—If you're hosting a party without help, ask a friend to help replenish trays as needed. Most guests are pleased to assist.

Special Sirloin Dinner
(Buffet Dinner for Eight)

Creme Vichyssoise or Cream of Broccoli Soup
Braised Sirloin Tips with Almond Rice
Beets in Orange Sauce
Chinese-Style Green Peas
Mint Delight Salad
Brandy Peaches
Coffee   Tea

CREME VICHYSSOISE

    4 leeks with tops or 1½ cups minced
        onion
    3 cups peeled, sliced potatoes
    3 cups boiling water
    4 chicken bouillon cubes
    3 tablespoons butter or margarine
    1 cup half-and-half or whipping cream
    1 cup milk
    1 teaspoon salt
    ¼ teaspoon pepper
    2 tablespoons minced chives
    ¼ teaspoon paprika

Finely chop leeks and green tops. Cook leeks and potatoes, uncovered, in boiling water about 10 minutes or until tender. Do not drain.

Press mixture through a fine sieve into a double boiler. Add next 6 ingredients. Mix well; reheat. Chill thoroughly. Serve very cold, and top with chives and paprika. Yield: 8 servings.

CREAM OF BROCCOLI SOUP

    2 cups chopped broccoli
    1 small onion, thinly sliced
    1 leek or green onion, thinly sliced (white
        portion only)
    1 small stalk celery, sliced
    1 tablespoon butter or margarine
    ½ cup water
    2 teaspoons salt
        Pinch of cayenne pepper
    3 tablespoons uncooked regular rice
    2 cups chicken broth, divided
    ½ cup half-and-half

Cook broccoli in a small amount of boiling water; drain, reserving liquid. Set aside.

Combine onion, leek, celery, butter, and water in 2-quart saucepan; place over medium heat and simmer slowly for 2 minutes. Add salt, cayenne pepper, rice, and 1 cup broth; simmer for 15 minutes. Do not boil.

Place broccoli, onion mixture, and remaining 1 cup broth into blender; blend until smooth. Combine half-and-half and soup mixture in a saucepan; heat and serve. If a thinner soup is desired, add broccoli liquid. Yield: 8 to 10 servings.

BRAISED SIRLOIN TIPS WITH ALMOND RICE

1½ pounds fresh mushrooms, sliced
¼ cup melted butter or margarine, divided
1 tablespoon salad oil
1 (3-pound) sirloin steak, cut into 1-inch cubes
¾ cup beef bouillon
¾ cup red wine
2 tablespoons soy sauce
2 cloves garlic, minced
½ onion, grated
2 tablespoons cornstarch
⅓ cup beef bouillon
½ (10¾-ounce) can cream of mushroom soup, undiluted
Salt to taste
Almond Rice

Sauté mushrooms in 2 tablespoons butter until lightly browned; spoon into a 3-quart casserole. Add remaining butter and salad oil to skillet; add meat, and brown on all sides. Spoon over mushrooms.

Combine ¾ cup bouillon, wine, soy sauce, garlic, and onion; add to skillet, scraping bottom to salvage all particles.

Blend cornstarch with ⅓ cup bouillon; stir into wine mixture. Cook, stirring constantly, until smooth and thickened. Spoon over meat, stirring gently to mix. Cover and bake at 275° for 1 hour. Add mushroom soup, stirring until smooth. Add salt to taste. Bake 10 to 15 minutes longer. Serve over Almond Rice. Yield: 8 servings.

Almond Rice:

½ cup slivered blanched almonds
3 tablespoons melted butter
1½ cups uncooked regular rice
4½ cups water
Salt to taste

Sauté almonds in butter until golden. Add rice and stir until thoroughly coated; add water and salt. Bring mixture to a brisk boil; stir briefly, and boil until water barely disappears from surface.

Lower heat immediately; cover tightly, and cook about 20 to 30 minutes or until rice is tender. Check for doneness after about 20 minutes, and quickly stir with a fork.

If rice is not to be served immediately, it can be held for 15 to 20 minutes over low heat or in a 200° oven. Yield: 8 servings.

BEETS IN ORANGE SAUCE

16 to 20 small beets, cooked and peeled, or 2 (16-ounce) cans small whole beets
2 tablespoons cornstarch
1¼ cups firmly packed light brown sugar
1 (6-ounce) can frozen orange juice concentrate, undiluted
¾ cup cider vinegar
1 tablespoon butter or margarine

Drain beets, reserving ¾ cup juice; set beets aside. Combine cornstarch, brown sugar, orange juice, vinegar, and reserved beet liquid. Cook until thick and clear, stirring constantly; stir in butter. Add beets, and heat thoroughly. Yield: 8 servings.

CHINESE-STYLE GREEN PEAS

¼ cup olive oil
¼ cup salad oil
3 (10-ounce) packages frozen peas,
    thawed
3 medium onions, chopped
1½ cups coarsely chopped celery
1 (8½-ounce) can water chestnuts,
    drained and sliced
4 teaspoons cornstarch
1 cup beef broth
1 teaspoon soy sauce
    Salt to taste

Heat olive oil and salad oil in a large skillet over medium heat; do not let oil get too hot. Add peas, onion, celery, and water chestnuts. When peas start sputtering, cover and turn heat to low. Cook 10 to 15 minutes, stirring occasionally. Do not overcook vegetables; they must remain crisp.

Dissolve cornstarch in ¼ cup broth; combine with remaining broth, stirring well. Gradually pour over vegetables and cook, stirring constantly, until slightly thickened and transparent. Add soy sauce and salt; cook 1 minute longer. Serve at once. Yield: 8 to 10 servings.

MINT DELIGHT SALAD

¾ cup mint jelly
1 cup salad dressing or mayonnaise
1 cup miniature marshmallows
1 cup diced pears
1 (15¼-ounce) can pineapple chunks,
    drained
1 cup whipping cream, whipped

Melt jelly over low heat; add salad dressing, blending well. Stir in marshmallows, pears, and pineapple. Fold in whipped cream. Pour into an 8-inch square pan, and freeze until firm. Cut into squares to serve. Yield: 8 to 10 servings.

BRANDY PEACHES

16 canned cling peach halves (reserve
    syrup)
1 cup maple syrup
1 cup firmly packed brown sugar
⅓ cup melted butter or margarine
    Ground cinnamon
⅓ cup brandy
    Vanilla ice cream (optional)

Place peach halves, cavity side up, in a shallow baking pan; pour some of peach syrup around halves.

Pour 1 tablespoon maple syrup over each peach half, and put 1 tablespoon brown sugar and 1 teaspoon butter in each cavity. Sprinkle with cinnamon. Bake, uncovered, at 325° about 20 minutes or until thoroughly heated.

At this point, peaches may be refrigerated until needed (they'll keep at least a week). To serve, pour brandy over peaches and top with ice cream, if desired. Yield: 8 servings.

Save refrigerator space—Use insulated ice chests to keep bottled drinks and other items cold. This saves refrigerator space.

Be willing to alter your shopping and eating habits. Learn less-expensive nutritional alternatives and substitute whenever possible. For example, substitute reconstituted dry milk for whole milk in cooking and baking.

Stuffed Flounder Feast
(Dinner for Eight to Ten)

Helvetia Soup
Crab-Stuffed Flounder
Tomatoes Stuffed with Mushrooms
Dilly Artichoke-Rice Salad
Parmesan French Bread
Blueberry Cheesecake or Frozen Lemon Pudding
Wine   Coffee

HELVETIA SOUP

  1 cup chopped onion
1/3 cup melted butter or margarine
  6 cups small dry bread cubes
  6 cups chicken broth
  2 egg yolks, beaten
  1 cup half-and-half
1 1/2 cups shredded Swiss cheese
    Salt to taste
    White pepper to taste
    Grated nutmeg

Sauté onion in butter until tender; add bread cubes, stirring until well coated and lightly browned. Stir in chicken broth, and simmer over low heat 8 minutes. Cool slightly.

    Pour broth mixture in blender; puree. Pour into saucepan; add egg yolks, half-and-half, and cheese, mixing well. Season with salt, pepper, and nutmeg. Heat thoroughly. Yield: 8 to 10 servings.

CRAB-STUFFED FLOUNDER

  4 (1 1/2-pound) flounder or
    1 (6- to 8-pound) flounder
1/3 cup minced onion
1/3 cup minced green pepper
  1 cup melted butter
1 1/2 pounds crabmeat
    Salt and pepper to taste
1/4 cup chopped parsley
  2 tablespoons lemon juice
    Dash of hot sauce
    Additional melted butter
    Additional lemon juice
    Parsley
    Notched lemon halves
    Paprika
    Seafood Sauce

Lay each fish flat on a cutting board, light side down; slit lengthwise, beginning 3/4 inch from head and cutting down center of fish to tail. Make a crosswise slit in flounder near head. Cut flesh along both sides of backbone to the tail, allowing the knife to run over the rib bones to form a pocket for stuffing.

Sauté onion and green pepper in 1 cup melted butter in a large skillet over medium heat; cook until onion is transparent. Remove from heat. Add crabmeat, salt, pepper, chopped parsley, 2 tablespoons lemon juice, and hot sauce; mix thoroughly.

Brush pocket of fish with melted butter, and sprinkle with salt and pepper. Stuff fish loosely with crabmeat mixture, and place on a greased baking sheet. Bake at 350° for 40 to 60 minutes (depending on size of fish) or until fish flakes easily when tested with a fork; baste frequently with additional butter and lemon juice as fish bakes.

Remove fish to serving platter, and garnish with parsley and notched lemon halves dipped in paprika. Top with Seafood Sauce before serving. Yield: 8 to 10 servings.

Seafood Sauce:

6 tablespoons melted butter
6 tablespoons all-purpose flour
 Fish Stock
 Salt and pepper to taste
⅓ cup chopped shrimp
⅓ cup crabmeat

Combine butter and flour in a saucepan, blending until smooth. Place over medium heat; cook, stirring constantly, 2 to 3 minutes or until frothy. Heat 3 cups Fish Stock to boiling, and gradually add to flour mixture; cook until thickened, stirring constantly. Add remaining ingredients, and simmer 5 minutes. Yield: about 3 cups.

Fish Stock:

2 pounds fish trimmings (heads, bones, or skin)
 About 4 cups water
⅓ cup sliced carrot
⅓ cup sliced onion
⅓ cup sliced celery
1 bay leaf
½ teaspoon dried parsley
¼ teaspoon salt
⅛ teaspoon pepper

Combine all ingredients in a saucepan. Simmer, uncovered, 30 minutes; let liquid cook down to about 3½ cups. Strain stock, discarding residue; cool and skim off fat. Cover and refrigerate. If stock will not be used immediately, store in freezer; keeps well several weeks. Yield: about 3 cups.

TOMATOES STUFFED WITH MUSHROOMS

8 to 10 firm, ripe tomatoes
1½ pounds mushrooms, sliced
½ cup melted butter or margarine
1 (8-ounce) carton commercial sour cream
4 teaspoons all-purpose flour
1 (3-ounce) package Roquefort cheese
¼ teaspoon ground oregano
1 teaspoon chopped parsley
2 tablespoons dry sherry
 Salt and pepper to taste
 Paprika

Cut a slice from top of each tomato; scoop out pulp, leaving shells intact. Invert tomato and drain. Sauté mushrooms in butter until tender; drain.

Combine sour cream, flour, cheese, oregano, parsley, and sherry; cook over low heat until smooth and thickened, stirring constantly. Add mushrooms, salt, and pepper; stir well.

Spoon mixture into tomato shells, and place in a shallow baking pan. Sprinkle with paprika. Bake at 375° for 15 minutes. Yield: 8 to 10 servings.

DILLY ARTICHOKE-RICE SALAD

2 cups chicken broth
1 cup uncooked regular rice
⅓ cup chopped green onion
⅓ cup chopped green pepper
⅓ cup sliced stuffed olives
1 (7-ounce) jar marinated artichoke hearts, drained and chopped
⅓ cup chopped celery
½ cup mayonnaise
¾ teaspoon dillweed
  Salt and pepper to taste
  Lettuce
  Sliced stuffed olives

Bring chicken broth to a boil. Add rice and cook over low heat 20 minutes or until rice is tender and broth is absorbed; remove from heat. Cool.

Combine rice and next 8 ingredients; chill well. Serve on lettuce, and garnish with sliced olives. Yield: 8 to 10 servings.

PARMESAN FRENCH BREAD
(see Index)

BLUEBERRY CHEESECAKE

2 (8-ounce) packages cream cheese, softened
2 cups cottage cheese
1½ cups sugar
4 eggs, slightly beaten
6 tablespoons cornstarch
6 tablespoons all-purpose flour
1½ tablespoons lemon juice
1 teaspoon vanilla extract
½ cup melted margarine, cooled
1 pint commercial sour cream
  Graham Cracker Crust
  Blueberry Glaze

Combine cream cheese and cottage cheese; beat until smooth and creamy. Gradually add sugar, beating well. Add eggs, and beat until well mixed. Add cornstarch, flour, lemon juice, and vanilla; blend well. Add margarine and sour cream, beating until smooth.

Pour filling into a 10-inch springform pan prepared with Graham Cracker Crust. Bake at 325° for 1 hour and 10 minutes or until firm around edges. Turn off oven; let cheesecake stand in oven 2 hours. Remove from oven; let cool completely. Remove from pan; chill. Top with Blueberry Glaze. Yield: 10 to 12 servings.

Graham Cracker Crust:

1½ cups graham cracker crumbs
¼ cup melted margarine
1 teaspoon sugar

Combine all ingredients, and press into bottom of a 10-inch springform pan. Yield: one 10-inch crust.

Blueberry Glaze:

1 cup sugar
2 tablespoons cornstarch
1 cup water
1 pint fresh blueberries, divided

Combine sugar and cornstarch in a small saucepan; blend thoroughly. Gradually stir in water.

Crush ½ cup blueberries; add to sugar mixture. Cook over medium heat, stirring constantly, until mixture thickens and boils. Continue to boil about 2 minutes or until mixture is clear. Cool.

Arrange remaining blueberries over top of chilled cheesecake. Pour cooled glaze over berries. Yield: about 1⅓ cups.

FROZEN LEMON PUDDING

4 tablespoons lemon juice
3 eggs, separated
½ cup sugar
  Grated rind of 1 lemon
½ pint whipping cream, whipped
½ cup graham cracker crumbs

Combine lemon juice, egg yolks, sugar, and lemon rind in top of a double boiler; cook until smooth and thickened, stirring constantly. Cool. Fold stiffly beaten egg whites and whipped cream into lemon mixture.

Sprinkle graham cracker crumbs in a 9-inch square pan; pour in lemon mixture. Freeze until firm. Cut into squares to serve. Yield: 8 to 10 servings.

If utensils are to be stored for any length of time between use, rub a light film of oil over interior. Wipe off film before using, and wash in clear water.

With an electric blender it's easy to make breadcrumbs from dry bread slices and leftover hamburger and hotdog buns. Break up bread and buns, and blend at medium speed for a few seconds. Store crumbs in an airtight container, and freeze.

A Pork Chop Flambé

(Dinner for Six)

Pork Chops Flambé
Savory Rice
Broccoli Soufflé
Hot Curried Fruit
Onion-Dill Bread or Commercial French Rolls
Relish Tray
Kentucky Derby Pie
Wine　　Coffee

PORK CHOPS FLAMBÉ

1½ teaspoons salt
¼ teaspoon pepper
¾ teaspoon dry mustard
6 (¾- to 1-inch-thick) pork chops
¼ cup melted butter or margarine
1 medium onion, thinly sliced
1½ teaspoons tomato paste
¾ cup white wine
¼ cup brandy

Combine salt, pepper, and mustard; coat chops with seasoning mixture, and sauté in butter until browned. Remove chops from skillet, and sauté onion in remaining butter until golden brown; blend in tomato paste and wine. Return chops to skillet; cover and simmer 45 minutes.

Heat brandy in a small saucepan over medium heat. Do not boil. Ignite and pour over chops. After flames die down, serve immediately. Yield: 6 servings.

SAVORY RICE

4 slices bacon
1 onion, thinly sliced
1 cup sliced mushrooms
1½ cups uncooked regular rice
1 cup chicken or game bird broth
½ cup dry white wine
2 teaspoons sage
Salt and pepper to taste
1 egg, slightly beaten

Cook bacon until crisp; drain, reserving drippings.

Sauté onion and mushrooms in bacon drippings until onion is transparent but not brown; add rice and cook until golden. Stir in broth, wine, and seasonings; mix well. Simmer until rice is tender. Add egg, mixing lightly; crumble in bacon. Yield: 6 servings.

Note: Rice may be used as a stuffing for poultry and game birds.

BROCCOLI SOUFFLÉ

3 tablespoons melted butter or margarine
3 tablespoons all-purpose flour
1 cup milk
½ teaspoon salt
⅛ teaspoon white pepper
1 cup mayonnaise
2 cups cooked chopped broccoli
   Onion salt or juice to taste
6 eggs

Combine butter and flour, blending until smooth; cook over low heat until bubbly. Gradually add milk; cook, stirring constantly, until smooth and thick. Add salt, pepper, and mayonnaise, stirring until well blended.

Combine sauce, broccoli, and onion salt. Beat eggs until light and fluffy; gradually fold into broccoli mixture.

Spoon into a lightly greased 2-quart casserole. Bake at 300° for 45 to 55 minutes or until firm. Yield: 6 to 8 servings.

HOT CURRIED FRUIT

½ cup melted margarine
¾ cup firmly packed brown sugar
1½ teaspoons curry powder
1 (29-ounce) can pear halves, drained
1 (20-ounce) can pineapple tidbits, drained
1 (30-ounce) can apricot halves, drained
1 (29-ounce) can sliced peaches, drained
1 (8-ounce) jar maraschino cherries, drained
2 bananas, sliced

Combine margarine, sugar, and curry powder; heat, stirring until well blended. Combine fruit in a shallow 2-quart casserole; add sauce. Bake at 300° for 1 hour. Yield: 8 to 10 servings.

ONION-DILL BREAD
(see Index)

RELISH TRAY

An assortment of crisp vegetables for a relish tray might include: carrot or celery sticks, radishes, cauliflowerettes, and yellow squash or zucchini slices. Add ripe or green olives, Italian peppers, or your favorite pickles.

KENTUCKY DERBY PIE

½ cup melted butter
1 cup sugar
1 cup light corn syrup
4 eggs, beaten
1 to 2 tablespoons bourbon
½ cup chocolate morsels
1 cup chopped pecans
1 unbaked 9-inch pastry shell
   Whipped cream

Combine first 7 ingredients, mixing well; pour into pastry shell. Bake at 350° for 40 to 45 minutes or until firm. Serve warm with whipped cream. Yield: one 9-inch pie.

A Gourmet Debut

(Dinner for Eight to Ten)

Avocado Mousse
Croquettes de la Viandes Variées
Armenian Rice
Gourmet Baked Spinach
Sherried Fruit
Rich Dinner Rolls   Butter
Coffee Ice Cream Dessert or Chocolate Cream Dream
Wine   Coffee

AVOCADO MOUSSE

  2 envelopes (2 tablespoons) unflavored
     gelatin
  ¼ cup cold water
  2 (3-ounce) packages lime-flavored gelatin
  4 cups boiling water
  2 cups mashed avocado
  1 cup mayonnaise
  ½ pint whipping cream, whipped
     Lettuce leaves

Dissolve unflavored gelatin in cold water. Dissolve lime-flavored gelatin in boiling water; add unflavored gelatin. Chill until slightly thickened; fold in avocado, mayonnaise, and whipped cream. Spoon into an 8-cup mold and chill until firm. Serve on lettuce leaves. Yield: 10 to 12 servings.

CROQUETTES DE LA VIANDES VARIÉES

  1 pound lean ground pork
  1 pound ground chicken breast
  1 pound ground veal
  ¼ cup butter, softened
  1 tablespoon monosodium glutamate
  1 teaspoon salt
  ½ teaspoon pepper
  ½ onion, grated
  1 clove garlic, minced, or dash of garlic
     powder
  ¾ cup breadcrumbs
  ¼ cup Parmesan cheese
  6 tablespoons clarified butter
  2 cups sliced mushrooms
  1 teaspoon monosodium glutamate
     Juice of ½ lemon
  ¼ cup melted butter
  1 cup dry vermouth
  1 cup whipping cream
  3 tablespoons all-purpose flour
  2 to 3 tablespoons water
     Salt and pepper to taste

Combine pork, chicken, and veal; work ¼ cup soft butter into meat. Add 1 tablespoon monosodium glutamate, salt, pepper, onion, and garlic.

Combine breadcrumbs and cheese; place on waxed paper. Shape meat into thick patties; coat with breadcrumb mixture. Cook patties in clarified butter over medium heat, turning frequently, 15 to 20 minutes or until well done.

Combine mushrooms, 1 teaspoon monosodium glutamate, lemon juice, and ¼ cup melted butter in a saucepan; sauté until mushrooms are barely tender.

Remove meat patties from skillet and keep warm. Gradually add vermouth to pan drippings, stirring well over medium heat; add whipping cream, and blend well.

Combine flour and water; add to sauce, and mix well. Cook, stirring constantly, until slightly thickened. Stir in seasonings and sautéed mushrooms. Serve sauce over patties. Yield: 8 to 10 servings.

ARMENIAN RICE

    1 medium onion, chopped
    1 cup broken vermicelli
    ½ cup melted butter or margarine
    2 cups uncooked regular rice
      Salt and pepper to taste
    4 cups beef consommé

Sauté onion and vermicelli in butter until onion is browned; stir in remaining ingredients. Bring to a boil, and boil 10 minutes. Lower heat and simmer 45 minutes or until done, stirring occasionally. Yield: 10 to 12 servings.

GOURMET BAKED SPINACH

    3 (10-ounce) packages frozen chopped
      spinach
    3 tablespoons minced onion
  4½ tablespoons butter or margarine
    6 to 8 tablespoons all-purpose flour
    3 cups milk
    4 hard-cooked eggs, finely chopped
    ⅛ teaspoon ground nutmeg
      Salt and pepper to taste
    ¾ cup shredded American cheese
    ¾ cup buttered breadcrumbs
      Paprika

Cook spinach according to package directions; drain well. Sauté onion in butter until tender; blend in flour. Gradually stir in milk, and cook until smooth and thickened. Add spinach, eggs, nutmeg, salt, and pepper. Pour into a buttered 2½-quart baking dish.

Combine cheese and breadcrumbs; spread evenly over top. Sprinkle with paprika. Bake at 375° for 20 minutes or until lightly browned. Yield: about 12 servings.

SHERRIED FRUIT

    ¼ cup melted margarine
    2 tablespoons all-purpose flour
    ½ cup sugar
    1 cup sherry
    1 (29-ounce) can pear halves, drained
    1 (29-ounce) can peach halves, drained
    1 (20-ounce) can pineapple chunks,
      drained
    1 (14-ounce) can spiced red apple rings,
      drained
    1 (8-ounce) jar maraschino cherries,
      drained
    1 (17-ounce) can apricot halves, drained

Combine margarine and flour. Place over low heat; blend until smooth. Stir in sugar. Slowly add sherry; cook, stirring constantly, until slightly thickened.

Combine sauce and fruit in a 2-quart casserole; cover and refrigerate overnight. Bake at 350° for 30 minutes. Yield: 8 to 10 servings.

RICH DINNER ROLLS
(see Index)

COFFEE ICE CREAM DESSERT

2½ cups vanilla wafer crumbs, divided
1 cup butter or margarine, softened
3 cups powdered sugar
3 ounces unsweetened chocolate, melted
1 teaspoon vanilla extract
3 egg whites, stiffly beaten
1 cup chopped pecans
½ gallon coffee ice cream, slightly softened

Spread 2 cups of vanilla wafer crumbs in bottom of 13- x 9- x 2-inch dish. Combine butter, sugar, chocolate, and vanilla; fold in egg whites and pecans. Spread mixture over wafer crumbs, and top with ice cream. Sprinkle remaining ½ cup vanilla wafer crumbs over top.

Place dish on large baking sheet and freeze until firm. To freeze for longer periods, wrap in freezer wrap. Yield: 15 to 18 servings.

CHOCOLATE CREAM DREAM

1 (12-ounce) package semisweet chocolate pieces
½ teaspoon ground cinnamon
3 tablespoons water
4 eggs, separated
3 tablespoons sugar
2 cups whipping cream, whipped
¼ cup chopped pecans
1 small angel food cake, broken into pieces
Additional whipped cream
Pecan halves

Melt chocolate in a double boiler over hot (not boiling) water; beat in cinnamon and water until smooth. Beat in egg yolks, one at a time; cook over hot water until thickened. Pour into a large bowl; cool 15 minutes.

Beat egg whites until frothy; add sugar, 1 tablespoon at a time, beating until stiff peaks form. Fold into chocolate mixture along with whipped cream and chopped pecans.

Arrange cake pieces in a lightly buttered 3-quart mold or springform pan. Pour a small amount of chocolate mixture over cake, stirring to coat cake. Pour additional chocolate mixture over cake, reserving 1 cup to frost top and sides.

Refrigerate 24 hours. Unmold; frost with reserved chocolate mixture. Garnish with additional whipped cream and pecan halves. Yield: 12 to 16 servings.

Party Lamb Dinner

(Dinner for Four)

Curry Dip   Raw Vegetables
Party Lamb Steaks
Turnip Puff or Potatoes Deluxe
Sweet-and-Sour Green Beans
Crème de Menthe Salad Ring
Commercial Hard Rolls   Butter
Orange Meringue Pie
Coffee   Tea

CURRY DIP

1 cup mayonnaise
1 tablespoon horseradish
1 tablespoon tarragon vinegar
1 tablespoon minced onion
¼ teaspoon curry powder
⅛ teaspoon turmeric

Combine all ingredients; mix well. Chill. Serve with crisp raw vegetables. Yield: about 1 cup.

PARTY LAMB STEAKS

4 (½-inch-thick) lamb steaks
1 clove garlic, halved
Salt and pepper to taste
¼ cup melted butter or margarine
2 tablespoons minced green onions or shallots
½ cup dry white wine
1 (8-ounce) can mushroom stems and pieces, undrained
1 (8-ounce) can tomato sauce
½ teaspoon tarragon
1 tablespoon chopped parsley

Rub steaks with garlic, and season with salt and pepper. Brown steaks in butter, and remove from skillet.

Add onion to pan drippings, and sauté until tender. Add wine, mushrooms, tomato sauce, tarragon, and parsley; bring to a boil. Add steaks; cover and simmer 12 to 15 minutes or until tender. Yield: 4 servings.

TURNIP PUFF

2 cups cooked, mashed turnips, cooled
1 cup breadcrumbs
½ cup melted margarine
½ teaspoon sugar
½ teaspoon salt
¼ teaspoon pepper
2 eggs, separated

Combine turnips, breadcrumbs, margarine, sugar, salt, pepper, and beaten egg yolks.

Beat egg whites until stiff; fold into turnip mixture. Spoon into lightly greased 1-quart casserole. Bake at 350° for 40 minutes. Yield: 4 to 6 servings.

POTATOES DELUXE

4 medium potatoes, peeled and cooked
1 cup milk
2 cups shredded Cheddar cheese, divided
2 teaspoons finely chopped green onion tops
½ teaspoon salt
5 slices bacon, cooked and crumbled

Mash potatoes and set aside. Scald milk; add 1 cup cheese, onion, and salt, stirring until cheese is melted. Add milk mixture and bacon to potatoes; blend well.

Spoon mixture into a greased 1-quart casserole; sprinkle with remaining cheese. Bake at 350° for 10 minutes or until cheese melts. Yield: 4 to 6 servings.

SWEET-AND-SOUR GREEN BEANS

1 pound fresh green beans, cut into 1-inch pieces
2 tablespoons bacon drippings
1 cup boiling water
½ teaspoon salt
1 tablespoon cornstarch
3 tablespoons vinegar
¼ cup cold water
3 tablespoons sugar
1 tablespoon soy sauce
4 tablespoons sweet pickle relish

Combine beans, bacon drippings, boiling water, and salt in a saucepan; bring to a rapid boil. Cover and simmer 15 to 20 minutes or until beans are crisp-tender. Do not drain.

Combine cornstarch and vinegar, stirring to blend. Add cold water, sugar, soy sauce, and pickle relish, stirring well. Pour over beans; cook over low heat, stirring constantly, until smooth and thickened. Yield: 4 servings.

CRÈME DE MENTHE SALAD RING

1 (3-ounce) package lime-flavored gelatin
¾ cup boiling water
1 (8¼-ounce) can crushed pineapple
3 tablespoons crème de menthe liqueur
½ cup commercial sour cream
1 cup diced pears, fresh or canned
1 (8-ounce) carton plain yogurt
1 cup commercial sour cream
2 teaspoons lime juice
Lime slices

Dissolve gelatin in boiling water. Drain pineapple, reserving juice. Combine juice with crème de menthe and enough water to equal ¾ cup liquid; add to gelatin. Chill until mixture starts to thicken. Add ½ cup sour cream and beat mixture until light and creamy; fold in pears and pineapple. Pour mixture into a greased 4-cup ring mold and chill until set.

Combine yogurt, 1 cup sour cream, and lime juice; blend well. Pour dressing into center of unmolded ring, and garnish with lime slices. Yield: 6 servings.

ORANGE MERINGUE PIE

1 cup sugar
5 tablespoons cornstarch
1 cup fresh orange juice
1 cup orange sections, cut into pieces
2 tablespoons grated orange rind
3 egg yolks, beaten
2 tablespoons lemon juice
2 tablespoons melted butter or margarine
1 baked 9-inch pastry shell
Meringue

Combine sugar and cornstarch. Add orange juice, orange sections, and orange rind; cook over low heat, stirring constantly, until clear.

Add a small amount of orange mixture to egg yolks, blending well; add to remaining orange mixture. Cook over low heat, stirring constantly, about 5 minutes or until thickened. Remove from heat; blend in lemon juice and butter.

Pour into pastry shell, and top with Meringue. Bake at 400° for 10 minutes or until Meringue is lightly browned. Yield: one 9-inch pie.

Meringue:

3 egg whites
¼ teaspoon cream of tartar
6 tablespoons sugar

Combine egg whites and cream of tartar; beat until frothy. Add sugar, a small amount at a time, and continue beating until thick and glossy. Yield: meringue for one 9-inch pie.

Ideal conditions for storing chocolate are a temperature of 60° to 70° and a humidity reading of 50%. Keep chocolate away from moisture, and do not store in the refrigerator. During hot weather keep chocolate in a cool place.

Read labels to learn the weight, quality, and size of food products. Don't be afraid to experiment with new brands. Store brands can be equally good in quality and nutritional value, yet lower in price. Lower grades of canned fruits and vegetables are as nutritious as higher grades. Whenever possible, buy most foods by weight or cost per serving rather than by volume or package size.

Flank Steak from the Grill
(Dinner for Eight)

Blue Cheese Shrimp or Crab-Stuffed Mushrooms
Grilled Flank Steak
Sesame Potato Sticks
Crusty Broiled Tomatoes
Spinach-Avocado Salad
Dilly Bread
Fabulous Cheesecake
Wine   Coffee

BLUE CHEESE SHRIMP

1 (3-ounce) bag crab boil
2½ pounds fresh shrimp
   About 2 tablespoons salad oil
1 medium onion, thinly sliced
   Salt and pepper
6 ounces blue cheese, crumbled
   Crackers

Place crab boil bag in a large saucepan with 4 to 5 quarts water; bring to a boil. Add shrimp; return to a boil, and boil 1 to 2 minutes. Drain, cool, and peel shrimp.

Toss shrimp with oil to coat lightly. Combine shrimp with remaining ingredients except crackers; mix thoroughly. Cover and refrigerate 2 days, stirring often. Serve with crackers. Yield: about 8 servings.

CRAB-STUFFED MUSHROOMS

20 medium mushroom caps
3 tablespoons melted butter
1 (6-ounce) package frozen crabmeat,
   thawed and drained
½ cup breadcrumbs
1 heaping teaspoon salad dressing
1 heaping teaspoon mayonnaise
1 teaspoon lemon juice
½ teaspoon curry powder
   Pimiento strips

Coat mushrooms with butter; place, upside down, in a shallow pan. Spoon ¼ teaspoon butter into each cap.

Combine crabmeat, breadcrumbs, salad dressing, mayonnaise, lemon juice, and curry; spoon into mushroom caps, and drizzle with remaining butter. Place a pimiento strip on each, and broil 5 minutes. Yield: about 8 servings.

GRILLED FLANK STEAK

Garlic powder
3 pounds flank steak
½ cup soy sauce
¼ cup Worcestershire sauce
¼ cup salad oil

Sprinkle garlic powder lightly on both sides of steak. Prick both sides of steak with fork.

Combine soy sauce, Worcestershire sauce, and oil; pour over steak. Marinate 6 to 8 hours at room temperature, turning frequently.

Remove steak from marinade. Cook over medium heat about 7 minutes for medium rare. Slice across grain in thin slices. Yield: about 8 servings.

Note: Marinade may be refrigerated and used again.

SESAME POTATO STICKS

6 to 8 medium baking potatoes, peeled
¾ cup sesame seeds
½ cup melted butter or margarine
Salt
Paprika

Cut potatoes into strips 1 inch thick. Sprinkle sesame seeds in a thin layer on waxed paper. Dip potato sticks in butter; coat one side of sticks with sesame seeds. Place sticks, seed side up, on a well-greased baking sheet. Sprinkle with salt and paprika. Bake at 400° about 40 minutes or until done. Yield: about 8 servings.

CRUSTY BROILED TOMATOES

4 medium tomatoes
Dijon-style mustard
Salt
Freshly ground pepper
Cayenne pepper
6 tablespoons melted butter or margarine
½ cup seasoned breadcrumbs.
½ cup grated Parmesan cheese

Cut tomatoes in half. Spread cut side with mustard; sprinkle with salt, pepper, and cayenne pepper to taste.

Combine butter, breadcrumbs, and cheese. Spoon crumb mixture on top of each tomato half. Broil until crumbs are brown and tomatoes are tender. Yield: 8 servings.

SPINACH-AVOCADO SALAD

2 pounds fresh spinach, torn
1 large head Boston lettuce, torn
3 ripe avocados, peeled and sliced
Lemon juice
Honey-Lime Dressing

Combine salad greens in a large bowl. Brush avocados with lemon juice; add to salad. Toss with Honey-Lime Dressing. Yield: about 8 servings.

Honey-Lime Dressing:

¼ cup lemon juice
3 tablespoons lime juice
¼ cup salad oil
¼ cup honey
½ teaspoon salt
¼ teaspoon dry mustard

Combine all ingredients; blend well. Chill. Yield: about 1 cup.

DILLY BREAD

1 package yeast
¼ cup warm water (105° to 115°)
1 cup creamed cottage cheese
2 tablespoons sugar
1 tablespoon minced onion
1 tablespoon melted butter or margarine
2 teaspoons dillseeds
1 teaspoon salt
¼ teaspoon soda
1 egg
2¼ to 2½ cups all-purpose flour
    Softened butter or margarine

Soften yeast in warm water; set aside. Heat cottage cheese to lukewarm in a saucepan. Combine cottage cheese, sugar, onion, melted butter, dillseeds, salt, soda, and egg in a large bowl. Stir in yeast. Add flour to make a stiff dough; beat well.

  Cover and let rise in a warm place until doubled in bulk, about 50 to 60 minutes. Stir down dough. Spoon into a well-greased 2-quart round baking dish. Let rise in a warm place until doubled in bulk, about 30 to 40 minutes. Bake at 350° for 30 to 40 minutes or until golden brown. Brush with softened butter. Yield: about 8 servings.

FABULOUS CHEESECAKE

1½ cups graham cracker crumbs
¼ cup butter or margarine, melted
2 cups sugar, divided
3 eggs
3 (8-ounce) packages cream cheese, softened
6 tablespoons half-and-half or milk
2 cups commercial sour cream
1 tablespoon vanilla extract
    Fresh strawberries (optional)
    Mint sprigs (optional)

Combine crumbs, butter, and ½ cup sugar. Press into an 11¾- x 7½- x 1¾-inch baking dish; set aside.

  Beat eggs and 1 cup sugar until thick. Blend in cream cheese. Add half-and-half and beat until smooth. Pour into crust. Bake at 350° for 45 minutes. Turn off oven; leave cake in oven 30 minutes. Remove and cool at least 30 minutes.

  Combine sour cream, vanilla, and remaining ½ cup sugar; mix well. Spread over cheesecake. Bake at 450° for 10 minutes. Cool. Garnish each serving with a fresh strawberry and a sprig of mint, if desired. Yield: 12 to 15 servings.

Cooking vegetables with the least amount of water possible will preserve vitamins and maintain flavor. Save the cooking liquid, and add to soup stock or gravy for additional food value and flavor.

Make 1 cup sour milk by combining 1 tablespoon lemon juice or vinegar and enough regular milk to make 1 cup.

Seafood in a Chafing Dish

(Buffet Dinner for Eight to Ten)

Sherried Seafood or Easy Lobster Newburg
Rice   Broiled Tomato Cups
Broccoli with Lemon Butter or Southern Green Beans
Tossed Salad with French Dressing
Commercial French Rolls   Butter
Ladyfinger Cake
Wine   Coffee

SHERRIED SEAFOOD

  2 cups oysters
  5 tablespoons melted margarine, divided
  1 cup sliced mushrooms
  4 cups cooked, peeled, and deveined
     shrimp
  1 cup cooked, chopped chicken
  2 (10¾-ounce) cans cream of mushroom
     soup, undiluted
  1 tablespoon grated onion
  ½ teaspoon pepper
  1 teaspoon salt
  1 tablespoon finely chopped parsley
  2 tablespoons sherry
  ¼ teaspoon cayenne pepper
    Hot cooked rice

Sauté oysters in 3 tablespoons margarine until edges curl; drain and set aside. Sauté mushrooms in remaining 2 tablespoons margarine; drain.

Combine all ingredients except rice; simmer over low heat 5 minutes, stirring occasionally. Transfer to a chafing dish set on low heat. Serve over rice. Yield: 8 to 10 servings.

EASY LOBSTER NEWBURG

  ½ cup melted butter or margarine
  ½ cup all-purpose flour
  1 teaspoon dry mustard
  1 teaspoon paprika
  1½ cups milk
  ½ pint whipping cream
  2 pounds cooked lobster, cut into chunks
  1 cup sliced mushrooms
  2 teaspoons salt
  ½ cup sherry
    Hot cooked rice

Combine butter, flour, mustard, and paprika; cook over low heat 2 to 3 minutes. Gradually add milk and cream; cook, stirring constantly, until smooth and thickened. Stir in lobster, mushrooms, salt, and sherry.

Transfer to a chafing dish set on low heat. Serve over rice. Yield: 8 to 10 servings.

BROILED TOMATO CUPS

6 tomatoes
½ cup commercial sour cream
½ cup mayonnaise
¼ cup grated Parmesan cheese
1 teaspoon garlic salt
  Juice of 1 lemon
1 teaspoon chopped parsley
3 green onions, chopped

Cut tomatoes in half crosswise. Combine remaining ingredients, blending well. Top each tomato half with small amount of mixture. Broil tomatoes until bubbly. Yield: 12 servings.

BROCCOLI WITH LEMON BUTTER

2 bunches broccoli
½ cup butter or margarine
½ cup lemon juice

Trim off large leaves of broccoli. Remove tough ends of lower stalks, and wash broccoli thoroughly. If stalks are more than 1 inch in diameter, make lengthwise slits in stalks. Cook broccoli, covered, in a small amount of boiling salted water for 12 to 15 minutes or until crisp-tender. Drain.

Melt butter; add lemon juice, mixing well. Pour over hot broccoli just before serving. Yield: 8 to 10 servings.

SOUTHERN GREEN BEANS

4 slices bacon
  About 5 cups water
3 pounds fresh green beans
½ teaspoon sugar
  Dash of hot sauce
  Salt and pepper (optional)

Place bacon in large saucepan with water. Bring to boiling; reduce heat; cover and simmer 30 minutes. Wash beans and trim ends; break into 1-inch pieces. Add beans, sugar, and hot sauce to bacon. Cover and cook over very low heat 2 to 3 hours. If necessary, from time to time add water just to keep beans from sticking. Taste during last hour of cooking and add salt and pepper if needed. Yield: 10 servings.

TOSSED SALAD WITH FRENCH DRESSING

5 to 6 cups salad greens, broken into
    bite-size pieces
1 cup fresh spinach, broken into bite-size
    pieces
½ cup chopped celery
½ cup diced carrots
½ cup onion rings
½ cup coarsely chopped green pepper
1 cup cauliflower flowerets
  Commercial French dressing

Prepare vegetables and dry well. Cover and chill until just before serving. When ready to serve, add desired amount of French dressing and toss gently. Serve at once. Yield: 8 to 10 servings.

LADYFINGER CAKE

1 cup butter or margarine, softened
2 cups powdered sugar
4 eggs
1 (13¼-ounce) can crushed pineapple,
    well drained
1 cup chopped pecans
2 dozen ladyfingers, split
½ pint whipping cream, whipped

Cream butter and sugar until light and fluffy. Add eggs, one at a time, beating well after each addition. Add pineapple and pecans, stirring to mix.

Line a 13- x 9- x 2-inch pan with half of ladyfingers; spread with half of pineapple mixture. Repeat layers and top with whipped cream. Refrigerate 12 to 24 hours. Yield: 10 to 12 servings.

The Ultimate in Dining—Beef Wellington
(Dinner for Twelve)

Cold Cream of Spinach Soup
Beef Wellington
Artichokes la Primavera or Asparagus Deluxe
Broiled Tomato Cups
Commercial Hard Rolls   Butter
Melon Compote or Crêpes Suzette
Wine   Coffee

COLD CREAM OF SPINACH SOUP

    2 (10-ounce) packages frozen chopped
        spinach
    4 teaspoons finely chopped onion
    ¼ cup melted butter or margarine
    ½ cup all-purpose flour
    2 teaspoons salt
    ¼ teaspoon white pepper
    2 quarts milk, divided
    6 tablespoons lemon juice

Cook spinach according to package directions; drain well and set aside.

Sauté onion in butter; stir in flour, salt, and pepper. Cook over low heat, stirring constantly, until smooth and bubbly. Gradually stir in 2 cups milk; heat until mixture is thick.

Blend cream sauce and spinach; add remaining milk and lemon juice, and blend well. Cover and refrigerate at least 4 hours. Stir gently. Serve in chilled bowls or mugs. Yield: 12 to 16 servings.

BEEF WELLINGTON

    Pastry
    1 (5- to 5½-pound) beef tenderloin
    2 (4¾-ounce) cans liver pâté
    1 egg, beaten
    1 teaspoon cold water

Prepare pastry; chill at least 1 hour.

Trim fat from tenderloin; reserve. Tuck small end of meat underneath tenderloin; tie securely with string at 2-inch intervals. Place meat on rack in an open pan. Lay pieces of fat on top of meat. (Do not add water, and do not cover.) Roast at 425° for 20 to 25 minutes for rare; 25 to 30 minutes for medium.

Remove meat from oven, and discard fat. Let stand 30 minutes to cool. Remove string; keep small end of meat tucked underneath.

Roll pastry into an 18- x 14-inch rectangle on a lightly floured board or pastry cloth. Spread pâté over pastry to within 1 inch of edge.

Place tenderloin lengthwise, top side down, in middle of pastry. Bring long sides of pastry up to overlap on underside of tenderloin. Combine egg and water; brush seam with egg mixture to seal. Trim ends of pastry and fold over; brush with egg mixture to seal.

Place meat, seam side down, on a lightly greased baking sheet. Brush with egg mixture.

Roll pastry timmings; cut into decorative shapes and arrange on top of tenderloin. Brush with remaining egg mixture. Bake at 425° for 30 minutes or until pastry is golden. Let stand 10 minutes before slicing. Garnish as desired. Yield: 12 to 14 servings.

Pastry:

  3 cups all-purpose flour
  ½ teaspoon salt
  ¾ cup shortening
  ½ to ¾ cup cold water

Combine flour and salt; cut in shortening with pastry blender until mixture resembles coarse cornmeal. Add water, 1 tablespoon at a time, stirring with a fork until dough holds together. Shape into a ball. Wrap in waxed paper and chill until ready to use.

ARTICHOKES LA PRIMAVERA

12 medium artichokes
    Lemon slices
    Salt
  4 tablespoons salad oil
  6 cups diced carrots
  6 tablespoons melted butter
2¼ teaspoons sugar
1½ cups water
  1 cup half-and-half
  6 egg yolks
  2 to 4 tablespoons lemon juice

Wash artichokes well, and trim stem even with base. Slice about ¾ inch off top of artichoke, and remove discolored leaves at base. Trim off thorny leaf tips.

Tie string around each artichoke from top to bottom to hold leaves in place during cooking. (If not cooking immediately, place artichokes in a bowl containing 1 tablespoon lemon juice to 1 quart water to prevent discoloration.)

Place artichokes in 2 inches water in a deep saucepan. Add a few lemon slices, salt, and salad oil. Cover and cook over medium heat 25 to 40 minutes or until leaves pull out easily.

Remove artichokes from water using tongs; place upside down to drain. Untie string, and gently spread center leaves apart; pull out center leaves, and scrape off the fuzzy thistle center (choke) with a spoon.

Sauté carrots in butter about 5 minutes; add 1½ teaspoons salt, sugar, and 1½ cups water. Cover and simmer 10 to 15 minutes or until carrots are tender. Do not drain.

Combine half-and-half and egg yolks; beat well. Add egg yolk mixture to carrots; cook over low heat, stirring constantly, until slightly thickened. Stir in lemon juice. Spoon carrot mixture into center of each artichoke. Serve immediately. Yield: 12 servings.

ASPARAGUS DELUXE

  9 tablespoons butter, melted
  9 tablespoons cornstarch
  3 (10½-ounce) cans asparagus spears
    Milk
  6 hard-cooked eggs, thinly sliced
  3 cups shredded Cheddar cheese
    Buttered breadcrumbs

Combine butter and cornstarch; stir over medium heat until mixture is smooth and bubbly. Drain asparagus and reserve juice; add enough milk to reserved juice to make 4½ cups. Add milk mixture to sauce; cook, stirring constantly, until mixture begins to thicken. Layer asparagus, eggs, cheese, and sauce in a greased 2½-quart casserole dish. Repeat layers. Top with buttered breadcrumbs. Bake at 325° for 30 minutes. Yield: 12 to 14 servings.

BROILED TOMATO CUPS
(see Index)

MELON COMPOTE

1 cup sugar
½ cup water
½ cup kirsch or Cointreau
10 cups melon balls, chilled
Mint leaves

Combine sugar and water; bring to a boil. Remove from heat, and add kirsch; chill. Place melon balls in sherbet glasses; pour kirsch mixture over fruit. Garnish with mint. Yield: 12 servings.

CRÊPES SUZETTE

1¼ cups all-purpose flour
Pinch of salt
2 tablespoons sugar
3 eggs, beaten
1½ cups milk
2 tablespoons melted butter
½ teaspoon lemon, rum, or brandy extract
Orange Butter
Orange Sauce
3 tablespoons Grand Marnier or other
orange-flavored liqueur

Combine flour, salt, sugar, and eggs; mix well. Blend in milk, butter, and flavoring; beat until smooth. Refrigerate batter at least 2 hours (this allows flour particles to swell and soften so crêpes are light in texture). Prepare Orange Butter and Orange Sauce while batter is chilling.

Place domed crêpe pan over medium heat; allow pan to heat until water sizzles when sprinkled on surface. Pour batter into pieplate.

Dip heated pan (domed side down) into batter. Place pan (domed side up) over medium heat; cook crêpe about 1 minute or until lightly browned on bottom. Lift edge of crepe to test for doneness. (It is not necessary to cook both sides of crêpe; the lighter side is either filled or folded inward.) Remove crêpe from pan.

Crêpes can be made in advance and stacked between layers of waxed paper to prevent sticking.

Spoon about 1 tablespoon Orange Butter on each crêpe, spreading evenly to outer edges. Fold crêpe in half, then in quarters. Spoon half of Orange Sauce into chafing dish; arrange crêpes in sauce. Spoon remaining sauce over crêpes; place over low heat until thoroughly heated.

Heat Grand Marnier in a small saucepan over medium heat. (Do not boil.)

Pour over crêpes and ignite. After flames die down, serve immediately. Yield: 12 to 15 servings.

Orange Butter:

¾ cup unsalted butter, softened
½ cup sugar
⅓ cup Grand Marnier or other
orange-flavored liqueur
¼ cup grated orange rind

Cream butter and sugar until light and fluffy. Add Grand Marnier and orange rind, beating until well blended. Yield: about 2 cups.

Orange Sauce:

½ cup unsalted butter, melted
¾ cup sugar
2 tablespoons grated orange rind
⅔ cup orange juice
2 oranges, peeled and sectioned
¼ cup Grand Marnier or other
orange-flavored liqueur

Combine butter, sugar, orange rind, and orange juice in a skillet or saucepan. Cook over low heat about 10 minutes, stirring frequently. Add orange sections and Grand Marnier. Keep warm. Yield: about 2¾ cups.

Note: If you prefer using a 6- or 7-inch skillet or standard crêpe pan for cooking the crêpes, follow this procedure: Brush bottom of skillet lightly with salad oil; place over medium heat until just hot, not smoking. Pour 2 tablespoons batter in pan; quickly tilt pan in all directions so batter covers the pan in a thin film. Cook about 1 minute.

Lift edge of crêpe to test for doneness. Crêpe is ready for flipping when it can be shaken loose from pan. Flip the crêpe, and cook about 30 seconds on the other side.

OUTDOOR PARTIES AND COOKOUTS

Ham over the Coals

Feast by the Pool

Dinner from the Grill

Seaside Oyster Roast

Hot off the Coals

Grilled Fish Feast

A Picnic from the Grill

Barbecue with an Eastern Flair

Pork Kabob Supper

A Good-Neighbor Cookout

Meal-on-a-Skewer

Spicy Sparerib Special

Backyard Barbecue

Carnival Cookout

Steak-on-a-Stick

Crowd-Pleasing Patio Party

Outdoor cooking and eating is a natural for Southern living. The beautiful sunny outdoors is a lovely place to entertain during much of the year in the South. Whether it's a garden party, a picnic at the lake, or a family gathering in the backyard, dining alfresco reflects the carefree life-styles of warm-weather days.

Since outdoor dining can be as simple as a spur-of-the-moment wiener roast or as elaborate as a poolside feast, put your grill to use with some of our outdoor specialties. We offer menus and recipes for sixteen perfect outdoor gatherings. The side dishes we've included team well with the foods sizzling on the grill and complete an easy outdoor feast.

Ham over the Coals

(Dinner for Eight)

Ham on the Grill
Zucchini-Tomato Kabobs   Savory Succotash
Island Fruit Boats
Garlic Bread
Hawaiian Cheesecake
Sunshine Punch

HAM ON THE GRILL

1 (1¾-inch-thick) slice fully cooked
center-cut ham (about 3½ pounds)
Whole cloves (optional)
½ cup dry sherry
¼ cup melted butter or margarine

Score ham in a diamond pattern at ½-inch intervals; stud with whole cloves, if desired. Place ham in a heavy-duty plastic bag in a shallow pan; add sherry, and fasten bag securely. Refrigerate overnight, turning once. Drain, reserving sherry for basting during grilling.

Brush ham with melted butter, and place on grill 4 to 6 inches from coals. Grill 15 to 20 minutes on each side, basting frequently with butter and reserved sherry. Yield: 8 servings.

ZUCCHINI-TOMATO KABOBS

½ pound fresh mushrooms
1½ pounds small zucchini, cut into 1-inch
slices
12 to 18 large cherry tomatoes
Commercial Italian salad dressing
9 (1-inch) fresh pineapple chunks

Clean mushrooms with a damp cloth; remove stems. Combine mushrooms, zucchini, tomatoes, and salad dressing; cover and marinate in refrigerator 4 hours or overnight.

Drain vegetables, and reserve marinade; thread vegetables alternately with pineapple onto 3 long skewers. Cook on grill over medium heat 10 minutes, turning occasionally and basting frequently with reserved marinade. Yield: 8 servings.

SAVORY SUCCOTASH

3 (10-ounce) packages frozen succotash
3 tablespoons butter or margarine
Ground savory to taste
¾ teaspoon salt
Pepper to taste

Prepare succotash according to package directions; add remaining ingredients. Simmer about 2 minutes. Yield: 8 servings.

What better way to celebrate summer than with a handsome feast, a carefree afternoon, and good company to enjoy it all. Our Ham over the Coals Menu is above.

ISLAND FRUIT BOATS

4 small fresh pineapples
4 oranges, peeled and sectioned
4 unpeeled apples, cut into wedges
1 cup sliced celery
1 (6-ounce) can frozen lemonade
    concentrate, thawed and undiluted

Cut pineapples in half lengthwise; scoop out pulp, leaving shells intact. Cut pineapple pulp into chunks, and set aside 2 cups (use remaining pineapple chunks as desired).

Combine 2 cups pineapple with remaining ingredients; chill well. Drain and spoon into pineapple shells. Yield: 8 servings.

GARLIC BREAD

1 (1-pound) loaf French bread
1 clove garlic, crushed
½ cup butter or margarine, softened

Cut bread into 1-inch slices, not quite through bottom crust. Combine garlic and butter; spread between slices and on top of bread.

Wrap loaf in heavy-duty aluminum foil; place on grill over coals about 15 minutes or until well heated. Yield: 8 servings.

HAWAIIAN CHEESECAKE

2 cups flaked coconut
3 tablespoons melted butter
1 (8¼-ounce) can crushed pineapple

Appetites soar after a day around the pool, so a menu featuring Sesame Seed Chicken, Saffron Rice, and Baked Squash is the order of the day. Our Feast by the Pool Menu is on page 164.

2 eggs, separated
¾ cup sugar, divided
¼ teaspoon salt
1 tablespoon lemon juice
1 envelope (1 tablespoon) unflavored
    gelatin
¼ cup cold water
2 (3-ounce) packages cream cheese,
    softened
½ pint whipping cream, whipped
    Toasted coconut

Combine 2 cups coconut and butter; press in bottom and about 1 inch up sides of an 8-inch springform pan. Bake at 350° about 10 minutes or until lightly browned.

Drain pineapple, reserving juice. Add enough water to pineapple juice to make 1 cup liquid. Beat egg yolks; add ½ cup sugar, salt, lemon juice, and pineapple liquid. Place over low heat; cook stirring constantly, until slightly thickened.

Sprinkle gelatin over cold water; add to cooked mixture, stirring until dissolved. Beat cream cheese until smooth; slowly add cooked mixture, beating until smooth. Chill until slightly thickened; fold in pineapple.

Beat egg whites until foamy; gradually add remaining ¼ cup sugar, beating until stiff. Fold into cream cheese mixture. Spoon filling into prepared crust, and chill until firm. Top with whipped cream, and sprinkle with toasted coconut. Yield: 8 servings.

SUNSHINE PUNCH

1 (46-ounce) can orange-pineapple juice,
    chilled
1 (28-ounce) bottle ginger ale or
    lemon-lime carbonated beverage,
    chilled
    Orange slices
    Lemon slices

Combine juice and ginger ale in a punch bowl. Serve over ice cubes, and garnish with orange and lemon slices. Yield: 8 servings.

Note: For delicious variations, 1 pint of pineapple sherbet or vodka to taste may be added to punch.

Feast by the Pool
(Dinner for Eight)

Salmon Tomato Bites
Toasted Cheese Appetizers
Pineapple Cheese Ball
Hawaiian Party Drink
Sesame Seed Chicken
Saffron Rice
Baked Squash
Tossed Spinach-Orange Salad
Rolls
Fresh Strawberry Pie
Iced Tea

SALMON TOMATO BITES

12 cherry tomatoes
1 (7¾-ounce) can red salmon, drained
   and flaked
¼ cup mayonnaise
1 tablespoon finely chopped celery
1 tablespoon finely chopped onion
   Salt to taste
   Monosodium glutamate to taste
   Paprika or parsley flakes

Cut a slice from top of each tomato; scoop out pulp, leaving shells intact. Invert tomatoes to drain. Reserve pulp for soups or sauces.

Combine salmon, mayonnaise, celery, onion, salt, and monosodium glutamate; blend well. Spoon mixture into tomato shells; chill. Sprinkle with paprika. Yield: 1 dozen.

TOASTED CHEESE APPETIZERS

1 cup shredded sharp Cheddar cheese
¼ cup mayonnaise
1 to 2 teaspoons grated onion
¼ teaspoon red pepper
8 slices bread

Combine cheese, mayonnaise, onion, and pepper; mix until smooth. Spread a small amount on each slice of bread; roll up jellyroll fashion, and secure with toothpicks.

Slice each roll into thirds, and place on cookie sheet. Bake at 400° for 8 to 10 minutes or until lightly browned. Yield: 2 dozen.

PINEAPPLE CHEESE BALL

2 (8-ounce) packages cream cheese, softened
1 (8½-ounce) can crushed pineapple, drained
¼ cup finely chopped green pepper
2 tablespoons chopped onion
1 tablespoon seasoned salt
2 cups chopped pecans, divided
  Crackers

Combine first 5 ingredients; add 1 cup pecans, and mix well. Refrigerate until firm, and shape into a ball. Roll in remaining pecans before serving. Garnish as desired. Serve with an assortment of crackers. Yield: about 3 cups.

HAWAIIAN PARTY DRINK

1 (46-ounce) can pineapple juice
1½ cups vodka or rum
  Coconut Syrup

Combine all ingredients; stir well, and serve over ice cubes. Yield: 8 cups.

Coconut Syrup:

1½ cups flaked coconut
¾ cup water
½ cup light corn syrup

Combine coconut and water in a saucepan; simmer over low heat, uncovered, 20 minutes. Let stand 15 minutes. Drain well, reserving liquid; discard coconut. Combine reserved liquid and corn syrup, stirring well. Yield: about 1 cup.

SESAME SEED CHICKEN

1 teaspoon salt
½ teaspoon pepper
¾ cup all-purpose flour, divided
4 whole chicken breasts, split and boned
4 eggs, beaten
4 tablespoons milk
6 tablespoons sesame seeds
  Hot salad oil
  Supreme Sauce

Combine salt, pepper, and ¼ cup flour in a bag. Add chicken, and shake to coat. Combine eggs and milk in a small bowl; set aside. Combine remaining flour and sesame seeds in a small bowl.

Dip each chicken breast in egg mixture; then coat with sesame seed mixture. Heat salad oil to 350°; add chicken, and sauté about 15 minutes or until golden brown. Serve with Supreme Sauce. Yield: 8 servings.

Supreme Sauce:

6 tablespoons butter or margarine
4 tablespoons all-purpose flour
3 cups chicken broth
2 egg yolks, beaten

Melt butter in a small saucepan over low heat; add flour, blending until smooth. Gradually add chicken broth; cook, stirring constantly, until slightly thickened. Gradually add about ½ cup hot mixture to egg yolks; then beat yolk mixture into remaining hot mixture. Cook over low heat, stirring constantly, until sauce is thickened and smooth. Yield: about 2 cups.

Outdoor Parties and Cookouts   165

SAFFRON RICE

2 (5-ounce) packages saffron rice
2 (4-ounce) cans button mushrooms,
    drained
2½ tablespoons chopped pimiento, divided

Prepare rice according to package directions. Set aside several mushrooms for garnish. Stir remaining mushrooms and 2 tablespoons pimiento into rice; heat thoroughly. Garnish with reserved mushrooms and ½ tablespoon pimiento. Yield: 8 servings.

BAKED SQUASH

2 pounds yellow squash, cut into ½-inch
    slices
3 tablespoons chopped onion
3 eggs, beaten
½ teaspoon hot sauce
2 teaspoons parsley flakes
    Salt and pepper to taste
½ cup melted margarine
2 cups round buttery cracker crumbs,
    divided

Cook squash in a small amount of boiling water until tender; drain well. Add remaining ingredients except 1 cup cracker crumbs; stir gently.

Spoon mixture into a lightly greased 1½-quart casserole; sprinkle with remaining cracker crumbs. Bake at 350° for 35 to 40 minutes. Yield: about 8 servings.

TOSSED SPINACH-ORANGE SALAD

1½ cups torn lettuce
1½ cups torn fresh spinach
3 medium oranges, peeled and sliced
1 tablespoon sugar
    Salt to taste
¼ cup Tomato Salad Dressing
½ onion, sliced into rings
    Additional orange slices

Combine lettuce, spinach, orange slices, sugar, and salt in a large bowl. Add ¼ cup Dressing (more, if desired); toss. Garnish with onion rings and additional orange slices. Yield: 8 servings.

Tomato Salad Dressing:

1 (10¾-ounce) can tomato soup,
    undiluted
¾ cup vinegar
½ cup salad oil
¼ cup sugar
1 tablespoon Worcestershire sauce
3 tablespoons grated onion
1 teaspoon salt
1 tablespoon dry mustard
1 teaspoon paprika
2 cloves garlic

Combine all ingredients except garlic in a quart jar; shake well. Add garlic; let stand about 1 hour for flavor to develop. Chill. Remove garlic before serving. Yield: 1 quart.

FRESH STRAWBERRY PIE

1 quart fresh strawberries, divided
1 cup water
¾ cup sugar
3 tablespoons cornstarch
    Red food coloring (optional)
1 baked 9-inch pastry shell
    Whipped cream

Wash and cap strawberries. Crush 1 cup strawberries in a small saucepan; add water, and cook 2 minutes. Strain through a sieve, reserving liquid; discard pulp.

Combine sugar and cornstarch; stir into strawberry liquid. Bring to a boil, and cook until mixture thickens, stirring constantly. Add red food coloring, if desired.

Place 1½ cups strawberries in pastry shell; pour half of sauce over top. Repeat with remaining strawberries and sauce. Chill.

Top pie with whipped cream before serving. Yield: one 9-inch pie.

Dinner from the Grill
(Cookout for Eight)

Tropical Cooler
Beer-Barbecued Pork Chops
Mediterranean Chicken
Vegetable Kabobs
Savory Bread
Bean Salad
Strawberry Angel Pie
Iced Tea   Beer

TROPICAL COOLER

1 (6-ounce) can frozen orange juice
    concentrate, undiluted
1 (6-ounce) can frozen lemonade
    concentrate, undiluted
1 quart apple juice
2 quarts ginger ale, chilled

Combine orange juice, lemonade, and apple juice; mix well. Just before serving, stir in ginger ale. Serve over crushed ice. Yield: about 3 quarts.

BEER-BARBECUED PORK CHOPS

8 (¾-inch thick) pork chops
    Garlic salt to taste
2 (12-ounce) cans beer
1⅓ cups catsup
1 cup water
⅔ cup lemon juice
2 teaspoons celery salt
4 teaspoons Worcestershire sauce
2 bay leaves
1 teaspoon pepper
½ teaspoon basil
⅛ teaspoon hot sauce

Place chops in a shallow pan; sprinkle with garlic salt. Pour beer over chops and marinate in refrigerator 4 hours.

Combine remaining ingredients in a saucepan; bring to a boil. Simmer over low heat 10 minutes.

Remove chops from marinade. Grill 30 to 45 minutes or to desired doneness, basting frequently with sauce. Yield: 8 servings.

MEDITERRANEAN CHICKEN

½ cup olive oil
½ cup white wine
¼ cup honey
¼ cup white wine vinegar
2 teaspoons garlic salt
½ teaspoon ground oregano
2 (2-pound) broiler-fryer chickens
1 lemon, thinly sliced
1 orange, thinly sliced

Combine oil, wine, honey, vinegar, garlic salt, and oregano; blend well. Pour over chickens; marinate in refrigerator overnight. (Turn occasionally, if possible.)

Center chickens securely on spit of rotisserie. Cook over low heat 1 hour or until chicken is tender and brown; baste frequently with marinade.

Add lemon and orange slices to remaining marinade; heat and serve with chicken. Yield: 8 servings.

VEGETABLE KABOBS

2 cups salted water
½ teaspoon oregano
3 medium zucchini squash
6 small tomatoes, cut into wedges
½ cup melted butter or margarine
2 tablespoons grated Parmesan cheese
   Salt and pepper to taste

Combine salted water and oregano; add zucchini, and boil 4 to 5 minutes. Drain. Cut zucchini diagonally into 1-inch-thick slices.

Thread zucchini slices and tomato wedges on skewers; cook on grill over medium heat 10 minutes. Turn occasionally, basting frequently with butter. Sprinkle with cheese, salt, and pepper just before removing from grill. Yield: 8 servings.

SAVORY BREAD
(see Index)

BEAN SALAD

2 (15½-ounce) cans French-style green
   beans, drained
1 (16-ounce) can cut green beans, drained
1 (17-ounce) can peas, drained
1 cup finely chopped celery
¼ cup chopped onion
1 medium pepper, finely chopped
¼ cup chopped pimiento
¼ cup sliced water chestnuts
½ cup cider vinegar
½ cup salad oil
1¼ cups sugar

Combine vegetables. Combine vinegar, oil, and sugar; mix well. Pour over vegetables, and toss gently to coat thoroughly. Refrigerate overnight. Drain well before serving. Yield: 8 servings.

STRAWBERRY ANGEL PIE

3 egg whites
1 teaspoon vanilla extract
¼ teaspoon cream of tartar
   Dash of salt
1 cup sugar
1 (3-ounce) package strawberry-flavored
   gelatin
1 cup boiling water
1 cup sliced strawberries
1 cup whipping cream, whipped
   Strawberry halves

Beat egg whites until frothy. Add vanilla, cream of tartar, and salt; beat slightly. Gradually add sugar, beating well after each addition; continue beating until stiff and glossy. Do not underbeat.

Spoon meringue into a well-greased 9-inch pieplate. Using a spoon, shape meringue into a pie shell, swirling sides high. Bake at 275° for 1 hour. Turn off oven; leave meringue in oven with door closed 2 hours.

Dissolve gelatin in boiling water; chill until consistency of unbeaten egg white. Fold in sliced strawberries and whipped cream; spoon into meringue shell. Chill until firm. Garnish with strawberry halves. Yield: 8 servings.

Seaside Oyster Roast

(Cookout for Eight)

Spanish Soup
Roasted Oysters
Indian Roasted Corn
Cheese-Stuffed Eggs
Sweet 'n Sour Coleslaw
French Bread
Milk Chocolate Pound Cake
Beer

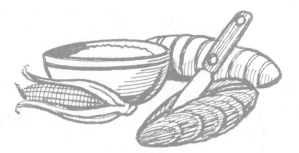

SPANISH SOUP

  1 (15-ounce) can tomato sauce
  1 (18-ounce) can tomato juice
  ¾ cup finely chopped celery
  ¾ cup finely chopped cucumber
  ½ cup finely chopped onion
  ½ cup chopped avocado
  ¼ cup finely chopped green pepper
  1 tablespoon parsley flakes
  3 tablespoons wine vinegar
  2 tablespoons olive oil
  1 teaspoon salt
  ¼ teaspoon pepper
  ½ teaspoon Worcestershire sauce
  ⅛ teaspoon garlic powder
  2 drops hot sauce

Combine all ingredients, mixing well. Cover and refrigerate overnight. Yield: 8 servings.

ROASTED OYSTERS

Build a fire and let burn about 1½ hours or until coals are very hot. Place a metal plate or grill over the fire.

A bushel of oysters will generally serve 10 people, but if you're feeding oyster connoisseurs, count on a bushel to serve 5 people. Rinse oyster shells to remove all mud and debris.

When fire has burned down to a bed of hot coals, place a quarter of a bushel of oysters on the hot metal plate. Cover oysters completely with wet burlap sacks (make certain that sacks have not contained chemical products). The heat hitting the wet sacks produces steam, which cooks the oysters.

In 5 to 10 minutes, the oyster shells will start popping open. Remove steaming oysters from fire; open shells with oyster knife or screwdriver. Cook remaining oysters in the same manner. Serve with melted butter, lemon slices, or cocktail sauce.

Note: A small amount of oysters can be roasted on a barbecue grill. Place oysters on hot grill, and cover with a wet towel.

INDIAN ROASTED CORN

8 ears fresh corn
3 tablespoons salt
Softened butter or margarine

Remove large outer husks from corn; turn back inner husks, and remove silk. Pull husks back over ears, and tie with heavy twine or fine wire. Dissolve salt in enough cold water to cover corn. Soak corn in salt water for 1 hour (a weight may be necessary to keep corn submerged).

Drain corn, and place on grill over hot coals 15 to 20 minutes, turning frequently. Serve at once with butter. Yield: 8 servings.

CHEESE-STUFFED EGGS

8 hard-cooked eggs
6 tablespoons crumbled blue cheese
1 (6-ounce) roll pasteurized process sharp cheese spread, softened
¼ cup mayonnaise
Lemon juice to taste
Salt to taste
Paprika

Cut eggs in half lengthwise, and remove yolks. Mash yolks; add cheese, mayonnaise, lemon juice, and salt, blending well. Stuff whites with yolk mixture. Sprinkle with paprika. Yield: 8 servings.

SWEET 'N SOUR COLESLAW

1 small head cabbage, shredded
1 onion, thinly sliced
½ cup sugar
½ cup vinegar
1 teaspoon salt
1 teaspoon dry mustard
1 teaspoon celery seeds or dillweed
½ cup salad oil

Combine cabbage and onion; set aside. Combine remaining ingredients in a saucepan; bring to a boil, stirring constantly. Pour dressing over vegetable mixture; toss lightly to mix. Chill. Yield: 8 servings.

MILK CHOCOLATE POUND CAKE

1 cup butter or margarine, softened
1½ cups sugar
4 eggs
8 (1⅛-ounce) milk chocolate candy bars, melted
1 cup buttermilk
2½ cups all-purpose flour
Pinch of salt
¼ teaspoon soda
1 cup chopped pecans
1 (5½-ounce) can chocolate syrup
2 teaspoons vanilla extract
Powdered sugar (optional)

Cream butter and sugar until light and fluffy. Add eggs, one at a time, beating well after each addition. Add melted candy bars and buttermilk, and mix well.

Combine flour, salt, and soda; add to chocolate mixture, mixing well. Add pecans, chocolate syrup, and vanilla, blending well.

Spoon batter into a greased and floured 10-inch tube or Bundt pan. Bake at 325° for 1 hour and 15 minutes or until done. When cake is cool, sift powdered sugar over cake, if desired. Yield: one 10-inch cake.

Hot off the Coals
(Cookout for Eight)

Whiskey Sour Punch
Tangy Barbecued Pork Chops
Barbecued Creamed Potatoes
Grilled Bacon and Mushrooms
Sauerkraut Salad
Grilled Cheese Bread
Southern Strawberry Pie
Iced Tea

WHISKEY SOUR PUNCH

   2 cups bourbon
   2 (6-ounce) cans frozen lemonade
      concentrate, thawed and undiluted
   1 quart apple juice
   1 quart ginger ale
      Ice ring

Combine bourbon, lemonade, apple juice, and
ginger ale; stir well. Pour over ice ring. Yield:
about 3 quarts.

TANGY BARBECUED PORK CHOPS

   ½ cup maple syrup
   ½ cup catsup
   1 tablespoon Worcestershire sauce
   1 tablespoon steak sauce
   1 tablespoon vinegar
   1 tablespoon prepared mustard
   1 tablespoon salad oil
   1 tablespoon melted butter or margarine
   1 teaspoon lemon juice
      Dash of ground cloves
      Salt and pepper to taste
   8 pork chops

Combine all ingredients except pork chops in
a small saucepan; bring to a boil. Simmer over
low heat 5 to 10 minutes.
   Grill chops over medium heat 30 to 45 minutes
or to desired doneness, basting frequently with
sauce. Yield: 8 servings.

BARBECUED CREAMED POTATOES

3 tablespoons butter or margarine
3 tablespoons all-purpose flour
1½ teaspoons salt
2 cups milk
½ teaspoon hot sauce
1 tablespoon chopped parsley
2 tablespoons chopped pimiento
4 cups cooked, diced potatoes
½ cup soft breadcrumbs
1 tablespoon butter or margarine, melted
½ cup shredded American cheese
¼ teaspoon paprika

Melt butter in a medium saucepan; add flour and salt, stirring until smooth. Add milk slowly; cook, stirring constantly, until mixture thickens and comes to a boil. Stir in hot sauce, parsley, and pimiento; add potatoes. Spoon into a 1½-quart casserole.

Combine breadcrumbs, butter, cheese, and paprika; sprinkle over casserole. Bake at 400° for 30 minutes. Yield: 8 servings.

Note: This casserole may be made ahead of time and refrigerated. Bake at 350° for 50 minutes or until heated through.

GRILLED BACON AND MUSHROOMS

16 slices bacon
1 pound medium mushrooms
4 eggs, beaten
4 teaspoons water
Dash of ground allspice
½ teaspoon salt
2 cups dry breadcrumbs

Cook bacon until transparent; drain and cool. Clean mushrooms; remove stems, leaving caps intact.

Combine eggs, water, allspice, and salt; blend well. Dip mushrooms into egg mixture; then coat with breadcrumbs. String bacon on short skewers alternately with mushrooms. Grill over hot coals, turning occasionally, until bacon is lightly browned. Yield: 8 servings.

SAUERKRAUT SALAD

⅔ cup vinegar
⅓ cup salad oil
⅓ cup water
1¼ cups sugar
2 (16-ounce) cans sauerkraut, drained
1 cup diced celery
1 cup chopped green onion
1 (8-ounce) can water chestnuts, drained and sliced
1 cup diced green pepper
2 tablespoons chopped pimiento (optional)
¼ cup grated carrot (optional)

Combine vinegar, salad oil, water, and sugar; stir well. Combine sauerkraut, celery, onion, water chestnuts, and green pepper; stir in pimiento and carrot, if desired.

Pour dressing over sauerkraut mixture; stir to coat all vegetables. Cover and refrigerate overnight. Yield: 10 to 12 servings.

Note: Sauerkraut Salad keeps well in refrigerator for several days.

GRILLED CHEESE BREAD

1 (1-pound) loaf French bread
1 (3-ounce) package cream cheese, softened
½ cup shredded Cheddar cheese
2½ tablespoons toasted sesame seeds
1½ tablespoons chopped green onion
1½ tablespoons milk
2 teaspoons Dijon-style mustard

Diagonally slice bread in 1-inch slices, not quite through the bottom crust. Cream together remaining ingredients; spread mixture between slices of bread. Wrap loaf in heavy-duty aluminum foil; place on grill over coals 10 to 15 minutes, turning once. Yield: about 8 servings.

SOUTHERN STRAWBERRY PIE

¾ cup sugar
2 tablespoons cornstarch
2 tablespoons light corn syrup
1 cup water
3 tablespoons strawberry-flavored gelatin
1 quart whole fresh strawberries
1 baked 9-inch pastry shell

Combine sugar, cornstarch, corn syrup, and water in a saucepan; bring to a boil. Cook, stirring constantly, until clear and thickened. Add gelatin, stirring until dissolved. Cool.

Place strawberries in pastry shell; pour in gelatin mixture. Chill until firm. Yield: one 9-inch pie.

A meat thermometer inserted so that the bulb doesn't touch bone or fat is the most accurate way to test doneness of large pieces of meat. For a roast, insert thermometer in the center. Beef will be rare when the internal temperature is 140°, medium at 160°, and well-done at 170°. Fresh pork should be cooked until the internal temperature is 180°. For poultry, the thermometer should be inserted in the thickest part of the thigh, close to the body. Poultry is done when the thermometer registers 180° to 185°.

Precooking spareribs in the kitchen cuts down on cooking time on the grill and also helps to remove some of the fat, eliminating flareups on the grill. Boil in a small amount of water or bake at 350° about 30 minutes. Drain well before putting on the grill, and baste with sauce as ribs cook.

Grilled Fish Feast

(Cookout for Eight)

Grilled Fish Steaks
Company Rice
Grilled Tomatoes
Hawaiian Spinach Salad
Savory Bread
Lemon Mousse
Iced Tea

GRILLED FISH STEAKS

  8 (¾-inch-thick) fish steaks
½ cup soy sauce
½ cup cooking sherry
1 tablespoon lime or lemon juice
1 clove garlic, crushed
¼ cup salad oil

Arrange fish in shallow pan. Combine remaining ingredients in a jar, and shake well; pour over fish. Cover and marinate in refrigerator at least an hour, turning frequently.

Drain fish slightly, and place in a wire basket. Grill over medium coals 6 to 9 minutes, basting frequently with marinade. Turn and cook until fish flakes easily when tested with a fork. Turn only once during grilling. Yield: 8 servings.

COMPANY RICE

1 cup uncooked regular rice
1 cup chopped onion
½ cup melted butter or margarine
½ cup seedless raisins
1 (4-ounce) can sliced mushrooms, drained
2 (10½-ounce) cans consommé
¼ to ½ cup chopped peanuts
½ cup chopped celery

Lightly brown rice and onion in butter. Combine rice mixture, raisins, mushrooms, consommé, peanuts, and celery; mix well. Pour into a 2-quart casserole.

Bake, uncovered, at 350° for 50 to 60 minutes or until rice is done. Yield: 8 servings.

GRILLED TOMATOES

8 firm ripe tomatoes
  Salt and pepper to taste
  Ground oregano
  Shredded Cheddar cheese or grated
    Parmesan cheese
  Butter or margarine

Cut each tomato in half crosswise; sprinkle cut surfaces with salt, pepper, and oregano. Place each tomato half on a square of heavy-duty aluminum foil. Sprinkle with cheese, and dot with butter. Fold foil securely around tomato halves.

Cook on grill over moderate heat 10 to 15 minutes or until tomatoes are tender and cheese is melted. Yield: 8 servings.

HAWAIIAN SPINACH SALAD

1½ pounds spinach
  1 (15½-ounce) can cut yellow wax beans,
    drained
  1 (15½-ounce) can pineapple chunks,
    drained
  ½ cup sugar
  1 cup honey
  1 teaspoon grated onion
  6 tablespoons tarragon vinegar
  3 tablespoons lemon juice
  1 cup salad oil
  1 teaspoon dry mustard
  1 teaspoon paprika
  ¼ teaspoon salt
  2 teaspoons poppy seeds
  1 teaspoon curry powder

Wash spinach, and tear into bite-size pieces. Combine spinach, beans, and pineapple; chill.

Combine remaining ingredients in a jar, and shake thoroughly. (Dressing keeps indefinitely in refrigerator.) When ready to serve, pour dressing over spinach salad. Yield: 8 servings.

SAVORY BREAD

1 (1-pound) loaf French bread
½ cup butter or margarine, softened
¼ cup chopped parsley
¼ cup chopped green onion

Slice bread in 1-inch slices, not quite through the bottom crust. Combine butter, parsley, and onion; spread mixture between slices and on top of bread. Wrap loaf in heavy-duty aluminum foil; place on grill over coals 15 minutes. Yield: 8 servings.

LEMON MOUSSE

1 (13-ounce) can evaporated milk
1 cup sugar
  Juice of 3 lemons
  Grated rind of 1 lemon
2 cups vanilla wafer crumbs, divided

Place evaporated milk in a bowl in freezer until milk starts to freeze. Remove and whip until stiff; gradually add sugar, and continue whipping. Add lemon juice and rind.

Line bottom of an 8-inch square pan with 1¾ cups vanilla wafer crumbs. Pour milk mixture over crumbs; sprinkle with remaining ¼ cup crumbs. Freeze and serve. To freeze for longer periods, wrap in freezer wrap. Cut in squares. Yield: 9 servings.

A Picnic from the Grill

(Cookout for Six to Eight)

Stuffed Hamburgers
Florentine Franks
Marinated Vegetables
Buffet Beans
Picnic Potato Salad
Butterscotch Squares
Lemonade

STUFFED HAMBURGERS

2 tablespoons butter or margarine
1¼ cups herb-seasoned stuffing
1 egg, beaten
1 (4-ounce) can chopped mushrooms, drained
⅓ cup beef broth
¼ cup sliced green onion
¼ cup chopped toasted almonds
1 teaspoon lemon juice
3 pounds ground beef
1 teaspoon salt

Melt butter in a saucepan over low heat; remove from heat. Add stuffing, egg, mushrooms, beef broth, green onion, almonds, and lemon juice; mix well, and set aside. Combine ground beef and salt; shape into 16 patties.

Top 8 patties with stuffing mixture, using ¼ cup per patty. Cover with remaining patties; pinch edges together to seal. Place patties in greased grill basket. Grill over medium coals for 10 to 12 minutes on each side. Yield: 6 to 8 servings.

FLORENTINE FRANKS

2 tomatoes, peeled, chopped, and drained
4 tablespoons shredded sharp American cheese
2 small cloves garlic, crushed
½ teaspoon crushed oregano leaves
Salt to taste
8 frankfurters
8 slices bacon
8 hotdog buns, split and toasted

Combine tomato, cheese, garlic, oregano, and salt; mix well. Split frankfurters lengthwise, cutting almost through; stuff with tomato mixture.

Wrap each frankfurter with a bacon strip, securing ends with toothpicks. Place franks over medium coals; grill 10 to 15 minutes or until bacon is crisp, turning occasionally. Serve in buns. Yield: 6 to 8 servings.

MARINATED VEGETABLES

6 tablespoons lemon juice
6 tablespoons vinegar
6 tablespoons olive oil
¼ cup garlic salt
⅔ cup salad oil
4 teaspoons salt
1 teaspoon sugar
  Dash of pepper
½ head cauliflower
3 stalks celery, cut into sticks
3 to 4 carrots, cut into sticks
10 to 15 cherry tomatoes, halved

Combine all ingredients except vegetables; mix well, and set aside.

Cut cauliflower flowerets 1 inch from top of stalks; then cut into bite-size pieces.

Arrange vegetables on a serving platter, and pour marinade over all. Marinate 6 hours before serving. Yield: 6 to 8 servings.

BUFFET BEANS

1 (10¾-ounce) can tomato soup, undiluted
1 tablespoon Worcestershire sauce
2 strips bacon, diced
6 tablespoons chopped onion
½ cup chopped green pepper
¼ cup finely chopped celery
1 tablespoon prepared mustard
½ cup light molasses
2 (16-ounce) cans pork and beans

Combine all ingredients except pork and beans; let stand 15 minutes. Add pork and beans, mixing well. Spoon into a greased 2-quart shallow baking dish. Bake at 325° for 1½ hours. Yield: 6 to 8 servings.

PICNIC POTATO SALAD

5 pounds potatoes, cooked and cubed
1 cup sliced green onions
½ cup commercial Italian dressing
1 cup mayonnaise or salad dressing
¼ cup prepared mustard
3 teaspoons salt
2 cups sliced celery
4 hard-cooked eggs, chopped
½ cup sweet pickle relish
  Parsley
  Green pepper rings

Combine potatoes, onion, and Italian dressing; toss gently to coat. Cover and chill 1 hour. Combine mayonnaise, mustard, and salt; pour over potato mixture; toss gently to coat. Add celery, eggs, and relish; toss lightly. Chill several hours. Garnish with parsley and green pepper rings. Yield: 10 to 12 servings.

BUTTERSCOTCH SQUARES

½ cup butter, softened
2 cups firmly packed dark brown sugar
2 eggs
2 cups all-purpose flour
2 teaspoons baking powder
½ teaspoon salt
1 teaspoon vanilla extract
1 cup chopped pecans
1 cup flaked coconut
1 (6-ounce) package butterscotch pieces

Cream butter and sugar until light and fluffy; add eggs, one at a time, beating well after each addition. Combine flour, baking powder, and salt; add to creamed mixture, mixing until smooth. Stir in vanilla, pecans, coconut, and butterscotch pieces.

Spread batter evenly in a lightly greased 9-inch square pan. Bake at 350° for 30 to 35 minutes. Cut into bars while warm. Yield: 25 (1½-inch) bars.

Barbecue with an Eastern Flair

(Cookout for Four)

Barbecued Chicken with Curry
Brown Rice
Broccoli with Orange Sauce
Tomato and Lima Bean Salad
French Bread
Peach Pie Parfait
Wine

BARBECUED CHICKEN WITH CURRY

4 teaspoons salt
1 cup warm water
1 (3-pound) broiler-fryer chicken, cut in quarters
1½ teaspoons curry powder
2 tablespoons lemon juice
½ cup melted butter
¼ teaspoon pepper

Combine salt and warm water. Grill chicken 25 minutes over low heat, basting with salt water every 5 minutes.

Combine curry powder, lemon juice, butter, and pepper; blend well. Grill chicken an additional 20 minutes, turning frequently and basting with sauce. Yield: 4 servings.

BROWN RICE

1 large onion, chopped
1 clove garlic, crushed
¼ cup salad oil
1 cup uncooked regular rice
1 (10½-ounce) can consommé
1¼ cups water
1 (6-ounce) can sliced mushrooms, drained
Salt and pepper to taste

Lightly brown onion and garlic in salad oil; stir in rice, consommé, water, mushrooms, salt, and pepper. Bring to a boil; then lower heat. Cover and cook about 40 minutes or until rice is tender and liquid is absorbed; stir occasionally. Yield: about 4 servings.

BROCCOLI WITH ORANGE SAUCE

About 1½ pounds fresh broccoli
2 tablespoons margarine
2 tablespoons all-purpose flour
1 cup orange juice
2 teaspoons sugar
⅛ teaspoon salt
Paprika

Wash broccoli; cook in a small amount of salted water until crisp-tender, about 5 to 7 minutes; drain.

Melt margarine in a saucepan; blend in flour, and cook until bubbly. Add orange juice, sugar, and salt; cook, stirring constantly, until thick and smooth. Pour sauce over hot broccoli, and sprinkle with paprika. Yield: 4 to 5 servings.

TOMATO AND LIMA BEAN SALAD

1 (10-ounce) package frozen baby lima beans
4 large tomatoes
1 tablespoon chopped parsley
1 small onion, grated
½ cup finely chopped pecans
2 tablespoons minced celery
Salt and pepper to taste
½ cup commercial French dressing
Lettuce leaves

Cook lima beans according to directions on package; drain, and set aside to cool.

Slice top and scoop out pulp from each tomato; set shells aside, and chop pulp. Combine parsley, onion, pecans, celery, salt, pepper, French dressing, tomato pulp, and lima beans, stirring to mix well. Fill tomatoes with bean mixture. Serve on lettuce leaves. Yield: 4 servings.

Note: Any salad dressing may be used. Additional dressing may be poured over salad or served separately. The tomatoes may be peeled and cut in thick slices and lima mixture served over slices, if preferred.

PEACH PIE PARFAIT

1 (29-ounce) can sliced peaches
1 (3-ounce) package orange-flavored gelatin
½ cup cold water
1 pint French vanilla ice cream, softened
1 baked 9-inch pastry shell
1 (8-ounce) carton frozen whipped topping, thawed

Drain peaches, reserving syrup. Set aside several peach slices for garnish. Add enough water to peach syrup to make 1 cup liquid; heat to boiling. Add gelatin, stirring to dissolve; add cold water.

Add ice cream to gelatin mixture, stirring to melt. Chill about 20 minutes or until partially set. Fold in peaches.

Pour into pastry shell; chill until firm. Garnish with whipped topping and reserved peach slices. Yield: one 9-inch pie.

Pork Kabob Supper

(Cookout for Six)

Zesty Bloody Mary
Glazed Pork Kabobs
Onion Potatoes
Savory Green Beans
Mexican Corn Salad
Commercial Crusty Rolls   Butter
Chocolate Marble Cheesecake
Iced Tea

ZESTY BLOODY MARY

1¼ cups vodka
2¼ cups tomato juice
 ½ to 1 teaspoon hot sauce
 ½ teaspoon monosodium glutamate
 ¾ teaspoon celery salt
 ¼ teaspoon garlic powder
1½ teaspoon Worcestershire sauce
   Juice of 3 limes or lemons
 6 stalks celery

Combine all ingredients except celery in a
pitcher, mixing well. Serve over ice cubes in tall
glasses; garnish with celery stalk. Yield: 6 servings.

GLAZED PORK KABOBS

 ½ cup apricot preserves
 ½ cup tomato sauce
 ¼ cup firmly packed brown sugar
 ¼ cup dry red wine
 3 tablespoons lemon juice
 2 tablespoons salad oil
 1 teaspoon onion juice
 4 large carrots, cut into 1-inch slices
1½ pounds lean boneless pork, cut into
   1-inch cubes
   Fresh pineapple chunks
   Salt and pepper

Combine apricot preserves, tomato sauce, brown
sugar, wine, lemon juice, salad oil, and onion
juice; boil, uncovered, 10 to 15 minutes.
   Parboil carrots about 5 minutes. Alternate
pork, pineapple, and carrots on skewers; season
with salt and pepper. Grill 10 minutes over
medium heat, turning occasionally. Baste with
apricot sauce, and grill 5 additional minutes.
Yield: 6 servings.

ONION POTATOES

½ cup butter or margarine, softened
1 (1⅜-ounce) envelope onion soup mix
6 medium baking potatoes

Combine butter and soup mix; blend well, and set aside.

Scrub potatoes thoroughly. Working with one potato at a time, cut each into slices ½ inch thick. Spread one side of each slice with butter mixture, and reassemble potato. Wrap in heavy-duty aluminum foil.

Cook potatoes on grill over moderate heat 45 minutes to 1 hour or until done, turning once. Yield: 6 servings.

SAVORY GREEN BEANS

3 tablespoons melted butter or margarine
3 tablespoons all-purpose flour
2 cups milk
  Salt and pepper to taste
½ pound Cheddar cheese, shredded and divided
3 cups cooked, seasoned, drained green beans
3 hard-cooked eggs, coarsely chopped
⅓ cup chopped onion

Combine butter and flour, blending until smooth; cook over low heat until bubbly. Gradually add milk; cook, stirring constantly, until smooth and thick. Season with salt and pepper.

Set ½ cup cheese aside, and stir remaining cheese into sauce.

Place beans in a shallow 2-quart casserole; cover with sauce. Stir in egg and onion; sprinkle with ½ cup cheese. Bake at 350° for 15 minutes or until bubbly. Yield: 6 servings.

MEXICAN CORN SALAD

1 (16-ounce) can whole kernel corn, drained
1 pimiento, chopped
1 onion, chopped
1 green pepper, chopped
1 small cucumber, chopped
½ cup commercial French dressing
  Lettuce

Combine all ingredients except lettuce; chill. Serve on lettuce. Yield: 6 servings.

CHOCOLATE MARBLE CHEESECAKE

1½ cups graham cracker crumbs
1 tablespoon sugar
⅓ cup melted butter or margarine
3 (8-ounce) packages cream cheese, softened
1¼ cups sugar, divided
6 eggs, separated
2 tablespoons Grand Marnier or other orange-flavored liqueur
1 teaspoon grated orange rind
½ teaspoon salt
1 (8-ounce) carton commercial sour cream
¼ cup all-purpose flour
½ teaspoon cream of tartar
6 (1-ounce) squares semisweet chocolate, melted and cooled

Combine graham cracker crumbs, 1 tablespoon sugar, and butter in a small bowl; mix well. Pour into a 9-inch springform pan; press mixture evenly on bottom and sides of pan.

Combine cream cheese and 1 cup sugar; beat until smooth. Add egg yolks, one at a time, beating well after each addition. Stir in Grand Marnier, orange rind, salt, sour cream, and flour.

Combine egg whites and cream of tartar in a mixing bowl; beat until foamy. Gradually add ¼ cup sugar, and continue beating until stiff; fold into cream cheese mixture.

Combine chocolate and 3 cups cream cheese mixture in a small mixing bowl, mixing well. Drop alternate spoonfuls of cream cheese mixture and chocolate mixture into crumb-lined pan, reserving about 1 cup cream cheese mixture and ¼ cup chocolate mixture. Cut through mixture in pan with a spatula to give a marblelike effect.

Spread remaining cream cheese mixture evenly over top; make 2 parallel lines down center of cake with remaining chocolate mixture. Run tip of knife at right angles to lines in opposite directions to create a feathered effect.

Bake at 300° for 1 hour; turn oven off, and let cake stand in oven 1 additional hour. Remove from oven; cool on wire rack, away from drafts. Cake will shrink slightly as it cools. When cool, loosen cake from side of pan with a spatula; remove side of pan and refrigerate cake. Yield: one 9-inch cake.

When grilling chicken halves, place bony or rib-cage side of chicken next to heat first. The bones act as an insulator and prevent chicken from browning too fast. Twist the drumstick to test for doneness; if the joint twists out of the socket easily, the meat is done.

When using skewers, select long, sturdy ones that reach completely across the grill. Place food on skewers, leaving space between each piece to allow for heat penetration and thorough basting. Unless some vegetables are parboiled, they may require a longer cooking time than meat cubes; therefore, you may want to put them on separate skewers.

Metric Measures

APPROXIMATE CONVERSION TO METRIC MEASURES

When you know . . .	Multiply by . . . Mass (weight)	To find . . .	Symbol
ounces	28	grams	g
pounds	0.45	kilograms	kg
	Volume		
teaspoons	5	milliliters	ml
tablespoons	15	milliliters	ml
fluid ounces	30	milliliters	ml
cups	0.24	liters	l
pints	0.47	liters	l
quarts	0.95	liters	l
gallons	3.8	liters	l

A Good-Neighbor Cookout
(Cookout for Twelve)

Stuffed Flank Steak
Luau Beans
Marinated Carrots
Cheese Deviled Eggs
Creamy Slaw
Onion-Dill Bread
Triple Lemon Treat
Sangría

STUFFED FLANK STEAK

4 (1½-pound) flank steaks
½ pound mushrooms, sliced, or
  3 (4-ounce) cans sliced mushrooms,
  drained
¼ cup butter or margarine
¼ cup crumbled blue cheese or Roquefort
  cheese
2 cloves garlic, crushed
2 teaspoons salt, divided
½ teaspoon pepper, divided

Cut a pocket in each steak. Sauté mushrooms in butter; stir in cheese, garlic, 1 teaspoon salt, and ¼ teaspoon pepper. Fill steak pockets with mushroom mixture; seal with skewers. Sprinkle with remaining salt and pepper.

 Broil 3 inches from heat 3 to 4 minutes on each side. Place on a warmed platter; cut into thin slices diagonally across the grain. Yield: 12 servings.

LUAU BEANS

½ pound sliced bacon, cooked and
  crumbled
2 medium onions, chopped
4 (16-ounce) cans pork and beans
1 (8½-ounce) can crushed pineapple,
  undrained
¼ cup chili sauce
2 tablespoons molasses
1½ teaspoons dry mustard
½ teaspoon salt

Combine all ingredients in a 3-quart Dutch oven. Cover and cook on grill over moderate heat 1 to 1½ hours, stirring occasionally. Yield: 12 to 14 servings.

MARINATED CARROTS

2 pounds carrots, sliced
1 medium onion, sliced
½ green pepper, sliced
1 (10¾-ounce) can tomato soup,
    undiluted
½ cup vinegar
½ cup salad oil
¾ cup sugar
1 tablespoon prepared mustard

Cook carrots until tender in a small amount of boiling salted water; drain. Combine carrots, onion, and green pepper; set aside.

Combine soup, vinegar, salad oil, sugar, and mustard; stir until well mixed. Pour over vegetables; toss lightly with a fork. Refrigerate overnight. Yield: 12 servings.

CHEESE DEVILED EGGS

12 hard-cooked eggs
⅓ cup shredded sharp Cheddar cheese
3 tablespoons vinegar
1 teaspoon prepared mustard
1 teaspoon salt
1 teaspoon pepper
4 tablespoons butter or margarine,
    softened

Slice eggs in half lengthwise, and carefully remove yolks. Mash yolks; blend in remaining ingredients. Stuff egg whites with yolk mixture. Yield: 12 servings.

CREAMY SLAW

10 cups shredded cabbage
1 cup shredded carrot
⅔ cup chopped green pepper
½ cup evaporated milk
½ cup mayonnaise
¼ teaspoon hot sauce
⅓ cup vinegar
2 teaspoons prepared mustard
1 tablespoon sugar
½ teaspoon celery seeds
1½ teaspoons salt

Combine cabbage, carrot, and green pepper; set aside. Combine milk and mayonnaise, blending until smooth. Add remaining ingredients to mayonnaise mixture, and blend well. Pour dressing over cabbage mixture; toss lightly to mix. Refrigerate overnight. Yield: 12 servings.

ONION-DILL BREAD

2 packages dry yeast
1¼ cups very warm water (105° to 115°)
1 egg, beaten
2 tablespoons sugar
3 tablespoons melted butter or margarine
1 teaspoon salt
1 medium onion, minced
2 teaspoons dillweed
1 cup lukewarm buttermilk
    About 7½ cups all-purpose flour

Dissolve yeast in very warm water in a mixing bowl; add egg, sugar, butter, salt, onion, dillweed, and buttermilk, mixing well. Gradually add about half the flour; beat until smooth. Gradually add remaining flour to make a soft dough.

Turn dough out onto a lightly floured board; knead until smooth and elastic, about 7 minutes. Place dough in a greased bowl, turning to grease all sides. Cover and let rise in a warm place free from drafts until doubled in bulk, about 1 hour.

Punch dough down; turn onto a lightly floured board and knead lightly. Divide in half; shape each half into a loaf and place in 2 greased 9¼-x 5¼- x 2¾-inch loafpans. Cover; let rise in a warm place until doubled in bulk, about 1 hour. Bake at 350° for 35 to 45 minutes. Yield: 2 loaves.

Note: To make rolls, shape dough into 1½-inch balls and place in 2 greased 9-inch round pans. Let rise until doubled in bulk, about 1 hour. Bake at 350° for 20 to 25 minutes. Yield: about 18 large rolls.

TRIPLE LEMON TREAT

½ cup margarine, softened
1 cup all-purpose flour
1 (8-ounce) package cream cheese, softened
1 cup powdered sugar
1 (13½-ounce) container frozen whipped topping, thawed and divided
2 (3¾-ounce) packages lemon instant pudding and pie filling mix
3 cups cold milk
Lemon juice (optional)
Chopped pecans

Using 2 knives or a pastry blender, cut margarine into flour until mixture resembles coarse crumbs; press crumbs into the bottom of a 13- x 9- x 2-inch pan. Bake at 350° for 10 minutes; cool.

Combine cream cheese and powdered sugar; mix until smooth. Fold in whipped topping, reserving 1 cup; spread mixture over cooled pastry.

Combine pudding mix and milk; beat until smooth and thickened. Add lemon juice if more tartness is desired. Spread over cream cheese mixture. Spread reserved 1 cup whipped topping over top; sprinkle with pecans. Yield: 12 servings.

SANGRÍA

1 cup sugar
½ cup water
4 (4/5-quart) bottles Beaujolais wine, chilled
1 (46-ounce) can pineapple juice, chilled
1 (12-ounce) bottle club soda, chilled
Maraschino cherries
Orange slices
Lemon slices
Pineapple slices, cut in half

Combine sugar and water in a small saucepan; stir over medium heat until sugar dissolves. Cool. Combine sugar syrup, wine, pineapple juice, and club soda; pour into a punch bowl with an ice ring. Garnish with cherries, and slices of orange, lemon, and pineapple. Yield: about 5½ quarts.

Meal-on-a-Skewer

(Cookout for Eight to Ten)

Chilled Avocado Soup
Lamb Kabobs with Brown Rice
Golden Carrots Supreme
Marinated Salad
Grilled Garlic Bread
Buttermilk Sherbet
Wine

CHILLED AVOCADO SOUP

　5 ripe avocados, peeled and coarsely
　　　chopped
　2 cups chicken broth
　2 cups half-and-half
　2 teaspoons salt
　½ teaspoon onion salt
　　Pinch of white pepper
　2 teaspoons lemon juice
　　Lemon slices

Combine avocado and chicken broth in blender.
Cover and blend until smooth. Remove from
blender container, and stir in half-and-half, salt,
onion salt, and white pepper. Cover and refrigerate overnight.
　Before serving, stir in lemon juice. Garnish
with lemon slices. Yield: 8 to 10 servings.

LAMB KABOBS WITH BROWN RICE

　6 tablespoons lemon juice
　¼ cup salad oil
　2 tablespoons grated onion
　½ teaspoon cayenne pepper
　1 teaspoon ginger
　1 clove garlic, crushed
　2 teaspoons curry powder
　1 tablespoon salt
　4 pounds lamb, cut into 1-inch cubes
20 fresh mushroom caps
　2 green peppers, cut into 1-inch squares
　2 tablespoons melted butter
20 cherry tomatoes
　4 onions, quartered
1½ cups pineapple chunks
　　Cooked brown rice

Combine lemon juice, salad oil, grated onion,
cayenne, ginger, garlic, curry powder, and salt;
add lamb cubes and marinate 24 hours.

Sauté mushrooms and green pepper in butter. Alternate meat, vegetables, and pineapple on skewers; brush with marinade. Grill 10 to 15 minutes over medium heat, basting with marinade and turning occasionally. Serve over brown rice. Yield: 8 to 10 servings.

GOLDEN CARROTS SUPREME

¼ cup melted butter or margarine
¾ cup chicken broth
2 teaspoons salt
⅛ teaspoon pepper
2 teaspoons sugar
5 cups diagonally sliced carrots
2 teaspoons lemon juice
¼ cup chopped parsley

Combine butter and chicken broth; bring to a boil. Add salt, pepper, sugar, and carrots; simmer, covered, 15 to 20 minutes or until tender. Stir in lemon juice and parsley. Yield: 8 to 10 servings.

MARINATED SALAD

1 cup vinegar
1 cup sugar
½ cup salad oil
1 (16-ounce) can French-style green
    beans, drained
1 (8-ounce) can peas, drained
2 carrots, thinly sliced
1 green pepper, finely chopped
1 red onion, thinly sliced
1 (2-ounce) jar chopped pimiento,
    drained
1 cucumber, thinly sliced
3 stalks celery, chopped

Bring vinegar to a boil in a small saucepan; stir in sugar and oil. Cool slightly. Combine remaining ingredients; add vinegar mixture. Cover and refrigerate overnight. Yield: 10 to 12 servings.

GRILLED GARLIC BREAD

½ cup softened butter or margarine
1 clove garlic, minced
1 teaspoon parsley flakes
¼ teaspoon oregano
¼ teaspoon dried dill, crushed
1 (1-pound) loaf French bread

Combine butter, garlic, parsley flakes, oregano, and dill. Put in covered container and keep in refrigerator. (Flavor is better if mixture is prepared several days before using.) Remove and allow 1 hour for mixture to soften before spreading on bread.

Cut bread in ¾-inch slices, not quite through the bottom crust. Spread butter mixture generously between slices. Wrap loosely in aluminum foil; heat on grill for 15 minutes. Yield: 8 to 10 servings.

BUTTERMILK SHERBET

1 quart buttermilk
¾ cup sugar
1 (8-ounce) can crushed pineapple,
    undrained
1 teaspoon vanilla extract
2 egg whites, stiffly beaten

Combine buttermilk, sugar, pineapple, and vanilla; blend well. Pour into freezer trays, and freeze to a thick mush.

Remove mixture from trays, and fold in egg whites. Return to trays, and freeze until firm. Yield: 8 to 10 servings.

Spicy Sparerib Special

(Cookout for Six)

Springtime Strawberry Cooler
Orange-Garlic Spareribs
Stuffed Zucchini Supreme
Herbed Tomatoes
Bibb Lettuce with Cucumber Salad Dressing
Garlic Toast
Peach Cobbler Supreme
Wine

SPRINGTIME STRAWBERRY COOLER

2½ cups fresh strawberries, divided
1½ cups water
½ cup sugar
2 tablespoons lemon juice
1 teaspoon grated lemon rind
½ cup white wine

Puree 2 cups strawberries in blender. Add water, sugar, lemon juice, lemon rind, and wine; blend well. Chill and pour into cups. Slice remaining berries; use for garnish. Yield: 6 servings.

ORANGE-GARLIC SPARERIBS

4 large cloves garlic, crushed
1 tablespoon salt
1 cup chicken broth
1 cup orange marmalade
¼ cup vinegar
¼ cup catsup
6 pounds spareribs

Combine garlic and salt; add broth, marmalade, vinegar, and catsup. Pour over ribs; marinate at least 12 hours, turning several times.

Grill ribs over low coals 1 to 1½ hours or until tender; baste with marinade during cooking. Yield: 6 servings.

STUFFED ZUCCHINI SUPREME

 4 medium zucchini squash
 2 tablespoons melted margarine
1½ cups soft bread cubes
 1 (1½-ounce) envelope sloppy Joe
  seasoning mix
 1 egg, slightly beaten
 1 (2-ounce) jar chopped pimiento,
  drained
 ¼ cup shredded Swiss cheese

Cut squash in half lengthwise; carefully scoop out pulp, leaving shells about ⅜ inch thick. Place shells cut side down in a shallow baking pan; add boiling water to a depth of ½ inch. Bake at 400° for 20 minutes.

 Chop squash pulp; sauté in margarine about 4 to 5 minutes or until tender. Add bread cubes, sloppy Joe seasoning mix, egg, and pimiento; blend well. Spoon into zucchini shells; sprinkle with cheese. Bake at 400° about 15 to 20 minutes or until tender. Yield: 6 to 8 servings.

HERBED TOMATOES

 ⅔ cup salad oil
 ¼ cup vinegar
  Pinch of thyme
 ½ cup chopped parsley
 ½ cup chopped chives
  Salt and pepper to taste
 6 tomatoes, quartered
  Lettuce

Combine salad oil, vinegar, and seasonings. Place tomatoes in a shallow dish, and add dressing; cover and refrigerate overnight.

 Remove tomatoes from dressing, and serve on a bed of lettuce; spoon on a small amount of dressing. Yield: 6 servings.

CUCUMBER SALAD DRESSING

 1 small cucumber, peeled and chopped
 1 small onion, chopped
  Lemon juice to taste
 2 cups mayonnaise
  Green food coloring (optional)
  Seasoned salt to taste
  Worcestershire sauce to taste
  Bibb lettuce

Combine first seven ingredients in blender; cover and blend until smooth. Chill well. Serve over Bibb lettuce. Yield: 4 cups.

GARLIC TOAST

 ½ cup soft margarine
 1 tablespoon grated Parmesan cheese
 1 teaspoon garlic powder
 2 tablespoons pasteurized process sharp
  cheese spread
 1 (1-pound) loaf French bread

Combine margarine, Parmesan, garlic powder, and cheese spread; whip until light and fluffy. Cut bread into 4-inch slices; then split slices horizontally. Toast outer crust. Spread cut side with cheese mixture; return to oven and toast until mixture is bubbly and edges are golden brown. Yield: 8 servings.

PEACH COBBLER SUPREME

　About 8 cups sliced fresh peaches
　2 cups sugar
　2 to 4 tablespoons all-purpose flour
　½ teaspoon ground nutmeg
　1 teaspoon almond extract
　⅓ cup melted butter or margarine
　Pastry for double crust 8-inch pie

Combine peaches, sugar, flour, and nutmeg; set aside until syrup forms. Bring peaches to a boil, and cook over low heat 10 minutes or until tender. Remove from heat; add almond extract and butter, blending well.

Roll out half of pastry to ⅛-inch thickness on a lightly floured board; cut into an 8-inch square. Spoon half of peaches into a lightly buttered 8-inch square pan; top with pastry square. Bake at 475° for 12 minutes or until golden brown. Spoon remaining peaches over baked pastry square.

Roll out remaining pastry, and cut into ½-inch strips; arrange in lattice design over peaches. Return to oven for 10 to 15 minutes or until lightly browned. Yield: 6 to 8 servings.

When using the rotisserie with your barbecue grill, make certain the rotisserie rod is inserted in the center of the meat lengthwise and that the spit forks are tight. This will keep the meat balanced, making the rotisserie turn evenly.

Punch bowl tip—Instead of using an ice block for your punch bowl, try this: Prepare a mixture of orange juice and any other fruit juice desired. The mixture should be quite strong. Pour into a mold or plastic container, and add strawberries or other fruit if desired; freeze. Place the frozen juice block in your punch bowl and pour punch over it. The block will prevent punch from becoming watery during a long serving period and will add to the flavor of the punch.

Backyard Barbecue

(Cookout for Six to Eight)

Dill Dip   Raw Vegetables
Creamy Cheese Ball   Crackers
Barbecued Chicken
Garlic Baked Grits
Summer Salad
French Bread   Butter
Three Fruit Sherbet
Light Wine Punch

DILL DIP

2 cups mayonnaise
2 cups commercial sour cream
3 tablespoons minced fresh parsley or
    1 tablespoon dried parsley
3 tablespoons grated onion
3 tablespoons dillweed
1½ tablespoons seasoned salt

Blend together all ingredients; chill several hours. Serve with raw vegetables such as whole cherry tomatoes, bite-size pieces of cauliflower, celery and carrot strips. Dip may be made several days ahead of time. Yield: 4½ cups.

CREAMY CHEESE BALL

6 (3-ounce) packages cream cheese,
    softened
½ pound sharp Cheddar cheese, shredded
2 teaspoons grated onion
2 teaspoons Worcestershire sauce
2 teaspoons finely minced garlic (garlic
    powder or dried onion flakes may be
    substituted)
Parsley sprigs
Crackers

Combine cheese, onion, Worcestershire sauce, and garlic, blending well. Refrigerate until firm; shape into a ball. Wrap in plastic or heavy-duty aluminum foil, and let ripen in refrigerator for at least 24 hours.

Remove from refrigerator at least 2 hours before serving. Garnish with parsley, and serve with crackers. Yield: about 3 cups.

BARBECUED CHICKEN

⅓ cup melted butter or margarine
⅓ cup salad oil
2 tablespoons lemon juice
2 teaspoons prepared mustard
⅓ teaspoon horseradish
3 drops liquid smoke
1 clove garlic, finely chopped
2 teaspoons commercial barbecue sauce
2 (3-pound) fryers, cut in half
  Ac´cent

Combine all ingredients except fryers and Ac´cent; bring sauce to a boil and simmer 5 minutes. Sprinkle fryers with Ac´cent. Brush both sides of chicken with sauce, and place on grill. Cook slowly 60 to 75 minutes, turning and basting often with sauce. Yield: 6 to 8 servings.

GARLIC BAKED GRITS

1 cup uncooked grits
4 cups water
2 eggs, slightly beaten
½ cup butter or margarine
1 (6-ounce) roll pasteurized process cheese
    food with garlic, cubed
  Dash of garlic salt

Cook grits in water according to package directions. Stir small amount of hot grits into eggs; add egg mixture to remainder of grits. Stir in butter, cheese, and garlic salt. Spoon mixture into a greased 2-quart casserole. Bake at 350° for 1 hour. Yield: 6 to 8 servings.

SUMMER SALAD

3 to 4 ripe tomatoes, cut in wedges
1 to 2 cucumbers, sliced
1 green onion, chopped
¼ green pepper, chopped
1 teaspoon Ac´cent
½ teaspoon basil
2 tablespoons salad oil
1 tablespoon vinegar
  Salt and pepper to taste
  Lettuce

Combine vegetables in a salad bowl. Combine Ac´cent, basil, salad oil, vinegar, salt, and pepper; pour over vegetables. Chill. Serve on a bed of lettuce. Yield: 6 to 8 servings.

THREE FRUIT SHERBET

3 bananas, sliced
1 (8¼-ounce) can crushed pineapple,
    undrained
  Juice of 3 lemons
2 cups sugar
1 quart milk

Combine bananas, pineapple, and lemon juice; stir in sugar. Chill well. Blend in milk; freeze in ice trays or an ice cream freezer. Yield: 6 to 8 servings.

LIGHT WINE PUNCH

1 quart strawberry-flavored wine
1 quart ginger ale

Combine wine and ginger ale; serve over ice. Yield: 6 to 8 servings.

Carnival Cookout

(Cookout for Eight)

Mystery Dip   Raw Vegetables
Carnival Sausage and Peppers
Sour Cream Potato Salad
Marinated Squash
Black-Bottom Cupcakes or Apricot Squares
Minted Lemonade

MYSTERY DIP

2 cups mayonnaise
1 (10-ounce) package frozen chopped
    spinach, cooked and well drained
½ cup chopped green onion
½ cup chopped fresh parsley
1 teaspoon salt
1 teaspoon pepper

Combine all ingredients, stirring well. Serve with cucumber, carrot, and celery sticks. Yield: about 3 cups.

CARNIVAL SAUSAGE AND PEPPERS

2 pounds Polish sausage, cut in 2-inch
    chunks
3 to 4 green peppers, cut into 2-inch
    strips
1 (15-ounce) can tomato-herb sauce
8 small French rolls

Thread sausage and green pepper alternately on skewers. Grill 6 inches from white-hot coals 10 minutes on each side; baste lightly with tomato sauce during cooking.

Split rolls lengthwise almost completely through; open and place cut side down on grill until lightly toasted. Place 3 pieces of sausage and green pepper on each roll. Heat remaining tomato sauce; spoon over sausage. Yield: 8 servings.

SOUR CREAM POTATO SALAD

4 hard-cooked eggs
⅔ cup mayonnaise
¾ cup commercial sour cream
1½ teaspoons prepared mustard with
    horseradish
½ pound bacon
⅓ cup chopped green onion
7 cups cooked cubed potatoes (about 8
    medium)
⅓ cup commercial Italian salad dressing
    Salt to taste
    Celery seeds to taste

Cut eggs in half and remove yolks. Mash yolks, and blend with mayonnaise, sour cream, and mustard.

Cook bacon until crisp; drain and crumble. Chop egg whites, and combine with bacon, onion, potatoes, and salad dressing. Fold in mayonnaise mixture, and season with salt and celery seeds. Yield: 8 to 10 servings.

MARINATED SQUASH

8 cups sliced raw yellow squash
2 onions, sliced and separated into rings
½ cup sliced stuffed olives
1 (8-ounce) bottle commercial Italian
    dressing
Salt and pepper to taste

Combine vegetables and olives; add dressing, and season with salt and pepper. Refrigerate overnight, gently stirring several times. Drain dressing from vegetable mixture, and arrange vegetables on serving platter. Yield: 8 to 10 servings.

BLACK-BOTTOM CUPCAKES

1 (8-ounce) package cream cheese,
    softened
2⅓ cups sugar, divided
1 egg, beaten
1⅛ teaspoons salt, divided
1 (6-ounce) package semisweet chocolate
    pieces
3 cups all-purpose flour
½ cup cocoa
2 teaspoons soda
2 cups water
⅔ cup salad oil
1 tablespoon vinegar
2 teaspoons vanilla extract

Combine cream cheese, ⅓ cup sugar, egg, and ⅛ teaspoon salt in small mixing bowl; beat until well blended. Add chocolate pieces, and set aside.

Combine flour, cocoa, 2 cups sugar, 1 teaspoon salt, and soda. Add water, oil, vinegar, and vanilla; beat until smooth. (Batter will be very thin.)

Place paper liners in muffin pans. Fill each muffin liner two-thirds full of batter; then drop a teaspoonful of cream cheese mixture in the center of each. Bake at 350° for 30 to 35 minutes. Cool on racks. Yield: 2 to 2½ dozen.

Note: These cupcakes freeze well when wrapped in aluminum foil.

APRICOT SQUARES

½ cup shortening
½ cup sugar
1 egg, beaten
½ teaspoon lemon extract
2 tablespoons milk
1½ cups all-purpose flour
1½ teaspoons baking powder
½ teaspoon salt
½ teaspoon ground cinnamon
¼ teaspoon ground cloves
¾ cup apricot jam

Cream shortening and sugar until light and fluffy. Add egg, lemon extract, and milk; beat well. Combine dry ingredients; add to creamed mixture, mixing well.

Spread half the batter in a greased 9-inch pan. Batter will be stiff. Spread jam over batter; top with remaining batter.

Bake at 400° for 25 minutes. Cut into 1-inch squares. These cookies freeze well. Yield: 3 dozen squares.

MINTED LEMONADE
(see Index)

Fresh Peach Ice Cream (page 102) is a favorite dessert of summer.

Steak-on-a-Stick

(Cookout for Six)

Orange-Champagne Cocktail
Spicy Beef Kabobs
Cheesy Potatoes   Green Beans Bourguignon
Mixed Fruit Toss
Garlic Toast
Cream Cheese Brownies   Homemade Vanilla Ice Cream
Iced Tea

ORANGE-CHAMPAGNE COCKTAIL

1 (4/5-quart) bottle champagne, chilled
1 (28-ounce) bottle ginger ale, chilled
2 cups orange juice, chilled
   Sliced fresh strawberries

Combine champagne, ginger ale, and orange juice. Place a few strawberries in glasses and pour in champagne mixture. Yield: 2 quarts.

The courtyard of the Hermann-Grima House in New Orleans is a natural setting for these oyster specialties (clockwise): Oysters on the Half Shell (page 74), Oyster Loaf (page 258), Oysters Commander (page 250), Oysters Rockefeller (page 89), Oysters Bienville (page 130), and Oysters en Brochette (page 258).

SPICY BEEF KABOBS

1 cup Burgundy
1 cup salad oil
2 tablespoons Worcestershire sauce
¼ cup catsup
2 tablespoons sugar
2 tablespoons vinegar
1 teaspoon marjoram
1 teaspoon rosemary
2 pounds sirloin steak, cut into 1-inch cubes
2 onions
12 fresh mushroom caps
2 green peppers, cut into 1-inch squares
2 tomatoes, cut into wedges
   Melted butter

Combine Burgundy, salad oil, Worcestershire sauce, catsup, sugar, vinegar, marjoram, and rosemary; add meat cubes, and marinate at least 4 hours in refrigerator.

Quarter onions and separate sections. Alternate meat and vegetables on skewers. Brush vegetables with butter. Grill 10 to 15 minutes over medium heat, basting with marinade and turning occasionally. Yield: 6 servings.

CHEESY POTATOES

   3 large baking potatoes, peeled and thinly
       sliced
   1 large onion, thinly sliced
     Salt to taste
     Coarsely ground pepper
   1 (8-ounce) package sharp Cheddar
       cheese, cubed
   4 to 5 slices bacon, cooked and crumbled
   ½ cup butter or margarine

Place potato slices on a large piece of heavy-duty aluminum foil; cover with onion slices. Season with salt and pepper. Sprinkle with cheese and bacon; dot with butter. Wrap foil tightly.

   Cook about 1 hour on grill or until potatoes are done, turning several times. Yield: 6 servings.

GREEN BEANS BOURGUIGNON

   2 pounds green beans, cut into 1-inch
       pieces
   6 tablespoons melted butter or
       margarine, divided
   4 teaspoons all-purpose flour
   1 cup beef broth
   ½ cup red wine
   1 tablespoon chopped parsley
   1 tablespoon chopped chives
     Juice of ½ lemon
     Salt and pepper

Cook beans in boiling salted water about 20 minutes or until tender; drain.

   Combine 3 tablespoons butter and flour; cook over low heat, stirring constantly, until bubbly. Heat broth and wine; gradually add to flour mixture. Cook, stirring constantly, until smooth and thickened.

   Combine 3 tablespoons butter, beans, parsley, and chives; cook 5 minutes. Add sauce; heat thoroughly, stirring constantly. Sprinkle with lemon juice; season to taste with salt and pepper. Yield: 6 servings.

MIXED FRUIT TOSS

   2 cups mandarin orange sections
   1 cup seeded purple grapes
   1 cup seedless green grapes
   1 cup strawberries
     Lettuce
     Poppy Seed Dressing

Combine fruit; chill. Arrange chilled fruit on lettuce, and serve with Poppy Seed Dressing. Yield: 6 servings.

Poppy Seed Dressing:

   ⅓ cup frozen lemonade concentrate,
       thawed and undiluted
   5 tablespoons honey
   ⅓ cup salad oil
   2 tablespoons lemon juice
   1 teaspoon poppy seeds

Combine all ingredients; beat until smooth. Yield: about 1 cup.

GARLIC TOAST
(see Index)

CREAM CHEESE BROWNIES

1 (4-ounce) package sweet chocolate
    squares
5 tablespoons butter or margarine,
    divided
1 (3-ounce) package cream cheese,
    softened
1 cup sugar, divided
3 eggs, divided
½ cup plus 1 tablespoon all-purpose flour,
    divided
1½ teaspoons vanilla extract, divided
½ teaspoon baking powder
¼ teaspoon salt
¼ teaspoon almond extract
½ cup coarsely chopped pecans

Melt chocolate and 3 tablespoons butter over
low heat, stirring constantly. Set aside to cool.

Cream remaining 2 tablespoons butter and
cream cheese; gradually add ¼ cup sugar, beating
until light and fluffy. Blend in 1 egg, 1 tablespoon
flour, and ½ teaspoon vanilla. Set aside.

In a large bowl, beat 2 eggs; add remaining
¾ cup sugar, beating until thick. Add baking
powder, salt, and ½ cup flour. Blend in chocolate,
almond extract, and 1 teaspoon vanilla. Stir in
pecans.

Set aside 1 cup chocolate batter. Spread
remaining chocolate batter in a greased 9-inch
square pan. Top with cream cheese batter.

Drop reserved chocolate batter onto cream
cheese batter; swirl with spatula to marble. Bake
at 350° for 35 to 40 minutes. Cool; cut into
squares. Yield: about 1½ dozen squares.

HOMEMADE VANILLA ICE CREAM

2 cups powdered sugar
1 cup whipping cream
3 tablespoons vanilla extract
2 quarts half-and-half

Combine powdered sugar, whipping cream, and
vanilla; stir until smooth. Add half-and-half. Pour
into freezer can of a 1-gallon hand-turned or
electric freezer. Freeze according to manufacturer's instructions. Yield: 1 gallon.

Build a fire only large enough for the amount
of food to be grilled; you don't need an inferno
to barbecue. Allow about 30 minutes for charcoal briquets to turn ash gray before putting food
on the grill. When using gas or electric heat,
preheat the grill.

When grilling outdoors, place meat 4 to 5 inches
above the heat unless instructions state other-
wise. Just before pieces of meat are completely
done, move them to the outer edge of the grill
where they'll finish cooking and remain hot but
won't cook as rapidly as cuts in the center over
direct heat.

Crowd-Pleasing Patio Party

(Cookout for Eight)

Marinated Chuck Roast
Beer Rice
Roasted Bermuda Onions
Zesty Marinated Vegetable Salad
Cheese-Topped French Bread
Apple Fromage
Quick Sangría

MARINATED CHUCK ROAST

1 (3- to 4-pound) boneless chuck roast
  Meat tenderizer
1 (5-ounce) bottle soy sauce
1½ cups water
1 tablespoon lemon juice
½ cup firmly packed brown sugar
1 teaspoon Worcestershire sauce
½ cup bourbon

Sprinkle roast with tenderizer, and prick with fork; place roast in a shallow pan. Combine remaining ingredients, stirring well. Pour marinade over roast. Cover and place in refrigerator at least 12 hours, turning at least once.

Remove roast from marinade, and place on grill; cook over hot coals 30 to 45 minutes, basting often with marinade. Yield: 8 servings.

BEER RICE

½ cup chopped onion
½ cup chopped green pepper
½ cup melted butter or margarine
2 chicken bouillon cubes
2 cups boiling water
1 cup uncooked regular rice
¾ cup beer
½ teaspoon salt
¼ teaspoon pepper
¼ teaspoon ground thyme

Sauté onion and green pepper in butter until tender. Dissolve bouillon in boiling water; add to onion and green pepper mixture. Stir in rice, beer, and seasonings.

Cover and simmer over low heat 30 to 40 minutes or until all liquid is absorbed. Yield: 8 servings.

ROASTED BERMUDA ONIONS

8 large Bermuda onions, peeled
Butter or margarine
Salt to taste

Make 2 crosswise cuts halfway through each onion. Place each onion on a square of heavy-duty aluminum foil. Place a pat of butter in each cut in onion; sprinkle with salt. Fold foil securely around onion. Cook on grill over moderate heat 45 minutes to 1 hour, turning once. Yield: 8 servings.

ZESTY MARINATED VEGETABLE SALAD

2 (10-ounce) packages frozen brussels sprouts
½ cup salad oil
¼ cup wine vinegar
2 tablespoons minced onion
2 teaspoons salt
1 teaspoon sugar
¼ teaspoon white pepper
1½ teaspoons prepared mustard
3 to 4 tomatoes, cut into wedges
1 (16-ounce) can whole new potatoes, drained (optional)
4 carrots, cut into strips
4 stalks celery, cut into strips
Lettuce

Cook brussels sprouts according to package directions; drain. Combine oil, vinegar, onion, salt, sugar, pepper, and mustard in a jar; shake well.
Combine all vegetables except lettuce; add marinade, and refrigerate at least 3 hours or overnight, stirring occasionally. Drain, and arrange on a lettuce-lined platter. Yield: 8 servings.

CHEESE-TOPPED FRENCH BREAD

1 (1-pound) loaf French bread
½ cup margarine
1 clove garlic, crushed
Grated Parmesan or shredded Cheddar cheese

Cut loaf of French bread in half, lengthwise. Combine margarine and garlic in small saucepan; stir and cook for 2 minutes. Brush bread halves generously with this mixture, and sprinkle liberally with Parmesan cheese. Put halves together and wrap in a double thickness of heavy-duty aluminum foil. Place on the grill for 10 to 12 minutes. To serve, slice crosswise. Yield: 8 servings.

APPLE FROMAGE

1 envelope (1 tablespoon) unflavored gelatin
2 tablespoons cold water
3 cups applesauce
2 teaspoons grated lemon rind
⅛ teaspoon ground mace
½ pint whipping cream, whipped
Fresh fruit

Soften gelatin in cold water. Place over boiling water, and stir until gelatin is dissolved. Add applesauce, lemon rind, and mace; chill 30 minutes. Fold whipped cream into applesauce mixture. Spoon into individual custard cups, and serve with fresh fruit. Yield: 8 servings.

QUICK SANGRÍA

2 (6-ounce) cans frozen pink lemonade concentrate, thawed and undiluted
4½ cups rosé, chilled
Juice of 1 lime
2 cups club soda, chilled
1 lemon, thinly sliced
1 orange, thinly sliced

Combine lemonade, rosé, and lime juice; stir until well blended. Slowly stir in soda. Garnish with lemon and orange slices. Yield: 8 servings.

DINNERS WITH A FOREIGN FLAVOR

South of the Border
Oriental Shrimp Dinner
Italian Pasta Dinner
Polynesian Feast
Dinner Italiano
Greek Easter Dinner

A Special Bavarian Dinner
A French Classic
Dinner from the Orient
A Night in Old Mexico
Grecian Classic Dinner

Take a trip to some faraway land, right in your own kitchen. Tease your appetite with an Oriental dip, a Greek appetizer tray, Bavarian liverwurst spread, or French onion soup. Then feast on enchiladas from Mexico, black bread from Germany, crêpes from France, spumoni from Italy. Whatever places your dreams take you, visit them first through these around-the-world menus.

South of the Border

(Dinner for Four)

Gazpacho
Chili Hot Dip   Corn Chips
Enchiladas
Refried Beans
Guacamole Mousse
Flan
Quick Sangría

GAZPACHO

½ cup diced celery
½ cup diced green pepper
½ cup diced onion
½ cup thinly sliced cucumber
1 cup diced tomatoes
1 (10¾-ounce) can tomato soup,
   undiluted
1 soup can water
1½ cups cocktail vegetable juice
1 tablespoon wine vinegar
1 tablespoon commercial Italian dressing
   Garlic salt to taste
¼ teaspoon salt
⅛ teaspoon pepper
4 dashes of hot sauce
   Dash of Worcestershire sauce

Combine all ingredients in a large bowl. Cover and refrigerate at least 4 hours. Stir gently. Serve in chilled bowls or mugs. Yield: 6 to 8 servings.

CHILI HOT DIP

1 (8-ounce) package cream cheese,
   softened
¼ to ½ cup hot green chili relish
2 dashes of hot sauce
⅛ teaspoon garlic salt
   Corn chips

Combine first four ingredients; blend well with electric mixer. Serve with corn chips. Yield: 1½ cups.

ENCHILADAS

1 cup chopped onion
1 cup chopped green pepper
½ cup vegetable oil, divided
2 pounds ground beef
1 (14½-ounce) can tomatoes
1 (8-ounce) can tomato sauce
2 (1½-ounce) packages enchilada sauce
    mix
½ cup water
2 (15-ounce) cans pinto beans, undrained
8 tortillas
1 cup shredded Cheddar cheese
1 medium tomato, chopped
1 cup shredded lettuce

Sauté onion and green pepper in 2 tablespoons oil until soft. Add 2 tablespoons oil and ground beef; cook slowly until lightly browned. Stir in tomatoes, tomato sauce, enchilada sauce mix, water, and beans; simmer, uncovered, 10 minutes.

Heat remaining oil in a small skillet; dip each tortilla into hot oil, and cook until just softened. Drain on paper towels.

Spoon about 1 cup meat sauce in a lightly greased 13- x 9-inch baking dish. Spread each tortilla with ¼ cup meat sauce; roll up and place, seam side down, in baking dish.

Spoon remaining sauce over tortillas; sprinkle with cheese and chopped tomato. Bake at 350° for 20 minutes or until cheese is melted. Before serving, arrange lettuce around edge of dish. Yield: 4 servings.

REFRIED BEANS (Frijoles Refritos)

2 cups cooked pinto beans
½ cup bacon drippings
¼ pound sharp Cheddar cheese, shredded
    (optional)
¼ cup finely chopped green onions and
    tops

Mash beans, or put through a food mill. Melt bacon drippings in heavy skillet. Add beans; cook and stir over medium heat until beans have turned dark and are crisp and brown around the edges.

Turn heat to low, spread beans over bottom of skillet, and add shredded cheese, if desired. Stir gently until cheese melts. Serve with chopped green onion. Yield: 4 to 6 servings.

GUACAMOLE MOUSSE

1 envelope (1 tablespoon) unflavored
    gelatin
1 cup cold water
1 chicken bouillon cube, crumbled
¼ teaspoon salt
1½ cups sieved avocado
½ cup commercial sour cream
3 tablespoons finely chopped green onion
2 tablespoons lemon juice
½ teaspoon hot sauce
    Carrot strips
    Celery
    Ripe olives

Soften gelatin in cold water in a small saucepan. Add bouillon cube and salt. Heat, stirring constantly, until gelatin and bouillon are dissolved; cool slightly.

Combine avocado, sour cream, green onion, lemon juice, and hot sauce; stir in gelatin mixture. Pour into a 3-cup mold and refrigerate until firm. Unmold, and garnish with carrots, celery, and olives. Yield: 4 servings.

FLAN

3 cups sugar, divided
½ cup boiling water
6 eggs
1 tablespoon anisette
1 teaspoon vanilla extract
Dash of nutmeg
Dash of salt
2 cups scalded milk

Melt 1 cup sugar in a heavy skillet over low heat, stirring constantly. When mixture is light brown, remove from heat and slowly add boiling water; stir and boil until caramel is dissolved. Pour into 8 custard cups.

Beat eggs until frothy. Add remaining sugar, anisette, vanilla, nutmeg, and salt; beat well. Add milk gradually. Pour mixture into caramel cups. Place cups in a pan of water and bake at 350° for 30 to 40 minutes or until custard is set. Cool; chill in refrigerator. When ready to serve, loosen edges with a spatula and turn mold upside down. The caramel tops the custard. Yield: 8 servings.

QUICK SANGRÍA
(see Index)

When grilling steaks, turn them only once. Always use tongs to turn steak; a fork will pierce the meat and allow juice to escape. To prevent steak from curling while grilling, score or slit the fat along the edge at about 1½-inch intervals before placing meat on the grill.

Food may be basted during the entire cooking time or during the last half hour, depending on the ingredients in the sauce. A sauce containing sugar (or other ingredients that burn readily) should be applied during the last 15 to 30 minutes of cooking time. A long-handled cotton dishmop works well for basting.

Oriental Shrimp Dinner

(Dinner for Six)

Ginger Dip or Tangy Oriental Dip
Raw Vegetables
Chinese Sweet-and-Sour Shrimp or Szechwan Shrimp
Stir-Fry Vegetables
Oriental Spinach Salad
Almond Treats
Tea

GINGER DIP

  1 cup mayonnaise
  4 teaspoons soy sauce
  1 teaspoon vinegar
  ¾ teaspoon ground ginger
  2 tablespoons chopped onion
    Carrot sticks
    Celery sticks

Combine all ingredients, mixing well; place in a covered container, and refrigerate at least 4 hours. Serve with carrot and celery sticks. Yield: 1¼ cups.

TANGY ORIENTAL DIP

  1 cup mayonnaise
  1 cup commercial sour cream
  1 tablespoon chopped onion
  2 tablespoons chopped parsley
  1 (8-ounce) can water chestnuts, drained
    and chopped
  ⅛ teaspoon salt
  ¼ teaspoon garlic salt
  ½ teaspoon soy sauce
  ½ teaspoon Worcestershire sauce

Combine all ingredients, mixing well. Serve with melba toast, raw vegetables, or chips. Yield: about 2½ cups.

CHINESE SWEET-AND-SOUR SHRIMP

½ cup all-purpose flour
¼ cup cornstarch
½ teaspoon baking powder
1 egg, beaten
½ teaspoon salt
½ cup less 1 tablespoon water
1 teaspoon salad oil
1 pound fresh shrimp, peeled and
    deveined
    Hot cooking oil
    Hot cooked rice
    Sweet-and-Sour Sauce

Combine flour, cornstarch, baking powder, egg, salt, water, and 1 teaspoon oil; mix well. Dip shrimp into batter, and cook in oil heated to 375° until golden brown. Keep warm in oven. Serve over rice, and top with Sweet-and-Sour Sauce. Yield: 6 servings.

Sweet-and-Sour Sauce:

½ cup sliced carrots
½ cup chopped green pepper
¾ cup sugar
⅓ cup catsup
1 tablespoon soy sauce
¼ teaspoon salt
¼ teaspoon monosodium glutamate
1 cup water, divided
3½ tablespoons cornstarch
½ cup vinegar
1 (15¼-ounce) can pineapple chunks,
    drained

Cook carrots in small amount of boiling water 1 to 2 minutes; add green pepper, and cook 1 additional minute. Drain and rinse vegetables in cold water.

Combine sugar, catsup, soy sauce, salt, monosodium glutamate, and ⅔ cup water in a saucepan; bring to a boil. Dissolve cornstarch in ⅓ cup water to make a paste. Gradually add cornstarch paste and vinegar to sauce mixture; cook, stirring constantly, until smooth and thickened. Combine sauce, pineapple, and vegetables. Keep warm until ready to serve. Yield: about 4 cups.

SZECHWAN SHRIMP

2 tablespoons salad oil
4 cloves garlic, minced
2 cups sliced green onion
2 green peppers, cut into 1-inch pieces
2 pounds shrimp, cooked, peeled, and
    deveined
½ cup catsup
¼ cup soy sauce
2 tablespoons dry vermouth or sherry
1 teaspoon sugar
½ teaspoon ground ginger
1 teaspoon red pepper
1 (6-ounce) package frozen pea pods,
    thawed and drained
    Hot cooked rice

Pour oil into an electric wok (or an electric skillet); heat to 350°. Place garlic, onion, and green pepper in oil, and stir-fry 1 minute; push up sides of wok. Add shrimp and stir-fry 2 minutes or until pink; push shrimp up sides of wok.

Combine catsup, soy sauce, vermouth, sugar, ginger, and red pepper; add to wok, and cook 1 minute. Add pea pods; stir-fry about 1 minute. Reduce heat to warm for serving, and gently stir all foods together with sauce. Serve over rice. Yield: 6 to 8 servings.

STIR-FRY VEGETABLES

4 cups shredded cabbage
1 green pepper, thinly sliced
2 large onions, thinly sliced
2 large tomatoes, cut into thin wedges
3 tablespoons salad oil
2 teaspoons sugar
¾ teaspoon salt
¼ teaspoon pepper

Combine vegetables, and toss lightly. Heat oil in a skillet; add vegetables, and sprinkle with sugar, salt, and pepper. Cover and cook 10 minutes over medium heat, stirring twice during cooking period. Yield: 6 servings.

ORIENTAL SPINACH SALAD

1 pound fresh spinach, cleaned and torn
    into bite-size pieces
1 (16-ounce) can bean sprouts, drained
½ cup sliced radishes
½ cup commercial French dressing
8 slices bacon, cooked and crumbled

Combine spinach, bean sprouts, and radishes; toss well. Toss with dressing; sprinkle bacon on top. Yield: 6 servings.

ALMOND TREATS

3 eggs, well beaten
½ cup melted shortening
¾ cup sugar
3 cups all-purpose flour
¼ teaspoon salt
3 teaspoons baking powder
½ cup coarsely chopped almonds
1 teaspoon vanilla extract
1 teaspoon almond extract

Combine eggs and shortening, beating well; gradually add sugar, mixing well. Combine flour, salt, and baking powder; gradually add to creamed mixture, blending well. Stir in almonds and flavorings.

Lightly grease hands, and shape dough into six 4-inch-long loaves. Place on a lightly greased cookie sheet. Bake at 325° for 20 to 25 minutes; remove carefully.

Cut each loaf into ½-inch slices. Place cookies, cut side down, on cookie sheets; bake an additional 15 minutes or until lightly browned. Remove to rack to cool. Yield: about 3 dozen cookies.

Italian Pasta Dinner

(Dinner for Ten to Twelve)

Party Antipasto Tray
Lasagna
Mozzarella-Stuffed Mushrooms
Green Salad   Cheese and Garlic Dressing
Commercial Hard Rolls   Butter
Italian Party Cake or Bisque Tortoni
Wine   Coffee

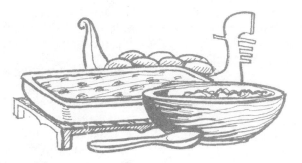

PARTY ANTIPASTO TRAY

½ medium head iceberg lettuce
1 small head endive
1 (3½-ounce) package thinly sliced
    pepperoni
1 (4-ounce) package thinly sliced Genoa
    salami, quartered
1 (3-ounce) package thinly sliced Italian
    ham
1 (15-ounce) can garbanzo beans, drained
1 (2-ounce) can anchovies with capers,
    drained
1 (8-ounce) jar peperoncini, drained
1 pound cherry tomatoes
    Radishes
    Carrot sticks
    Ripe olives
    Green olives
8 ounces provolone cheese, cubed
    Dressing

Shred lettuce and part of endive. Combine shredded salad greens; toss well and spread over bottom of serving tray.

Make a border of remaining endive leaves around edge of tray. Arrange meats, vegetables, and cubed cheese on top of shredded salad greens. Serve with Dressing. Yield: 10 to 12 servings.

Dressing:

2 tablespoons water
¼ cup wine vinegar
1 cup salad oil
1 tablespoon olive oil
1 clove garlic, crushed
1 teaspoon ground oregano
1 teaspoon basil
¼ teaspoon thyme
    Salt and pepper to taste (optional)

Combine all ingredients; mix well. Let stand several hours at room temperature. Yield: about 1½ cups.

LASAGNA

3 (16-ounce) cans stewed tomatoes
2 cloves garlic, crushed and divided
1¾ teaspoons salt, divided
¾ teaspoon pepper, divided
1 pound ground round steak
½ pound bulk pork sausage
1 tablespoon olive oil
1 medium onion, chopped
2 teaspoons seasoned salt
1 teaspoon basil leaves
¼ teaspoon ground oregano
¼ teaspoon dill-seasoned salt
1 teaspoon celery salt
1 tablespoon honey
3 tablespoons parsley flakes, divided
½ cup Burgundy
1 (2½-ounce) jar sliced mushrooms,
   drained
1 (14-ounce) package spinach lasagna
   noodles
2 (12-ounce) cartons small-curd cottage
   cheese
1 cup grated Parmesan cheese, divided
1 teaspoon oregano leaves
2 pounds mozzarella cheese, shredded
½ pound mild Cheddar cheese, shredded
½ pound Muenster cheese, shredded

Combine tomatoes, 1 clove crushed garlic, 1 teaspoon salt, and ¼ teaspoon pepper in a saucepan; simmer over low heat 2½ to 3 hours.

Brown round steak and pork sausage in olive oil in a large skillet; add remaining garlic, ½ teaspoon pepper, onion, seasoned salt, basil, and oregano. Cook until onion is tender; drain off drippings.

To meat add tomato mixture, dill-seasoned salt, celery salt, honey, 2 tablespoons parsley flakes, Burgundy, and mushrooms; simmer over low heat 8 hours or longer. (The sauce will be thick.)

Cook lasagna noodles according to package directions; drain. Combine cottage cheese, ½ cup Parmesan cheese, 1 tablespoon parsley flakes, ¾ teaspoon salt, and oregano leaves.

Reserve ¾ cup meat sauce; set aside. In a 13- x 9- x 2-inch baking dish, alternate layers of noodles, meat sauce, mozzarella, Cheddar, Muenster, and the cottage cheese mixture; repeat layers three times. Spread reserved meat sauce on top; sprinkle with remaining ½ cup Parmesan cheese.

Bake at 350° for 45 minutes; allow to stand 15 minutes before serving. Yield: 10 to 12 servings.

MOZZARELLA-STUFFED MUSHROOMS

1 pound fresh mushrooms
⅓ cup melted butter or margarine,
   divided
⅓ cup chopped onion
⅓ cup chopped pepperoni
⅓ cup shredded mozzarella cheese
½ cup Italian seasoning
¼ teaspoon garlic salt
⅓ cup seasoned breadcrumbs

Clean mushrooms with a damp cloth; remove stems, leaving caps intact. Chop stems. Brush caps with butter; set aside.

Sauté onion and mushroom stems in remaining butter; add pepperoni, mozzarella, seasonings, and breadcrumbs. Mix well, and spoon into mushroom caps. Place in a buttered baking dish. Bake at 350° for 15 minutes or until hot and bubbly. Yield: 10 to 12 servings.

CHEESE AND GARLIC DRESSING

1 (5-ounce) package Romano cheese,
   grated
4 cloves garlic, crushed
2 teaspoons salt
½ teaspoon pepper
4 teaspoons lemon juice
Salad oil

Combine cheese, garlic, salt, pepper, and lemon juice; add enough salad oil to make 3 cups dressing, and blend well. Yield: 3 cups.

ITALIAN PARTY CAKE

1 (10¾-ounce) frozen pound cake, thawed
1 (16-ounce) carton ricotta cheese
½ cup sugar
2 (1-ounce) squares unsweetened
  chocolate, grated
1 cup grated peeled apple
¼ teaspoon almond extract
1 cup whipping cream, whipped
½ cup finely chopped walnuts

Cut pound cake into thin slices. Combine cheese, sugar, chocolate, apple, and almond extract; mix well. Spread cheese mixture between cake slices; reassemble into a loaf. Chill overnight.

Just before serving, frost with whipped cream; sprinkle with walnuts. To serve, slice diagonally. Yield: 10 to 12 servings.

BISQUE TORTONI

3 eggs, separated
¼ cup sugar
1 dozen macaroon cookies, crushed
2 tablespoons crunchy nutlike cereal
  nuggets
1 tablespoon maraschino cherry juice
¼ teaspoon almond extract
½ cup chopped pecans
1 cup whipping cream, whipped

Combine egg yolks and sugar, beating until thick; stir in three-fourths of macaroon crumbs, cereal, cherry juice, almond extract, and pecans.

Beat egg whites until stiff; fold into macaroon mixture. Fold in whipped cream.

Spoon mixture into paper baking cups set in a muffin pan. Sprinkle with remaining macaroon crumbs; freeze until firm. Serve frozen. Yield: 10 to 12 servings.

Disposable pans for heating vegetables, bread, or other foods on the grill are easily made from heavy-duty aluminum foil: Just tear off a length of foil, and turn up edges to make 1½- to 2-inch sides; pinch corners to prevent leaking.

Frozen vegetables are delicious cooked on the grill. Remove from package, dot with butter, season, and wrap securely (while still frozen) in heavy-duty aluminum foil. Cook vegetables 30 to 40 minutes, turning once during cooking process.

Polynesian Feast
(Dinner for Six)

Chicken Tahitian
Polynesian Vegetables
Frozen Fruit Salad
Banana Bread
Guava Crisps
Mai Tais

CHICKEN TAHITIAN

  6 chicken breasts
    Salt and pepper to taste
  2 tablespoons salad oil
  1 (6-ounce) can frozen orange juice
      concentrate, thawed and undiluted
  6 tablespoons melted butter or margarine
1¼ teaspoons ground ginger
1¼ teaspoons soy sauce
    Hot cooked wild or regular rice
    Pineapple slices

Season chicken lightly with salt and pepper. Put oil in a shallow baking pan; add chicken, and bake at 350° for 30 minutes.

Combine orange juice concentrate, butter, ginger, and soy sauce; simmer 3 minutes. Baste chicken with sauce; bake an additional 35 minutes, basting frequently with sauce.

Place chicken under broiler until golden brown. Serve with rice and remaining sauce. Garnish with pineapple slices. Yield: 6 servings.

POLYNESIAN VEGETABLES

  2 (10-ounce) packages frozen
      Japanese-style vegetables
  2 tablespoons soy sauce
  1 teaspoon sherry
  1 tablespoon cornstarch
  1 cup chicken broth
½ teaspoon salt
⅓ cup sliced water chestnuts

Cook vegetables in a small amount of boiling salted water 5 minutes or until separated; drain.

Combine soy sauce and sherry in a saucepan; add cornstarch, blending until smooth. Add broth and salt; cook over low heat, stirring constantly, until slightly thickened and smooth.

Stir vegetables into sauce; simmer until vegetables are soft. Add water chestnuts; heat thoroughly. Yield: 6 servings.

FROZEN FRUIT SALAD

2 envelopes (2 tablespoons) unflavored
  gelatin
½ cup cold water
¾ cup orange juice
¾ cup pineapple juice
⅓ cup whipping cream, whipped
3 tablespoons mayonnaise
¾ cup drained pineapple chunks
½ cup halved orange sections
½ cup drained sliced peaches
2 bananas, sliced
¼ cup maraschino cherries
½ cup chopped pecans
¼ cup miniature marshmallows
  Lettuce

Soften gelatin in cold water. Combine fruit juices;
bring to a boil. Add gelatin, stirring until dissolved; chill until consistency of unbeaten egg
white.

Combine whipped cream and mayonnaise;
fold into gelatin mixture along with fruit, pecans,
and marshmallows. Spoon into a 4-cup mold;
freeze. Unmold on lettuce, and garnish as desired.
Yield: 6 servings.

BANANA BREAD

1 cup margarine, softened
1½ cups sugar
2 eggs
2 cups all-purpose flour
1 teaspoon soda
¼ teaspoon salt
3 ripe bananas, mashed

Cream margarine and sugar until light and fluffy.
Add eggs, one at a time, beating well after each
addition. Add dry ingredients; blend well. Add
bananas, mixing well.

Spoon batter into 2 greased and floured 8-inch
loafpans. Bake at 325° for 55 minutes. Cool and
slice. Yield: 2 loaves bread.

GUAVA CRISPS

¼ cup butter or margarine
⅓ cup guava jelly
2 tablespoons lemon juice
2 tablespoons sugar
¼ teaspoon salt
1 egg yolk, slightly beaten
¼ cup chopped macadamia nuts or
  almonds
  Pastry *(page 215)*

Combine butter, jelly, lemon juice, sugar, and
salt in top of a double boiler; heat until jelly
dissolves. Stir a small amount of jelly mixture
into egg yolk; mix well.

Slowly stir egg yolk mixture into jelly mixture
in double boiler; cook, stirring constantly, until
smooth and thickened. Add nuts, mixing well;
cool.

Place half of Pastry in an 8-inch square pan.
Spread filling evenly over Pastry; top with
remaining Pastry. Bake at 350° for 25 to 30
minutes. Cool and cut into 1½-inch squares.
Yield: 3 dozen squares.

Pastry:

  1 cup all-purpose flour
  ¼ teaspoon salt
  ½ teaspoon soda
  ½ cup firmly packed brown sugar
  ½ cup butter or margarine, softened
  1 cup quick-cooking oats

Combine flour, salt, soda, and brown sugar; cut in butter with 2 knives or a pastry blender until mixture resembles cornmeal. Add oats; mix well. Yield: about 3 cups.

MAI TAIS

  1 (6-ounce) can frozen orange juice
      concentrate
  3 cups pineapple juice
  ⅓ cup lemon juice
1½ cups rum
      Orange slices
      Mint leaves
      Maraschino cherries

Prepare orange juice according to directions; stir in pineapple juice, lemon juice, and rum. Serve over ice, and garnish with orange slices, mint, and cherries. Yield: about 2 quarts.

When food boils over in the oven, sprinkle the burned surface with a little salt. This will stop smoke and odor from forming and make the spot easier to clean. Also, rubbing damp salt on dishes in which food has been baked will remove brown spots.

Freeze extra parsley in plastic bags; just snip off sprigs of frozen parsley as needed.

Dinner Italiano

(Dinner for Ten)

Scampi
Chicken Cacciatore
Eggplant Parmesan
Garlic Toast
Italian Marinated Vegetables
Spumoni Mold
Wine

SCAMPI

2 pounds peeled and deveined shrimp
⅓ cup olive oil
½ cup vermouth
2 cloves garlic, crushed
¾ teaspoon salt
½ teaspoon pepper
3 tablespoons chopped parsley
3 tablespoons lemon juice

Sauté shrimp in hot oil. Add vermouth, garlic, salt, and pepper; simmer until liquid is almost absorbed. Sprinkle with parsley and lemon juice; stir gently to mix. Yield: about 10 to 12 appetizer servings.

CHICKEN CACCIATORE

2 (2½-pound) broiler-fryer chickens, cut up
Pepper
⅓ to ½ cup melted shortening
1 cup sliced onion
1 cup chopped celery
2 cloves garlic, minced
2 cups catsup
2 cups water
¼ cup chopped parsley
2 bay leaves
1 teaspoon salt
¼ cup red wine
Hot cooked noodles (optional)

Sprinkle chicken with pepper, and brown in hot shortening in a large skillet. Remove chicken from skillet. Sauté onion, celery, and garlic in drippings until lightly browned. Stir in next 6 ingredients. Add chicken. Simmer, uncovered, 30 minutes or until tender. Serve over noodles, if desired. Yield: 10 servings.

EGGPLANT PARMESAN

1 large eggplant
2 eggs, beaten
1¼ cups dry breadcrumbs
½ to ¾ cup salad oil
1 (8-ounce) package sliced mozzarella
    cheese
    Herb Tomato Sauce
2 tablespoons grated Parmesan cheese

Peel eggplant, and slice into ¼-inch slices. Dip slices into egg; then coat well with breadcrumbs. Sauté eggplant slices in hot salad oil about 3 minutes on each side or until golden brown; add more oil, if needed. Drain eggplant well on paper towels.

Place half of eggplant in a lightly greased 2-quart shallow baking dish. Top with half of mozzarella cheese and half of Herb Tomato Sauce. Repeat layers, and sprinkle with Parmesan cheese.

Bake, uncovered, at 400° for 20 minutes or until cheese melts and sauce is bubbly. Yield: 10 servings.

Herb Tomato Sauce:

1 tablespoon minced onion
1 tablespoon salad oil
3 (8-ounce) cans tomato sauce
1½ teaspoons oregano
    Pinch of basil
    Pinch of salt

Sauté onion in salad oil until tender; add remaining ingredients, and simmer 20 minutes. Yield: 3 cups.

GARLIC TOAST
(see Index)

ITALIAN MARINATED VEGETABLES

1 (14-ounce) can artichoke hearts,
    drained
1 (8-ounce) bottle commercial Italian
    dressing, divided
1 (16-ounce) jar small whole beets, drained
1 (16-ounce) can whole green beans,
    drained
1 (15-ounce) can green asparagus, drained
1 (15-ounce) can white asparagus, drained
1 (15-ounce) can small baby carrots,
    drained, or 4 fresh carrots, boiled
    and cut in 1-inch chunks
2 tablespoons finely chopped onion
½ teaspoon crushed basil leaves
1 large tomato, sliced
1 tablespoon chopped parsley

Combine artichoke hearts and 3 tablespoons salad dressing; cover and refrigerate 4 hours or overnight. Repeat procedure with beets. Arrange remaining vegetables except tomato in separate mounds in a 13- x 9- x 2-inch dish; sprinkle with onion and basil. Pour remaining dressing over vegetables; cover and refrigerate 4 hours or overnight.

To serve, arrange marinated vegetables and tomato on a large platter; spoon on dressing. Sprinkle with parsley. Yield: 10 servings.

SPUMONI MOLD

1 cup mixed candied fruit
½ cup chopped nuts
1 quart chocolate ice cream, softened
1 quart strawberry ice cream, softened
½ cup whipping cream, whipped and
    sweetened

Fold fruit and nuts into chocolate ice cream. Pour half into an 8-cup mold; freeze until firm. Keep remaining chocolate ice cream chilled.

Spoon strawberry ice cream over chocolate ice cream in mold; pack down lightly. Top with remaining chocolate ice cream; freeze. To serve, unmold and garnish with whipped cream on top and around base. Yield: 10 to 12 servings.

Greek Easter Dinner

(Dinner for Eight)

Magheritsa
Arni Psito
Manestra
Spanakopeta
Feta Cheese   Greek Olives
Kouloures
Kourambiethes or Koulourakia
Mavrodaphne (wine)

MAGHERITSA (Easter Soup)

3 pounds spring lamb (shin and shoulder)
1 lamb liver
4 quarts water
1 teaspoon salt
¾ cup uncooked regular rice
1 onion, finely chopped
1 tablespoon water
¼ cup salad oil
4 or 5 green onions, chopped (tops
   included)
2 tablespoons chopped parsley
½ teaspoon dried mint
¼ cup chopped fresh dill
   Salt and pepper
3 eggs, beaten
   Juice of 2 lemons

Boil lamb and liver in 4 quarts salted water about 1 hour or until done. Remove meat from broth and cut into pieces. Skim fat from broth and add enough water to broth to make 3 quarts; add rice and simmer for 15 minutes.

Sauté onion in 1 tablespoon water and salad oil until lightly browned; add green onions, parsley, mint, and dill. Sauté for 15 minutes.

Add meat, onion mixture, salt, and pepper to rice and broth; simmer about 15 minutes. Remove from heat.

Combine eggs and lemon juice; beat thoroughly until well blended. Slowly add 2 cups hot soup to egg-lemon mixture, beating constantly; gradually stir mixture into soup. Heat to boiling point and remove from heat immediately. Yield: 10 to 12 servings.

ARNI PSITO (Roast Spring Lamb)

1 (5- to 7-pound) leg spring lamb
3 cloves garlic, thinly sliced
1 tablespoon oregano
   Salt and pepper
¼ cup melted butter
   Juice of 3 lemons

Remove all fell (tissuelike covering) from lamb. Insert garlic in slits made with a sharp knife at 2- or 3-inch intervals on lamb. Combine oregano, salt, pepper, butter, and lemon juice; brush lamb with this mixture. Bake at 350° for 30 to 35 minutes per pound or until thermometer registers 175°. Yield: 8 servings.

MANESTRA (Pasta)

6 cups lamb or chicken broth
1 (16-ounce) package manestra or rice
1 (16-ounce) can tomato bits
½ cup grated Romano cheese

Combine lamb broth, manestra, and tomato bits; cook over medium heat for 20 minutes. Sprinkle with cheese, and serve. Yield: 8 to 10 servings.

SPANAKOPETA (Spinach Pie)

3 scallions, chopped
1 cup melted butter, divided
5 eggs, beaten
3 (10-ounce) packages frozen chopped
    spinach, thawed and pressed dry
1½ cups crumbled feta cheese
½ cup cottage cheese
16 pastry sheets or strudel leaves (filo)

Sauté scallions in 2 tablespoons melted butter; combine with eggs, spinach, and cheese. Place 8 pastry sheets, each brushed with melted butter, in a greased 13- x 9- x 2-inch pan.

Place spinach mixture evenly over pastry sheets. Top with remaining pastry sheets, having top sheet well buttered. Bake at 350° for 1 hour and 15 minutes. Cut into squares or diamond shapes. Serve hot. Spanakopeta freezes well. Yield: 12 to 15 servings.

KOULOURES (Easter Bread)

1 package dry yeast
½ cup warm water (105° to 115°)
½ cup boiling water
1 teaspoon ground cinnamon
¾ cup sugar
3 eggs
¼ cup melted butter
½ cup warm milk
1 teaspoon baking powder
½ teaspoon salt
5 cups all-purpose flour
1 egg yolk, beaten
  Sesame seeds
4 or 5 hard-cooked eggs (unshelled and
    dyed red)

Soften yeast in warm water and set aside. Combine boiling water and cinnamon; set aside. Combine sugar and eggs; beat well. Add melted butter to egg mixture and beat again. Skim off ¼ cup clear cinnamon water and add along with yeast and milk to egg mixture, blending well.

Combine dry ingredients and add to batter; knead until smooth and elastic, about 10 minutes. Shape dough to fit into 2 greased 8-inch round pans; crisscross 2 strips of dough over each loaf.

Cover and let rise in a warm place until doubled in bulk.

Brush loaves with beaten egg yolk and sprinkle with sesame seeds. Bake at 350° for 25 minutes or until brown. Push dyed eggs into bread immediately when loaves are removed from oven. Yield: 2 loaves bread.

KOURAMBIETHES
(Powdered Sugar Cookies)

    1 cup butter, softened
    ¼ cup powdered sugar
    1 egg yolk
    ½ teaspoon soda
    2 tablespoons whiskey
    3 to 3¼ cups all-purpose flour
    Whole cloves
    Powdered sugar

Cream butter and sugar until light and fluffy; add egg yolk. Combine soda and whiskey; add to creamed mixture. Add flour, 1 cup at a time; mix and knead by hand, adding enough flour to make a soft dough.

Shape as desired into crescents or oblong balls. Insert a whole clove in center of each cookie. Bake on ungreased cookie sheets at 350° for 20 to 25 minutes. Dust generously with powdered sugar while cookies are warm. Yield: 2½ dozen cookies.

KOULOURAKIA (Cookie Twists)

    1 cup butter, softened
    2¼ cups sugar
    10 eggs
    4 teaspoons vanilla extract
    4 teaspoons baking powder
    8½ to 9½ cups all-purpose flour
    1 egg, slightly beaten

Cream butter and sugar until light and fluffy. Add 10 eggs, one at a time, beating well after each addition; add vanilla.

Combine baking powder and flour; add enough flour to creamed mixture to make a pliable dough. Shape into twists. Brush tops of cookies with beaten egg. Bake on ungreased cookie sheets at 375° for 20 to 25 minutes. Yield: 10 dozen cookies.

Once pimientos have been opened, keep them in the refrigerator. Pour a little vinegar or water over them and cover tightly; they will stay fresh for days.

As a rule, thawed fish should not be held longer than a day before cooking; the flavor is better if it is cooked immediately after thawing.

A Special Bavarian Dinner

(Dinner for Six to Eight)

Liverwurst Pâté   Melba Toast
Wiener Schnitzel
Braised German Cabbage
German Potato Salad
Black Bread
Bavarian Apple Torte
Beer   Coffee

LIVERWURST PÂTÉ

1 (8-ounce) package liverwurst
6 slices bacon, cooked and crumbled
2 green onions, finely chopped
1 (3-ounce) package cream cheese,
    softened
1 tablespoon dry red wine

Combine all ingredients, blending well. Chill several hours; serve with melba toast. Yield: about 1½ cups.

WIENER SCHNITZEL

2 to 3 pounds (⅓-inch-thick) boneless
    veal cutlets
1 teaspoon salt
¼ teaspoon pepper
¾ cup all-purpose flour
2 eggs, beaten
1½ cups fine breadcrumbs
¼ cup butter or margarine
¼ cup shortening
    Lemon slices
    Parsley

Place veal on a sheet of waxed paper; using a meat mallet or rolling pin, flatten to ¼-inch thickness. If cutlets are too large for individual servings, cut into 2 or 3 pieces. Season cutlets with salt and pepper. Dredge in flour, and dip in eggs; then coat with breadcrumbs.

Heat butter and shortening in a large skillet over medium heat; add cutlets, and cook 1 minute on each side or until browned. Garnish with lemon slices and parsley; serve immediately. Yield: 6 to 8 servings.

BRAISED GERMAN CABBAGE

1 large head red cabbage, coarsely
    shredded
1 large onion, chopped
½ cup commercial French dressing
⅓ cup water
½ teaspoon caraway seeds
¼ teaspoon salt

Combine ingredients in a skillet; mix well. Cover; cook over low heat 20 to 25 minutes, stirring occasionally. Yield: 6 to 8 servings.

GERMAN POTATO SALAD

6 to 8 slices bacon, cooked and diced
6 medium potatoes, unpared
1 onion, finely chopped
1 teaspoon salt
⅛ teaspoon pepper
1 teaspoon dry mustard
¼ cup sugar
½ cup water
¼ to ½ cup vinegar
1 egg, slightly beaten
    Onion rings
    Crisp bacon

Cook bacon until crisp, reserving drippings. Cook potatoes until tender; remove skins while hot; slice potatoes. Combine bacon, potatoes, and onion. Add salt, pepper, dry mustard, sugar, water, vinegar, and beaten egg to bacon drippings. Cook mixture only until egg thickens. Pour over bacon-potato mixture and heat until liquid is absorbed. Garnish, if desired, with onion rings and additional pieces of crisp bacon. Yield: 6 to 8 servings.

BLACK BREAD

1 package dry yeast
2 cups warm water (105° to 115°)
2 tablespoons sugar
2 teaspoons salt
2 tablespoons shortening, melted and
    cooled
4 to 5 cups all-purpose flour, divided
3 tablespoons dark molasses
3 cups rye flour
1 tablespoon caraway seeds
1 tablespoon dillseeds
    Melted butter or margarine

Dissolve yeast in warm water in a large bowl. Add sugar, salt, shortening, and 3 cups all-purpose flour; beat well. Add molasses, rye flour, caraway seeds, and dillseeds. Stir in enough additional all-purpose flour to form a stiff dough.

Turn dough out on a floured surface, and knead until smooth and elastic (about 8 to 10 minutes). Place in a well-greased bowl, turning to grease top. Cover with plastic wrap or a towel. Let rise in a warm place (85°), free from drafts, until doubled in bulk, about 1 hour.

Divide dough in half, and shape each half into a smooth ball. Place each on a greased baking sheet, and lightly press to flatten bottom. Cover; let rise in a warm place, free from drafts, until doubled in bulk. Bake at 400° for 30 minutes or until loaves sound hollow when tapped. Brush hot loaves with melted butter. Remove from baking sheets; cool on wire racks. Yield: 2 loaves bread.

BAVARIAN APPLE TORTE

½ cup butter or margarine, softened
⅓ cup sugar
¼ teaspoon vanilla extract
1 cup all-purpose flour
    Cream Cheese Filling
    Apple Topping
½ cup chopped walnuts or pecans

Cream butter and sugar in a small mixing bowl; stir in vanilla. Add flour and mix well. Spread in bottom and 2 inches up sides of a greased 9-inch springform pan.

Spread Cream Cheese Filling evenly over pastry; spoon Apple Topping over Filling. Sprinkle with nuts. Bake at 450° for 10 minutes; reduce temperature to 400°, and continue baking 25 minutes. Cool before removing from pan. Yield: 8 to 10 servings.

Cream Cheese Filling:

1 (8-ounce) package cream cheese,
    softened
¼ cup sugar
1 egg
½ teaspoon vanilla extract

Combine cream cheese and sugar; add egg and vanilla, mixing well. Yield: about 1⅓ cups.

Apple Topping:

4 cups peeled, cored, and sliced apples
⅓ cup sugar
½ teaspoon ground cinnamon

Place apples in a large mixing bowl. Sprinkle sugar and cinnamon on top, and stir apples to coat. Yield: about 4 cups.

Pouring a strong solution of salt and hot water down the sink will help eliminate odors and remove grease from drains.

In comparison shopping, use the cost-per-serving rather than the cost-per-pound comparison. For example, a boneless smoked ham will yield five servings per pound, while a bone-in ham yields only three servings. If the boneless ham is selling for $2.09 per pound (about 42 cents per serving), it is a better buy than the bone-in ham selling for $1.49 per pound (about 50 cents per serving).

A French Classic

(Supper for Eight)

French Onion Soup or
Crab and Mushroom Quiche
Salade Niçoise
Commercial French Rolls or Crackers
Crêpes Fitzgerald
Wine

FRENCH ONION SOUP

 5 to 6 cups sliced Bermuda onions
¼ cup melted butter
   Salt and pepper to taste
½ teaspoon sugar
 2 to 3 tablespoons all-purpose flour
 2 quarts hot beef bouillon
½ cup dry vermouth or dry white wine
 1 cup shredded Swiss cheese
   Croutons

Sauté onion in butter until golden brown. Sprinkle with salt, pepper, sugar, and flour; stir well, and continue cooking 2 to 3 minutes. Add beef bouillon; cover and simmer 30 minutes. Add dry vermouth.

Spoon soup into ovenproof dishes; top with cheese and croutons. Place under broiler until cheese melts. Yield: 8 servings.

CRAB AND MUSHROOM QUICHE

 4 eggs, well beaten
 2 cups half-and-half
⅓ cup minced onion
 1 teaspoon salt
⅛ teaspoon cayenne pepper
 1 (6-ounce) package frozen crabmeat, thawed
¾ cup fresh mushrooms, sautéed in butter
 1 cup shredded mozzarella cheese
 1 unbaked 10-inch pastry shell
   Chopped parsley

Combine eggs, half-and-half, onion, salt, and cayenne pepper; blend until smooth, and set aside.

Drain crabmeat on paper towels until it's very dry. Sprinkle crabmeat, mushrooms, and cheese over bottom of pastry shell; pour in egg mixture and top with chopped parsley.

Bake at 425° for 15 minutes; reduce heat to 300° and bake 30 additional minutes or until a knife inserted into the quiche comes out clean. Let stand 15 minutes before serving. Yield: 8 servings.

SALADE NIÇOISE

3 cups salad oil
2 cups white wine vinegar
  Salt and pepper to taste
¼ cup chopped onion
  Garlic salt to taste
6 small new potatoes, cooked and thinly
  sliced
1 (16-ounce) can cut green beans,
  drained
2 cucumbers, peeled and sliced
1 small head Boston lettuce, torn into
  bite-size pieces
1 small head romaine, torn into bite-size
  pieces
4 hard-cooked eggs, quartered
1 (2-ounce) can rolled anchovy fillets,
  drained (optional)
1 (9¼-ounce) can chunk light tuna,
  drained and flaked
1 cup cooked, peeled, deveined shrimp,
  chilled
5 or 6 green onions or scallions, thinly
  sliced
3 tomatoes, quartered
1 green pepper, cut into rings
1 red onion, thinly sliced and separated
  into rings
  Niçoise Dressing

Combine oil, vinegar, salt, pepper, chopped onion, and garlic salt in a jar; shake well. Pour marinade over potatoes, beans, and cucumber; refrigerate in covered container overnight. Drain marinade from vegetables and set aside; discard marinade.

Place lettuce in bottom of a very large salad bowl. Arrange potatoes, beans, cucumber, eggs, anchovies, if desired, tuna, shrimp, and remaining vegetables in an attractive pattern on lettuce. Before serving, toss salad with Niçoise Dressing. Yield: 8 servings.

Niçoise Dressing:

½ cup olive or salad oil
⅓ cup white wine vinegar
2 teaspoons salt
½ teaspoon pepper
½ teaspoon oregano
½ teaspoon basil leaves
1 teaspoon garlic salt
3 tablespoons salad dressing or
  mayonnaise

Combine all ingredients in a jar; shake well. Yield: about 1 cup.

CRÊPES FITZGERALD

1 (8-ounce) package cream cheese,
  softened
¾ cup commercial sour cream
½ cup sugar, divided
2 teaspoons grated lemon rind
  Crêpes *(page 226)*
4 tablespoons butter
3 cups strawberries, sliced
  About ¼ cup strawberry liqueur
  About ¼ cup kirsch
½ cup whole strawberries

Combine cream cheese, sour cream, and 2 tablespoons sugar; beat until smooth and fluffy. Stir in lemon rind. Spoon mixture on Crêpes and roll up. Place on a platter and keep warm.

Combine remaining sugar and butter in a saucepan; cook until sugar has dissolved. Remove from heat, and stir in sliced strawberries. Transfer to chafing dish, and add strawberry liqueur and kirsch; ignite.

When flames die down, spoon sauce over Crêpes. Garnish with whole berries. Yield: 8 servings.

Crêpes:

¾ cup all-purpose flour
  Pinch of salt
1¼ cups milk
  1 egg
  1 egg yolk
  1 tablespoon melted butter
  Salad oil

Combine all ingredients except salad oil in blender; blend on medium speed for 10 seconds.

Brush the bottom of a 6- or 7-inch crêpe pan or heavy skillet lightly with salad oil, and heat pan over medium heat until just hot, not smoking.

Pour 2 tablespoons batter in pan and quickly tilt pan in all directions to run batter all over pan in a thin film. Cook about 1 minute. Lift edge of crêpe to test for doneness.

The crêpe is ready for flipping when it can be shaken loose from the bottom of pan. Flip the crêpe and cook about ½ minute on other side; this is rarely more than a spotty brown and is used as the side on which filling is placed.

Crêpes can be made in advance and stacked between layers of waxed paper to prevent sticking.

Crêpes can be frozen; heat them in a covered dish at 300° to thaw. Yield: 14 to 16 crêpes.

When baking a layer cake, don't let pans touch each other or sides of oven; stagger their placement so that heat can circulate evenly around pans.

For a successful cake, measure ingredients accurately, follow recipe without substitutions, and use size pans recommended.

Dinner from the Orient

(Dinner for Six to Eight)

Sukiyaki   Brown Rice
Oriental Cabbage   Shrimp Egg Rolls
Hot Mustard Sauce or Sweet-and-Sour Sauce
Orange-Ginger Cookies
Sake   Tea

SUKIYAKI

¼ cup peanut oil or salad oil
1 pound sirloin steak, diagonally cut into
    ¼- x 2-inch strips
2 medium onions, diagonally sliced
1 cup sliced celery, diagonally cut into
    ½-inch strips
½ pound fresh, sliced mushrooms or
    1 (8-ounce) can sliced mushrooms,
    drained
½ head Chinese or celery cabbage,
    diagonally cut into ½-inch slices
1 (10- to 12-ounce) can bamboo shoots,
    drained
2 (6-ounce) cans water chestnuts, drained
    and thinly sliced
8 scallions, cut into narrow strips
1 teaspoon monosodium glutamate
½ cup chicken broth or 1 chicken
    bouillon cube dissolved in ½ cup hot
    water
½ cup bean curd, cut into ½-inch cubes
1 green pepper, thinly sliced into strips
1 tablespoon brown sugar
1 teaspoon salt
½ cup soy sauce

3 cups fresh spinach, torn into large
    pieces
Cooked brown rice

Pour oil into wok or skillet; heat at 375° for 4 minutes. Place meat in hot oil and stir-fry for 2 minutes; push meat up sides of wok. Add onion and stir-fry for 2 minutes; push onion up sides of wok. Continue same procedure for celery, mushrooms, and Chinese cabbage, adding more oil if needed; stir-fry each ingredient for 2 minutes, push up sides of wok, and add next ingredient.

Combine bamboo shoots, water chestnuts, scallions, monosodium glutamate, and chicken broth; add to wok, stir once, cook for 2 minutes, and push up sides of wok. Add bean curd, green pepper, brown sugar, salt, and soy sauce; stir once and cook for 30 seconds. Do not push up sides of wok. Sprinkle spinach over all ingredients in wok, cover, and simmer for 2 minutes. Reduce heat to warm for serving. Serve immediately over cooked brown rice. Yield: 6 to 8 servings.

Note: Precise timing on stir-frying should be followed so vegetables will be cooked *al dente* (firm, but slightly undercooked). They will be crisp in texture and bright and translucent in color. Spinach or other greens will merely be somewhat wilted after stir-frying.

ORIENTAL CABBAGE

½ cup melted margarine
1 medium head cabbage, chopped
1 green pepper, cut into strips
2 stalks celery, chopped
2 carrots, thinly sliced
1 large onion, sliced into rings
¾ cup evaporated milk
   Salt and pepper to taste

Combine margarine and vegetables in a large skillet; cover and cook over medium heat 10 minutes. Stir in milk; heat thoroughly. Add salt and pepper to taste. Yield: 6 to 8 servings.

SHRIMP EGG ROLLS

1 cup all-purpose flour
1 teaspoon salt
3 eggs, beaten
1 cup water
   Salad oil
   Shrimp Filling
   Beaten egg

Combine flour, salt, and 3 beaten eggs; blend well. Gradually add water, stirring constantly until batter is smooth.

Brush the bottom of a 6- or 7-inch crêpe pan or heavy skillet lightly with salad oil; place over medium heat until just hot, not smoking.

Pour 2 tablespoons batter in pan; quickly tilt pan in all directions so batter covers the pan in a thin film. Cook egg roll wrapper about 1 minute. Lift edge to test for doneness.

Gently turn the wrapper, and cook about ½ minute on other side; this is rarely more than a spotty brown and is used as the side on which filling is placed. (Egg roll wrappers can be made in advance and stacked between absorbent towels to prevent sticking.)

Place 1 heaping tablespoon of Shrimp Filling off center on each egg roll wrapper. Fold two sides of wrapper over Filling; roll edge of wrapper nearest you over Filling. Brush exposed edge of wrapper with beaten egg. Finish rolling wrapper;

carefully seal end. Brush egg roll with beaten egg.

Place egg roll in 1 inch of oil heated to 375°. Cook until golden brown on both sides; drain well. Keep warm in oven. Yield: 1 dozen egg rolls.

Shrimp Filling:

1 tablespoon shredded celery
1 tablespoon chopped bean sprouts
1 tablespoon shredded carrot
1 tablespoon finely chopped onion
1 teaspoon sugar
½ cup ground cooked chicken
½ cup finely chopped cooked shrimp
⅛ teaspoon pepper
½ teaspoon salt

Combine celery, bean sprouts, and carrot. Cook in a small amount of boiling water until crisp-tender; drain. Combine vegetables and remaining ingredients, mixing well. Yield: about 1 cup.

HOT MUSTARD SAUCE

3 tablespoons dry mustard
2 tablespoons hot water

Combine dry mustard and water; let stand 10 minutes to develop flavor. Yield: about ¼ cup.

With the stir-frying technique of the wok, the vegetables in Sukiyaki retain a bright color, a crisp texture, and a fresh taste. Much of the preparation of Sukiyaki (page 227) can be done at the table in a party atmosphere.

SWEET-AND-SOUR SAUCE

½ cup vinegar
½ cup water
¼ cup firmly packed brown sugar
¼ cup sugar
¼ cup cornstarch
½ cup pineapple juice

Combine vinegar, water, and sugar; bring to a boil. Combine cornstarch and pineapple juice, blending well; add to sugar mixture. Cook, stirring constantly, until thickened. Yield: about 1¼ cups.

ORANGE-GINGER COOKIES

1 cup butter or margarine, softened
1½ cups sugar
1 egg
2 tablespoons light corn syrup
3 cups all-purpose flour
2 teaspoons soda
2 teaspoons ground ginger
½ teaspoon ground cloves
1 tablespoon grated orange peel

Cream butter and sugar until light and fluffy; add egg and corn syrup, beating well. Combine dry ingredients; add to creamed mixture, and mix well. Stir in orange peel.

Shape into two rolls about 9 inches long and 2 inches in diameter. Wrap in waxed paper; chill several hours or overnight.

Slice about ⅛ inch thick, and place 2 inches apart on greased cookie sheets. Bake at 400° for 5 to 6 minutes or until done. Yield: 8 dozen cookies.

Pineapple and green pepper enhance Sweet-and-Sour Pork served over rice. Recipe is on page 10.

A Night in Old Mexico

(Dinner for Six to Eight)

Nachos
Avocado Dip   Chips
Chalupas Compuestas   Relish Hot Sauce
Chiles Rellenos
Pralines
Sangría Blanca

NACHOS

1 (6-ounce) bag tortilla chips
1 to 2 cups shredded Cheddar cheese
5 to 6 jalapeño peppers, sliced into rings

Place chips on a cookie sheet or ovenproof platter. Top each with 1 to 2 teaspoons cheese and a slice of jalapeño pepper.

Bake at 400° for 2 to 3 minutes or until cheese melts. Serve immediately. Yield: about 6 to 8 servings.

AVOCADO DIP

6 ripe avocados, peeled and quartered
1 medium Spanish onion, minced
1 large tomato
2 tablespoons hot sauce
1 tablespoon Worcestershire sauce

Combine all ingredients in blender. Blend until smooth. Serve with chips. Yield: about 5 cups.

Note: Reserve 2 or 3 seeds from avocados. Place in dip to prevent mixture from darkening.

CHALUPAS COMPUESTAS

8 corn tortillas
Salad oil
Meat Filling
2 tomatoes, chopped
1 head lettuce, finely shredded
2 cups shredded Cheddar cheese
Sliced black olives
Commercial sour cream

Deep fry tortillas in oil until brown and crisp; drain on absorbent paper. Top each tortilla with Meat Filling, tomato, lettuce, cheese, olives, and sour cream. Yield: 8 servings.

Meat Filling:

1 pound ground beef
1 clove garlic, chopped
2 bunches green onions, chopped
15 black olives, chopped
2½ teaspoons chili powder
Salt and pepper to taste
¼ pound shredded Cheddar cheese
½ (16-ounce) can refried beans
Onion rings

Brown beef in a 10-inch skillet; stir in garlic, green onion, olives, chili powder, salt, and pepper. Cook until onion is tender. Stir in cheese and beans; heat thoroughly. Garnish with onion rings. Yield: about 3 cups.

RELISH HOT SAUCE

1 cup minced onion
½ cup chopped green pepper
1 clove garlic, minced
1 tablespoon salad oil
1 (7-ounce) can whole kernel corn,
    drained
1 (16-ounce) can tomatoes, drained and
    chopped
1 (4-ounce) can green chiles, undrained
    and chopped fine
4 tablespoons hot chili sauce
1 tablespoon chili powder
1 teaspoon salt
2 teaspoons pepper

Sauté onion, green pepper, and garlic in oil until wilted; stir frequently. Add remaining ingredients; heat well, stirring occasionally. Serve hot or cold. Store in refrigerator. Yield: about 1½ pints.

Note: May be served on chalupas, tacos, hamburgers, hot dogs, or as a dip.

CHILES RELLENOS

3 (4-ounce) cans green chiles, drained
8 ounces Monterey Jack or Cheddar
    cheese
4 eggs, separated
    Salt and pepper to taste
    All-purpose flour
    Salad oil
1 (16-ounce) can stewed tomatoes
    Green pepper rings

Rinse chiles, and remove seeds. Cut cheese into strips, and place inside chiles. Beat egg yolks with salt and pepper. Beat egg whites until stiff. Fold yolk mixture into egg whites.

Dip chiles into flour, then into egg mixture. Brown in a small amount of oil on both sides; drain on absorbent paper. Place in a shallow baking dish. Pour tomatoes over chiles. Bake at 350° for 30 minutes. Garnish with green pepper rings. Yield: 6 to 8 servings.

PRALINES

2 cups sugar
1 cup milk
8 large marshmallows
2 tablespoons butter or margarine
½ teaspoon vanilla extract
1 to 2 cups pecans

Combine sugar, milk, and marshmallows in a heavy 4-quart saucepan; cook over medium heat to 234° (soft ball stage), stirring constantly. Remove from heat; stir in butter and vanilla. Beat until creamy. Add pecans; beat just until mixture begins to thicken.

Working rapidly, drop mixture by tablespoonfuls onto lightly buttered waxed paper; cool. Store in an airtight container. Yield: about 15 (3-inch) pralines.

SANGRÍA BLANCA

2 (4/5-quart) bottles Riesling white wine
2 (6-ounce) cans frozen lemonade
    concentrate, thawed and undiluted
2 cups club soda
    Lime slices

Combine wine and lemonade concentrate; mix well. Add club soda and stir. Serve over ice cubes. Garnish with lime slices. Yield: 6 to 8 servings.

Grecian Classic Dinner
(Dinner for Ten to Twelve)

Skorthalia
Moussaka or Dolmathes Avgolemono
Salata
Tiropetes
Galatobourekos
Ouzo or Retsina (wine)

SKORTHALIA (Garlic Sauce)

1 (16-ounce) can small whole beets,
    drained
1 (6½-ounce) can artichoke hearts,
    drained
1 (4½-ounce) can medium shrimp,
    drained
1 cucumber, sliced
1 (3¾-ounce) can sardines, drained
    Fried eggplant wedges
    Fried zucchini slices
    Garlic Sauce

Arrange assortment of beets, artichoke hearts, shrimp, cucumber, sardines, eggplant, and zucchini on tray. Serve with Garlic Sauce as a dip. Yield: 10 to 12 servings.

Garlic Sauce:

  4 cloves garlic
  1 teaspoon salt
  1 egg
  4 tablespoons white vinegar
 12 slices white bread
  ½ cup olive oil or salad oil
     Hot water
  1 potato, cooked and mashed

Combine garlic cloves and salt, and mash to a paste with a mortar and pestle. Beat in egg and vinegar.

Remove crusts from bread and crumble slices into a mixing bowl; mix with olive oil and 2 or 3 tablespoons hot water. Add bread to garlic mixture and continue beating. Add additional hot water until mixture is consistency of whipped potatoes. Add mashed potato and beat until smooth. Yield: about 2 cups.

Note: 1 teaspoon garlic salt may be substituted for 4 cloves garlic and 1 teaspoon salt.

MOUSSAKA
(Baked Eggplant with Potatoes)

2 large eggplants
  Salt
3 potatoes
  Olive oil
2 large onions, chopped
1 pound ground beef
6 tablespoons melted butter, divided
½ cup parsley, chopped
1 cup tomato sauce
¼ cup breadcrumbs
⅓ cup all-purpose flour
2 cups milk
2 eggs, separated
¼ cup grated Romano cheese
  Dash of ground nutmeg

Slice eggplant and sprinkle with salt; set aside for 15 to 20 minutes. Pare and slice potatoes; dry eggplant slices. Brown eggplant and potato slices in olive oil. Drain on paper towels and set aside.

Sauté onion and ground beef in 2 tablespoons melted butter until brown; add parsley and tomato sauce and simmer for 10 minutes.

Dust a greased 13- x 9- x 2-inch baking dish with breadcrumbs. Place a layer of potatoes, eggplant, and meat mixture in pan; repeat layers, ending with eggplant.

Combine remaining butter and flour; cook over low heat, stirring constantly. Heat milk; gradually add to flour mixture, stirring constantly. Cook over low heat until thick; cool slightly.

Beat egg yolks, and combine with cheese and nutmeg; add to sauce. Beat egg whites until stiff and fold into sauce. Pour sauce over eggplant-meat layers. Bake at 350° for 45 to 55 minutes or until golden brown. Yield: 10 to 12 servings.

DOLMATHES AVGOLEMONO
(Stuffed Grapevine Leaves)

1 small onion, chopped
4 tablespoons melted butter
1 pound ground round steak
¼ cup uncooked regular rice
  Juice of 1 lemon
2 tablespoons chopped parsley
½ cup water
1 teaspoon salt
¼ teaspoon pepper
1 (16-ounce) jar grapevine leaves
  Avgolemono Sauce

Sauté onion in butter; add ground meat, rice, lemon juice, parsley, water, salt, and pepper. Wash and drain grapevine leaves. Put 1 teaspoon meat mixture in each leaf, fold in the ends, and roll up.

Place stuffed leaves in a 4-quart saucepan and barely cover with water. Weight leaves down with a heavy plate to prevent unfolding. Cover. Bring to a boil; reduce heat and simmer for 30 minutes. Remove leaves; reserve broth for Avgolemono Sauce. Pour Avgolemono Sauce over leaves and serve. Yield: 10 to 12 servings.

Avgolemono Sauce:

2 eggs, separated
  Juice of 1 lemon
  About ¼ cup broth from Dolmathes

Beat egg whites until stiff; add yolks and continue beating. Add lemon juice slowly and continue beating. Add broth, stirring constantly so as not to curdle. Yield: about 1 cup.

Note: Avgolemono Sauce may be omitted if Dolmathes are served as an appetizer.

Watch the price trends on fresh fruits and vegetables. Buy when they are in season and at their lowest price.

Crush leftover potato chips or pretzels, and use to top casseroles.

SALATA (Greek Salad)

2 cloves garlic, halved
2 heads lettuce, torn into bite-size pieces
1 cup chopped celery
6 tomatoes, cut into wedges
2 small onions or scallions
1 green pepper, sliced
10 to 12 radishes, sliced
  Salt and pepper
2 teaspoons oregano
½ cup olive oil
6 tablespoons vinegar
  Garnishes: ripe olives, anchovies, and
    feta cheese (crumbled)

Rub wooden salad bowl with clove of garlic. Wash and prepare vegetables; combine in bowl. Add seasonings, oil, and vinegar; toss. Add garnishes. Yield: 12 servings.

TIROPETES (Cheese Rolls)

6 eggs, separated
1 pound feta cheese, crumbled
1 (12-ounce) carton cottage cheese
¼ cup crumbled blue cheese (optional)
1 (16-ounce) package pastry sheets or
    strudel leaves (filo)
2 cups melted butter

Beat egg whites until stiff; add yolks and continue beating until well blended. Add cheese and mix well.

Cut pastry sheets into quarters or into 8- x 6-inch pieces. Brush pastry with hot melted butter. Place a teaspoon of cheese mixture in bottom center of pastry strip, folding over one-third on each side and brushing again with butter; roll like a jellyroll. Place on cookie sheets and bake at 350° for 20 minutes. Yield: 100 rolls.

Note: Tiropetes can be frozen before baking. Do not thaw; bake at 350° for 30 minutes.

GALATOBOUREKOS (Custard Tarts)

6 eggs
1 cup sugar
1 quart milk
6 tablespoons cornstarch
⅓ cup water
¼ cup butter or margarine
1 teaspoon vanilla extract
1 (16-ounce) package pastry sheets or
    strudel leaves (filo)
½ pound sweet butter, melted
  Powdered sugar

Beat eggs in saucepan; add sugar and beat thoroughly; slowly add milk. Cook over medium heat, stirring occasionally.

Dissolve cornstarch in water; slowly add to milk mixture before it comes to a boil. Cook until mixture thickens and comes to a hard boil. Remove from heat; add ¼ cup butter and vanilla.

Cut pastry sheets into thirds or into 9- x 5-inch pieces. Brush pastry with hot melted butter. Place about 1 tablespoon custard filling at bottom left corner of strip and fold the right bottom corner over it into a triangle. Continue folding back and forth into a triangle and brushing with butter to end of strip.

Place triangles, cut side down, on greased cookie sheet. Brush tops with melted butter and bake at 375° for 35 minutes. Dust with powdered sugar while warm. Yield: about 50 tarts.

Note: Custard can be refrigerated a few days before making tarts. These tarts can be frozen for 6 months. Bake frozen at 350° for 10 minutes; sprinkle with powdered sugar while warm.

DINNERS FOR TWO

Dinner for Two Italiano
Summertime Supper
Southern Seafare Special
Dinner for a Special Occasion
A Dinner Party for Two
Saucy Pork Chop Dinner

Elegant Dining for the Two of You
Little Chicken Pies
Seafood Dream Dinner
Hearty Salad Supper
Sunday Night Supper for Two

Singles and doubles describe a life-style as well as a tennis game, and cooking for this set presents a challenge. Perhaps you two are newlyweds, or parents of a grown family, or roommates, but the problems of cooking for two are common to all situations. Here are recipes planned for two that leave few if any leftovers. From a simple supper to an elegant event, these menus are designed especially for twosomes.

Dinner for Two Italiano

(Dinner for Two)

Stuffed Manicotti
Marinated Mushrooms
Tangy Spinach Salad
Garlic French Bread   Butter
Butterscotch Peaches with Ice Cream
Wine

STUFFED MANICOTTI

4 manicotti shells
3 quarts boiling water
Salt
½ pound ground chuck
1 small onion, finely chopped
½ green pepper, finely chopped
1 (15-ounce) can tomato sauce
2 teaspoons oregano
1 teaspoon thyme
1 bay leaf
1 cup shredded mozzarella cheese, divided

Cook manicotti shells in boiling salted water for 10 minutes; drain. Rinse in cold water; drain and set aside.

Sauté ground chuck, onion, and green pepper until brown; drain. Add tomato sauce, oregano, thyme, and bay leaf; simmer over low heat 10 minutes. Add ½ cup cheese, stirring until melted.

Arrange manicotti shells in a shallow baking dish; stuff with half of meat mixture. Pour remaining meat mixture over shells; sprinkle with remaining cheese. Bake at 300° for 30 minutes. Yield: 2 servings.

MARINATED MUSHROOMS

3 tablespoons olive oil
2 tablespoons wine vinegar
½ teaspoon black pepper
1 teaspoon salt
1 clove garlic, minced
1 small red or green pepper, chopped
1 teaspoon basil
3 green onions, sliced
1 (8-ounce) can whole mushrooms, drained

Combine first 7 ingredients in a pint jar; shake well. Add onions and mushrooms; marinate at room temperature 4 hours. Cover and refrigerate 3 to 4 days. Yield: 2 to 4 servings.

TANGY SPINACH SALAD

2 cups torn tender spinach leaves
1 cup torn lettuce
½ avocado, peeled and sliced
¾ cup orange sections
2 slices Bermuda onion, separated into
   rings
   Commercial Italian or French dressing

Combine all ingredients except salad dressing in a large salad bowl. Before serving, add Italian dressing; toss lightly. Yield: 2 servings.

BUTTERSCOTCH PEACHES WITH ICE CREAM

2 firm-ripe peaches, peeled and halved
2 tablespoons firmly packed brown sugar
   Butter or margarine
   Vanilla ice cream

Place peach halves, cavity side up, in a shallow baking pan. Put ½ tablespoon sugar in each cavity; dot with about 1 teaspoon butter. Bake at 325° for 15 to 20 minutes or until juice becomes syrupy. To serve, top with ice cream and a small amount of syrup. Yield: 2 servings.

Wine should be stored at an even temperature of 50 to 60 degrees. It is important that bottles of corked table wines be kept on their side so that the corks are kept moist and airtight. If the bottle has a screw cap, it may remain upright.

To use a griddle or frypan, preheat on medium or medium-high heat before adding the food. It is properly preheated when a few drops of water spatter when they hit the surface. Add food and reduce heat so that it cooks without spattering and smoking.

Summertime Supper

(Supper for Two)

Pepper Mates
Summertime Corn Pudding
Pickled Cauliflower
Just Peaches-and-Cream Pie
Iced Tea   Coffee

PEPPER MATES

    2 large green peppers
      Salt
 ½ pound mild bulk sausage
    1 small onion, chopped
    1 (8-ounce) can tomatoes, chopped
 1½ cups cooked rice
  ½ cup shredded sharp Cheddar cheese
    2 teaspoons Worcestershire sauce
      Pepper
      Parsley

Slice tops off green peppers, and remove seeds. Parboil peppers in boiling salted water 5 minutes; drain. Season cavity of each pepper with salt; set aside.

Brown sausage in a skillet; add onion, and cook until tender. Pour off drippings. Add tomatoes, rice, cheese, and Worcestershire sauce; season to taste with salt and pepper. Simmer 5 minutes.

Stuff peppers with sausage mixture, and place in a 1-quart casserole. Pack any extra stuffing around peppers. Bake at 350° for 30 minutes. Garnish with parsley. Yield: 2 servings.

SUMMERTIME CORN PUDDING

    1 tablespoon margarine
    1 tablespoon salad oil
  ½ cup chopped onion
    1 cup fresh corn cut from cob
  ½ teaspoon salt
  ⅛ teaspoon pepper
    1 tablespoon sugar
    3 eggs, separated
  ½ cup shredded Cheddar cheese

Heat margarine and salad oil in a skillet over medium heat; add onion, and sauté until golden. Stir in corn, salt, pepper, and sugar. Cook 5 minutes; cool slightly.

Add beaten egg yolks and cheese to corn mixture, mixing well; fold in stiffly beaten egg whites. Spoon into a greased 1-quart casserole. Bake at 350° for 30 to 40 minutes or until puffed and lightly browned. Yield: 2 servings.

PICKLED CAULIFLOWER

½ medium cauliflower
1½ tablespoons wine vinegar
1 tablespoon melted butter or margarine
1 tablespoon diced pimiento
1 tablespoon chopped green pepper
½ teaspoon sugar
⅛ teaspoon salt

Break cauliflower into flowerets; cook in a small amount of boiling salted water about 10 minutes; drain.

Combine remaining ingredients in a small saucepan; cook over low heat about 5 minutes. Pour over hot cauliflower. Serve either hot or cold. Yield: 2 to 3 servings.

When you need just a few drops of onion juice for flavor, sprinkle a little salt on a slice of onion; scrape the salted surface with a knife or spoon to obtain the juice.

JUST PEACHES-AND-CREAM PIE

¾ cup sugar
3 tablespoons cornstarch
1 cup boiling water
1 (3-ounce) package peach-flavored gelatin
2 cups sliced fresh peaches
1 baked 9-inch pastry shell
Frozen whipped topping, thawed

Combine sugar, cornstarch, and boiling water in a saucepan; cook over medium heat, stirring occasionally, until thickened (about 12 to 15 minutes). Remove from heat; add peach gelatin, mixing well. Cool until lukewarm.

Add peaches to gelatin, and pour into pastry shell. Chill. Top with whipped topping before serving. Yield: one 9-inch pie.

Most fruits are best stored in the refrigerator. Allow melons, avocados, and pears to ripen at room temperature; then refrigerate. Berries should be sorted to remove imperfect fruit before refrigerating; wash and hull just before serving.

Southern Seafare Special

(Dinner for Two)

Potato Soup
Shrimp Creole
Fancy Green Beans
Garlic Salad
Floating Island
Wine or Iced Tea

POTATO SOUP

2¼ cups milk, divided
  2 large potatoes, boiled and mashed
¼ teaspoon salt
    Dash of pepper
½ tablespoon butter or margarine,
    softened
¼ cup all-purpose flour
  1 egg, well beaten

Scald 2 cups milk; blend in potatoes, salt, and pepper.

Combine butter and flour in a small bowl, mixing well; stir in egg and remaining ¼ cup milk.

Drop batter by teaspoonfuls into hot mixture; cook, covered, about 10 minutes over low heat. Serve at once. Yield: 2 servings.

SHRIMP CREOLE

  1 medium onion, chopped
  1 clove garlic, minced
  1 green pepper, finely chopped
½ cup finely chopped celery
  2 tablespoons melted butter or margarine
  1 (8-ounce) can tomato sauce
½ cup water
  1 bay leaf, crushed
  1 teaspoon minced parsley
½ teaspoon salt
⅛ teaspoon cayenne pepper
  1 (8-ounce) package frozen shrimp,
    thawed
    Cooked rice

Sauté onion, garlic, green pepper, and celery in butter until tender. Stir in tomato sauce, water, and seasonings; simmer 10 minutes. Add additional water, if necessary. Stir in shrimp. Bring mixture to a boil; reduce heat, and simmer 5 minutes. Serve over rice. Yield: 2 servings.

FANCY GREEN BEANS

1 (16-ounce) can French-style green
   beans
1 slice bacon
½ medium onion, minced
½ teaspoon sugar
   Slivered almonds, toasted

Drain liquid from beans, reserving ¼ cup. Lightly brown bacon in a skillet; drain on paper towel, reserving excess drippings.

Sauté onion in bacon drippings; add beans, ¼ cup bean liquid, and sugar. Chop bacon, and add to bean mixture. Cook, uncovered, over low heat about 15 minutes or until liquid is absorbed. Top with almonds. Yield: 2 to 3 servings.

GARLIC SALAD

4 large lettuce leaves, torn in pieces
6 to 8 spinach leaves, torn in pieces
1 green onion, sliced
6 radishes, sliced
10 to 12 ripe olives, sliced
1½ tablespoons olive oil
1½ tablespoons lemon juice
   Salt and pepper to taste
1 small clove garlic, mashed

Combine lettuce, spinach, onion, radishes, and olives. Combine remaining ingredients; toss lightly with salad. Yield: 2 servings.

FLOATING ISLAND

2 egg yolks, beaten
5 tablespoons sugar, divided
   Pinch of salt
¾ cup milk
½ teaspoon vanilla extract
1 egg white

Combine egg yolks, 3 tablespoons sugar, and salt in a small bowl. Scald milk in top of a double boiler. Add a small amount of scalded milk to egg yolk mixture, and stir until blended; add to milk in double boiler, mixing well.

Place custard over boiling water; cook until slightly thickened, stirring constantly. Remove from heat, and beat 1 minute. Cool slightly, and stir in vanilla. Pour custard into individual serving dishes.

Beat egg white until foamy; gradually add 2 tablespoons sugar, and continue beating until stiff. Drop meringue islands onto custard. Chill well. Yield: 2 servings.

Separate raw eggs while still cold from the refrigerator, but let whites come to room temperature if they need to be stiffly beaten.

Compare costs of fresh, frozen, canned, and dried foods. To compute the best buy, divide the price by the number of servings. The lower price per serving will be the thriftiest buy.

Dinner for a Special Occasion

(Dinner for Two)

Cool Cucumber Soup
Glazed Cornish Hens
Golden Carrots
Bibb Lettuce with Roquefort Dressing
Commercial French Rolls   Butter
Quick Chocolate Mousse
Wine   Coffee

COOL CUCUMBER SOUP

  1 (10¾-ounce) can cream of celery soup,
    undiluted
½ medium cucumber, peeled and
    chopped
  1 tablespoon chopped parsley or
    watercress
½ green onion, chopped
  1 cup milk
    Commercial sour cream
    Paprika

Combine soup, cucumber, parsley, and onion in blender; cover and blend until cucumber is pureed. Remove from blender container, and stir in milk. Chill thoroughly.

Top each serving with a spoonful of sour cream, and sprinkle with paprika. Yield: 2 to 4 servings.

GLAZED CORNISH HENS

  2 Cornish hens
    Salt and pepper
    Wild Rice Stuffing
¼ cup melted margarine, divided
  1 (8¼-ounce) can pineapple slices
½ cup chicken broth
  2 tablespoons sugar
¼ teaspoon ground ginger
  1 teaspoon cornstarch

Season cavity of hens with salt and pepper; stuff lightly with Wild Rice Stuffing. Place hens, breast side up, in a shallow roasting pan; brush with half of margarine.

Drain pineapple, reserving juice. Add enough water to juice to make ½ cup liquid.

Combine ¼ cup pineapple liquid and chicken broth; pour over hens. Bake at 350° about 1 hour, basting every 15 minutes with remaining margarine and pan drippings.

Then place 2 pineapple slices on top of each hen. Combine sugar, ginger, cornstarch, and remaining pineapple liquid; spoon over hens. Increase temperature to 400°, and bake an additional 15 minutes. Serve pan liquid as sauce. Yield: 2 servings.

Wild Rice Stuffing:

½ cup uncooked wild rice
    Hot water
¼ cup melted margarine
¾ cup chicken broth
1 teaspoon salt
3 green onions, chopped
½ cup chopped celery
1 (2½-ounce) can sliced mushrooms, drained
½ teaspoon marjoram
    Dash of ground nutmeg

Soak wild rice in hot water to cover for 1 hour; drain.

Sauté rice in margarine until golden brown; add broth and salt. Cover and simmer about 25 minutes or until tender. Add green onion, celery, mushrooms, marjoram, and nutmeg; toss lightly to mix. Yield: about 1¼ cups.

GOLDEN CARROTS

1½ cups sliced carrots, cut ½ inch thick
2 tablespoons melted margarine, divided
1 tablespoon sugar
½ teaspoon grated orange rind
⅛ teaspoon salt
½ orange, thinly sliced

Cook carrots, covered, in unsalted water just until tender; drain.

Combine 1 tablespoon margarine, sugar, orange rind, and salt, blending well. Add to carrots; cook over medium heat, stirring often until lightly glazed. Top with remaining margarine, and garnish with orange slices. Yield: 2 servings.

ROQUEFORT DRESSING

¾ cup mayonnaise
⅓ cup commercial sour cream
1 (1½-ounce) package Roquefort cheese, crumbled
1 teaspoon Worcestershire sauce
    Dash of garlic powder
    Salt and pepper to taste

Combine all ingredients; chill thoroughly in a covered container. Stir well before serving on tossed salad. Yield: about 1 cup.

QUICK CHOCOLATE MOUSSE

½ cup semisweet chocolate pieces
1 tablespoon sugar
1 tablespoon boiling water
2 eggs, separated
½ teaspoon vanilla extract
    Pinch of salt
½ cup whipping cream, whipped
20 vanilla wafers
    Additional whipped cream

Combine chocolate pieces, sugar, and water in top of a double boiler; cook over boiling water until chocolate is melted. Remove from heat.

Beat egg yolks slightly; slowly stir in a small amount of melted chocolate. Add egg yolk mixture to remaining chocolate, stirring until well blended. Cool. Stir in vanilla.

Add salt to egg whites; beat until stiff. Fold egg whites and whipped cream into cooled chocolate mixture. Line a 9-inch pieplate with half of vanilla wafers; top with half of chocolate mixture. Repeat layers. Refrigerate 4 to 6 hours. Top with additional whipped cream. Yield: 2 servings.

A Dinner Party for Two

(Dinner for Two)

Stuffed Pork Chops
Spinach Sauté
Glazed Carrots and Onions
Harvest Salad
Apple Crisp
Wine   Coffee

STUFFED PORK CHOPS

  2 pork chops, cut with pocket
  1 tablespoon melted butter or margarine
  ½ cup chopped onion
  ¾ cup chopped celery
  1 (7-ounce) package cornbread stuffing
      mix
  1 cup water
  1 (8¾-ounce) can whole kernel corn,
      drained
  1 (0.75-ounce) package brown gravy mix

Brown pork chops in butter; remove from skillet, and set aside. Sauté onion and celery in drippings.

Remove vegetable seasoning packet and stuffing crumbs from package of cornbread stuffing mix. Combine 2 tablespoons vegetable seasoning and water; stir until well blended. Add half of stuffing crumbs, onion, celery, and corn; blend well. (Store remaining seasoning and crumbs for later use.)

Fill pocket of each chop with stuffing; place in a lightly greased shallow baking dish. Spoon remaining stuffing around chops.

Prepare gravy mix according to package directions; pour over chops and stuffing. Bake at 325° for 1½ hours or until chops are tender. Yield: 2 servings.

SPINACH SAUTÉ

  ½ pound fresh spinach
  1 small tomato, peeled and cut into thin
      wedges
  1 clove garlic, crushed
  1 to 1½ tablespoons salad oil
    Salt and pepper to taste

Wash spinach thoroughly and drain. Sauté tomato and garlic in salad oil in a large skillet. Add spinach; cover and cook over low heat 15 minutes, stirring once or twice. Add salt and pepper to taste. Cook, uncovered, 5 to 10 minutes longer, stirring occasionally. Yield: 2 servings.

GLAZED CARROTS AND ONIONS

4 small whole carrots, scraped
1 (8-ounce) can onions, drained
2 tablespoons sugar
⅛ teaspoon ground ginger
1½ to 2 tablespoons melted butter or
    margarine

Cook carrots 15 to 20 minutes in enough boiling salted water to cover; cool. Dry carrots and onions on paper towel.

Combine sugar and ginger. Roll vegetables in sugar mixture, being sure to coat well; then lightly brown in butter, turning frequently. Yield: 2 servings.

HARVEST SALAD

1 small head lettuce or assorted salad
    greens
1 (10½-ounce) can asparagus spears,
    drained
1 (8¼-ounce) can Harvard or pickled
    beets, drained and diced
Salad dressing of choice
Croutons

Tear lettuce into bite-size pieces. Combine lettuce, asparagus, and beets in a salad bowl. Add dressing, and toss lightly. Garnish with croutons. Yield: 2 servings.

APPLE CRISP

2 cups peeled, sliced apples
⅓ to ½ cup firmly packed brown sugar
¼ cup all-purpose flour
¼ cup regular or quick-cooking oats
½ teaspoon ground cinnamon
½ teaspoon ground nutmeg
3 tablespoons butter or margarine,
    softened
Whipped cream or ice cream (optional)

Place apples in a greased 9- x 5- x 3-inch loafpan. Combine remaining ingredients except whipped cream; mix until crumbly, and sprinkle over apples.

Bake at 350° for 30 to 35 minutes or until apples are tender and topping is golden brown. Serve warm with whipped cream, if desired. Yield: 2 servings.

Wash most vegetables; trim any wilted parts or excess leaves before storing in crisper compartment of refrigerator. Keep potatoes and onions in a cool, dark place with plenty of air circulation to prevent sprouting.

Store spices away from any direct source of heat as the heat will destroy their flavor.

Saucy Pork Chop Dinner

(Dinner for Two)

Pork Chops with Sour Cream Sauce
Spanish Rice
Sweet-and-Sour Beans Roquefort
Mixed Green Salad with Classic Salad Dressing
Biscuits for Two
Strawberries and Avocream Delight
Iced Tea   Coffee

PORK CHOPS WITH SOUR CREAM SAUCE

  2 (¾-inch-thick) loin pork chops
    Salad oil
  1 small onion, thinly sliced
  ¼ teaspoon caraway seeds
  ¼ teaspoon salt
  ¼ teaspoon paprika
  ⅛ teaspoon dillweed
    Dash of garlic powder
  ⅓ cup water
  ⅓ cup commercial sour cream

Brown pork chops in a small amount of hot oil; drain. Add onion, caraway seeds, salt, paprika, dillweed, garlic powder, and water; cover and simmer over low heat about 1 hour or until chops are tender.

Transfer chops to a warm platter. Add sour cream to meat drippings; blend well. Heat thoroughly, but do not boil; spoon over pork chops. Yield: 2 servings.

SPANISH RICE

  ½ small onion, chopped
  2 tablespoons chopped green pepper
  2 tablespoons chopped celery
  1 tablespoon melted butter or margarine
  1¼ cups cooked regular rice
  1 cup canned or cooked chopped
    tomatoes
  ¼ teaspoon salt
    Dash of pepper
  2½ tablespoons shredded Cheddar cheese

Sauté onion, green pepper, and celery in butter 5 minutes or until tender. Add rice, tomatoes, salt, and pepper; simmer 5 minutes.

Remove from heat; stir in cheese. Yield: 2 to 3 servings.

SWEET-AND-SOUR BEANS ROQUEFORT

1 (16-ounce) can cut green beans
2 slices bacon, chopped
1 small onion, chopped
2 teaspoons sugar
2 tablespoons vinegar
   Salt and pepper to taste
2 tablespoons crumbled Roquefort or
   blue cheese

Drain beans, reserving 2 tablespoons liquid. Cook bacon and onion until lightly browned; add reserved bean liquid, beans, sugar, vinegar, salt, and pepper; heat thoroughly. Spoon into a serving dish; sprinkle with cheese. Yield: 2 servings.

CLASSIC SALAD DRESSING

⅔ cup salad oil
¼ cup cider vinegar
2 tablespoons water
1 teaspoon salt
1 teaspoon sugar
¼ teaspoon pepper
2 cloves garlic, mashed
1 teaspoon prepared mustard
1 teaspoon creamy horseradish

Combine all ingredients in a jar, and shake well. Refrigerate at least 24 hours before using. Yield: about 1¼ cups.

BISCUITS FOR TWO

1 cup all-purpose flour
1 teaspoon baking powder
½ teaspoon salt
1 tablespoon salad oil
½ cup milk

Combine dry ingredients in a small bowl. Mix oil and milk; pour into dry ingredients, and stir until almost smooth. Turn dough out on a lightly floured board or pastry cloth; knead about 6 strokes.

Roll dough to about ½-inch thickness; cut with biscuit cutter, and place on a lightly greased baking sheet. Bake at 425° about 15 minutes or until golden brown. Yield: 6 biscuits.

STRAWBERRIES AND AVOCREAM DELIGHT

1 small avocado, peeled and chopped
2 tablespoons commercial sour cream
1 tablespoon honey
1 tablespoon Grand Marnier
1 pint fresh strawberries

Combine avocado, sour cream, and honey in blender; blend until smooth. Stir in Grand Marnier. Spoon over strawberries. Yield: 2 to 4 servings.

Keep bacon drippings in a covered container in the refrigerator; use for browning meats or seasoning vegetables.

Burned food can be removed from an enamel saucepan by using the following procedure: Fill the pan with cold water containing 2 to 3 tablespoons salt, and let stand overnight. The next day, cover and bring water to a boil.

Elegant Dining for the Two of You

(Dinner for Two)

Oysters Commander
Chicken with Olives
Lemon-Dill Potatoes
Baked Tomatoes
Savory Green Salad
Bread Pudding
Wine

OYSTERS COMMANDER

  8 oysters, divided
½ cup chopped green onions
¼ cup melted butter
1½ tablespoons all-purpose flour
  6 artichoke bottoms, sliced
1½ cups oyster liquid
    Salt and pepper to taste
  2 tablespoons grated Parmesan cheese

Chop 4 oysters and set aside. Sauté onion in butter, and blend in flour. Cook over medium heat, stirring until smooth. Add chopped oysters, artichokes, oyster liquid, salt, and pepper to flour mixture; simmer 10 minutes, stirring frequently.

Place whole oysters in a greased casserole dish. Spoon sauce over oysters, and sprinkle with Parmesan cheese. Place under broiler for 2 to 3 minutes or until lightly browned. Garnish as desired. Yield: 2 servings.

CHICKEN WITH OLIVES

  2 large chicken breasts, boned
  3 to 4 tablespoons olive oil
  3 to 4 tablespoons butter or margarine, melted
½ cup white wine, divided
  6 to 8 sliced pimiento-stuffed olives
    Parsley to taste

Wash and dry chicken breasts; brown on both sides in olive oil and butter. Cover and cook 8 to 10 minutes. Turn chicken, and add ¼ cup wine and olives; cook 10 minutes. Turn chicken again and cook until tender.

Remove chicken to serving platter; add remainder of wine and parsley to drippings. Bring mixture to a boil; serve hot over chicken. Yield: 2 servings.

LEMON-DILL POTATOES

6 small new potatoes
¼ cup butter or margarine, melted
1 teaspoon dillweed
1 teaspoon sugar
1 tablespoon lemon juice
  Salt to taste

Cook potatoes in boiling water until tender; drain. Cool slightly and peel. Combine remaining ingredients, and pour over potatoes. Yield: 2 servings.

BAKED TOMATOES

2 small tomatoes
  Onion salt
2 teaspoons grated Parmesan cheese
2 teaspoons chopped parsley

Cut tomatoes in half crosswise, and sprinkle with onion salt, cheese, and parsley. Bake at 350° for 20 minutes. Yield: 2 servings.

SAVORY GREEN SALAD

2 tablespoons salad oil
1½ tablespoons wine vinegar
1 clove garlic, crushed
¼ teaspoon salt
¼ teaspoon Ac'cent
¼ teaspoon pepper
¼ teaspoon thyme
1 small tomato, chopped
½ cup chopped green onion
½ cup chopped fresh parsley
3 cups torn lettuce
½ cup croutons

Combine first 7 ingredients, and let stand several hours to allow flavors to blend. Add tomato, onion, and parsley; mix until well coated. Add lettuce, and toss well. Sprinkle with croutons just before serving. Yield: 2 servings.

BREAD PUDDING

2 eggs, well beaten
2 to 3 tablespoons sugar
⅛ teaspoon salt
½ teaspoon ground cinnamon
½ teaspoon ground nutmeg
½ teaspoon vanilla extract
2 to 3 tablespoons raisins
2 cups breadcrumbs
1 cup hot milk
  Lemon Sauce

Combine eggs and sugar; blend in salt, spices, vanilla, raisins, breadcrumbs, and milk. Pour into a buttered 9- x 5- x 3-inch loafpan. Bake at 375° for 45 minutes. Serve with Lemon Sauce. Yield: 2 servings.

Lemon Sauce:

1 egg, beaten
1 cup sugar
  Juice of 2 lemons
  Grated rind of 1 lemon
1 tablespoon butter or margarine

Combine egg, sugar, lemon juice, and lemon rind in a saucepan over low heat; cook until thickened, stirring constantly. Add butter, and stir until melted. Yield: about 1½ cups.

Little Chicken Pies

(Supper for Two)

Little Biscuit-Topped Chicken Pies
Buttered Broccoli
Best Ever Tomato Aspic
Apple Crunch
Iced Tea   Coffee

LITTLE BISCUIT-TOPPED CHICKEN PIES

1 (5-ounce) can boned chicken
6 small white onions, peeled
1 cup biscuit mix
2 tablespoons melted butter or margarine
2 tablespoons all-purpose flour
¼ teaspoon salt
   Dash of pepper
¼ teaspoon Worcestershire sauce
1 chicken bouillon cube
½ cup milk
2 teaspoons sherry
½ cup minced celery
   Milk
   Parsley (optional)

Cut chicken into bite-size pieces; set aside. Cook onions, covered, in boiling salted water for 10 minutes or until tender; drain.

Prepare biscuit mix according to package directions; roll out dough and cut into 2-inch circles.

Combine butter and flour in top of double boiler; cook until bubbly. Add salt, pepper, Worcestershire sauce, bouillon cube, and ½ cup milk; cook, stirring constantly, until smooth and thick. Remove from heat, and blend in sherry.

Arrange chicken, onions, and celery in 2 individual casseroles or a 1-quart casserole; add sauce, and top with biscuits. Brush biscuits with milk. Bake at 425° for 30 minutes or until biscuits are browned. Garnish with parsley, if desired. Yield: 2 servings.

BUTTERED BROCCOLI

½ pound broccoli
2 tablespoons butter

Trim off large leaves of broccoli. Remove tough ends of lower stalks, and wash broccoli thoroughly. If stalks are more than 1 inch in diameter, make lengthwise slits in stalks. Cook broccoli, covered, in a small amount of boiling salted water for 12 to 15 minutes or until crisp-tender. Drain.

Melt butter. Pour over hot broccoli just before serving. Yield: 2 servings.

BEST EVER TOMATO ASPIC

1 (3-ounce) package lemon-flavored
    gelatin
1¼ cups boiling water
1 (8-ounce) can tomato sauce
1½ tablespoons lemon juice
    Dash of pepper
½ teaspoon salt
½ cup chopped olives or celery

Dissolve gelatin in boiling water; stir in tomato sauce, lemon juice, pepper, and salt. Chill until consistency of unbeaten egg white. Stir in olives. Pour into a 3-cup mold, and chill until firm. Yield: about 4 servings.

APPLE CRUNCH

4 cups sliced peeled apples
¼ cup water
¾ cup all-purpose flour
1 cup sugar
1 teaspoon ground cinnamon
½ teaspoon salt
½ cup margarine, softened
    Ice cream (optional)

Place apples in a lightly greased 10- x 6- x 1¾-inch baking dish; add water.
    Combine flour, sugar, cinnamon, and salt. Using 2 knives or a pastry blender, cut in margarine until mixture resembles coarse crumbs; sprinkle over apples. Bake at 350° for 40 minutes or until apples are tender. Top with ice cream, if desired. Yield: 6 servings.

Many gelatin molds do not have their size stamped on them. You can determine the capacity of a mold by measuring the number of cups of water it will hold.

When adding vegetables to homemade soup, remember that all vegetables should not be added at the same time. Vegetables that take the longest cooking time should be added first. These include green beans, potatoes (unless diced very thin), and corn. Canned vegetables need only to be heated, so add them last.

Seafood Dream Dinner

(Dinner for Two)

Sole Bonne Femme
Rice Casserole
Zucchini Italiano
Pineapple Fruit Bowl
Commercial Rolls   Butter
Peach Brandy Cooler
Wine   Coffee

SOLE BONNE FEMME

1½ pounds sole or flounder fillets
½ cup Sauterne
1 (10¾-ounce) can cream of mushroom
   soup, undiluted
2 tablespoons sherry
   Juice of 1 lemon
1 teaspoon prepared mustard
1 teaspoon Worcestershire sauce
1½ teaspoons onion salt

Roll fillets, using toothpicks to fasten; place in a shallow pan. Combine remaining ingredients, blending well; pour over fillets. Bake at 375° for 35 minutes. Yield: 2 servings.

RICE CASSEROLE

1 cup cooked regular rice, cold
3 eggs, separated
2 tablespoons melted butter or margarine
½ cup milk
   Salt to taste
1 cup shredded Cheddar cheese
   Paprika

Combine rice, egg yolks, butter, milk, salt, and cheese; mix well. Beat egg whites until stiff; fold into rice mixture. Pour into a lightly greased 1-quart casserole or soufflé dish. Sprinkle with paprika.

Bake, uncovered, at 325° for 30 to 40 minutes or until firm and golden brown. Yield: 2 to 4 servings.

ZUCCHINI ITALIANO

1 tablespoon melted margarine
⅛ teaspoon ground oregano
2 tablespoons chopped onion
2 tablespoons chopped green pepper
2 cups thinly sliced zucchini
½ teaspoon salt
1 small tomato, peeled and cut into thin
    wedges
½ cup shredded Cheddar cheese

Combine margarine and oregano; add onion and green pepper. Sauté until vegetables are tender. Add zucchini and salt; cover and cook over low heat 15 minutes or until tender. Add tomato; cook, covered, 2 to 3 minutes. Sprinkle with cheese; heat until cheese melts. Yield: about 4 servings.

PINEAPPLE FRUIT BOWL

1 fresh pineapple
¾ cup watermelon balls or cubes
¾ cup cantaloupe or honeydew melon
    balls
½ cup drained mandarin orange sections
½ cup seedless grapes
1 banana, sliced
2½ tablespoons frozen orange juice
    concentrate, thawed and undiluted

Slice each pineapple in half lengthwise. Using a grapefruit knife, carefully remove pineapple from shells. Reserve shells; cut pineapple into chunks.

Combine pineapple chunks, watermelon balls, cantaloupe balls, orange sections, grapes, and bananas; blend in orange juice. Chill about 30 minutes, stirring occasionally. Serve in pineapple shells. Yield: 2 servings.

PEACH BRANDY COOLER

1 pint vanilla ice cream
1 peach, peeled and cubed
1½ ounces peach-flavored brandy

Combine all ingredients in blender; blend until smooth. Serve in stemmed glasses. Yield: about 2 cups.

Hearty Salad Supper

(Supper for Two)

Hearty Tuna Salad
Cheese Soufflé
Buttermilk Muffins
Chocolate Morsel Pie
Iced Tea

HEARTY TUNA SALAD

1 (10-ounce) package frozen Italian green
    beans
1 (7-ounce) can tuna, drained and flaked
1 cup thinly sliced celery
½ cup mayonnaise or salad dressing
1 tablespoon lemon juice
1½ teaspoons soy sauce
    Dash of garlic powder
1 cup chow mein noodles
    Lettuce

Cook green beans according to package directions; drain and cool. Combine beans, tuna,
celery, mayonnaise, lemon juice, soy sauce, and
garlic powder; chill. Just before serving, stir in
chow mein noodles. Serve on bed of lettuce.
Yield: 2 to 3 servings.

CHEESE SOUFFLÉ

1 egg, separated
¼ cup breadcrumbs
1 teaspoon all-purpose flour
¼ teaspoon salt
    Dash of pepper
½ cup milk
1 tablespoon salad oil
¼ cup shredded Cheddar cheese

Combine beaten egg yolk, breadcrumbs, flour,
salt, pepper, milk, and oil; cook over low heat,
stirring constantly, until mixture begins to
thicken. Fold in cheese and stiffly beaten egg
white.

Spoon into 2 lightly greased custard cups, and
bake at 350° for 20 to 30 minutes. Serve immediately. Yield: 2 servings.

BUTTERMILK MUFFINS

1 cup buttermilk
¼ teaspoon soda
1 cup self-rising flour
1 egg, beaten

Combine buttermilk and soda; add flour, stirring until smooth. Blend in egg. Pour batter into well-greased muffin tins. Bake at 425° about 40 minutes (muffins will be very brown when done). Yield: about 9 muffins.

CHOCOLATE MORSEL PIE

1 cup sugar
½ cup all-purpose flour
2 eggs, beaten
½ cup melted butter or margarine
1 cup chopped pecans
1 (6-ounce) package chocolate morsels
1 teaspoon vanilla extract
1 unbaked 9-inch pastry shell

Combine sugar and flour, mixing well. Stir in eggs and butter. Add pecans, chocolate morsels, and vanilla; mix well. Pour into pastry shell. Bake at 350° for 40 to 45 minutes. Yield: one 9-inch pie.

Fish and onion odors can be removed from the hands by rubbing them with a little vinegar, followed by washing in soapy water.

Before putting the water in the saucepan used for cooking oatmeal, spray the inside with a no-stick cooking spray. Also spray the spoon used to stir the oatmeal. These sprays are also ideal for use in baking pans and casserole dishes.

Chopped onions have the best flavor if they are browned in shortening before being added to casserole dishes.

For efficient refrigerator storage, most foods should be wrapped or covered to protect against loss of flavor and moisture, absorption of moisture, and transfer of odors. An assortment of food wraps—aluminum foil, plastic film and bags, and waxed paper—is available for refrigerator storage.

Sunday Night Supper for Two

(Supper for Two)

Oyster Loaf or Oysters en Brochette
Tossed Salad   Emerald Dressing
Pink Strawberry Cloud or Lemon Soufflé
Iced Tea

OYSTER LOAF

½ cup yellow cornmeal
¾ teaspoon salt
¼ teaspoon pepper
   Dash of cayenne pepper
   About 1 dozen oysters, well drained
   Salad oil
1 (1-pound) loaf French bread
3 tablespoons melted butter
   Hot sauce (optional)
   Catsup or cocktail sauce (optional)

Combine cornmeal, salt, pepper, and cayenne. Roll each oyster in cornmeal mixture, coating evenly. Fry oysters in salad oil heated to 375°; cook about 2 minutes or until golden brown. Drain on absorbent paper.

Slice French bread in half lengthwise; brush with butter. Heat at 350° about 5 minutes. Arrange oysters on bottom half of loaf. Season with hot sauce or catsup, if desired. Cover with top half of loaf. Serve hot, and garnish as desired. Yield: 2 servings.

OYSTERS EN BROCHETTE

2 tablespoons melted butter
1 teaspoon lemon juice
4 fresh mushroom caps
4 cherry tomatoes
2 slices bacon, cut into 8 pieces
1 dozen oysters
½ green pepper, cut into 1-inch cubes

Combine butter and lemon juice. Alternate mushrooms, tomatoes, bacon, oysters, and green pepper on 2 skewers; brush with lemon butter.

Broil 3½ to 4 inches from source of heat about 3 minutes on each side. Brush with lemon butter. Garnish as desired. Yield: 2 servings.

EMERALD DRESSING

    1 cup salad oil
    ⅓ cup vinegar
    ¼ cup chopped onion
    ¼ cup minced parsley
    2 tablespoons finely chopped green
        pepper
    2 tablespoons powdered sugar
    1½ teaspoons salt
    2 teaspoons dry mustard
    ½ teaspoon red pepper

Combine all ingredients in a jar; shake until well blended. Refrigerate at least an hour. Shake well before using. Serve with seafood, cottage cheese, or tossed green salad. Yield: about 1½ cups.

PINK STRAWBERRY CLOUD

    1 (3-ounce) package strawberry-flavored
        gelatin
    ½ pint whipping cream, whipped
    1½ cups sliced strawberries
        Whole strawberries

Prepare gelatin according to package directions; chill until consistency of unbeaten egg white.

    Fold whipped cream and sliced strawberries into thickened gelatin. Pour into a 4-cup mold, and chill until firm. Unmold and garnish with whole strawberries. Yield: 4 servings.

LEMON SOUFFLÉ

    ¼ cup shortening
    1 cup sugar
    2 eggs, separated
        Juice and grated rind of 2 lemons
    ⅓ cup all-purpose flour
    ¼ teaspoon salt
    1 cup milk

Cream shortening and sugar until light and fluffy. Add egg yolks, lemon juice, and rind; beat well. Combine flour and salt; add to creamed mixture alternately with milk. Fold in stiffly beaten egg whites.

    Pour into a 1-quart soufflé dish; set in a pan of water. Bake at 350° for 40 to 45 minutes or until firm. Yield: 4 servings.

Most recipes for French bread call for placing a pan of hot water in the oven while loaves are baking. This makes the loaves crusty. Brushing the loaves with salt water as they bake thickens and hardens the crust.

Many recipes call for both the juice and rind of citrus fruits. Remember to wash and grate the fruit before juicing.

SOUTHERN FAVORITES

Hearty Meal in a Bowl

Southern Barbecue Special

Down Home Dinner

Pork Chop Dinner, Country-Style

Fresh-from-the-Garden Supper

Chicken in a Pie

Cajun Red Beans and Rice

When many people think about Southern dishes, they create images of country ham, turnip greens, and cornbread. Southern food is these favorites, but it's more—much more!

From our Southern Barbecue Special to our Fresh-from-the-Garden Supper, you'll enjoy a distinctive sampling of Southern cuisine.

You'll find pork, chicken, and seafood high on the list of main dish favorites. Fresh vegetables come to the table in a variety of ways—cooked and seasoned with salt pork, enjoyed in casseroles and soufflés, or even fried. Since hot bread is considered a necessity with each meal for many folks, we've included flaky biscuits, crusty cornbread, spoonbread, and fritters. The Southern hostess prides herself on her desserts, especially pies, cakes, and cobblers. Pecan pie, peach dumplings, and blackberry cobbler are among the treasured favorites.

The cuisine of the South reflects cherished recipes that have been handed down for generations, but many of our down-home favorites have been adapted for easy preparation using convenience foods and shortcuts.

Hearty Meal in a Bowl

(Dinner for Twelve to Fourteen)

Kentucky Burgoo or Seafood Gumbo
Pickled Okra
Corn Fritters
Old-Fashioned Stack Cake
Iced Tea

KENTUCKY BURGOO

1 (4- to 5-pound) hen
1 pound beef stew meat
1 pound veal stew meat
1½ to 2 pounds beef or knuckle bones
1 stalk celery
1 carrot, peeled
1 small onion, peeled
5 to 6 sprigs parsley
1 (10½-ounce) can tomato puree
4 quarts water
1 red pepper pod
¼ cup salt
1 tablespoon lemon juice
1 tablespoon Worcestershire sauce
1 tablespoon sugar
1½ teaspoons black pepper
½ teaspoon cayenne
6 onions, finely chopped
8 to 10 tomatoes, peeled, and chopped
1 turnip, peeled and finely chopped
2 green peppers, finely chopped
2 cups fresh butterbeans
2 cups thinly sliced celery
2 cups finely chopped cabbage
2 cups sliced fresh okra
2 cups fresh corn (3 to 4 ears)
½ unpeeled lemon, seeded

Combine first 17 ingredients in a large pot; bring to a boil. Cover and simmer 4 hours; cool. Strain meat mixture, reserving meat and stock; discard vegetables. Remove bone, skin, and gristle from meat; finely chop meat. Return meat to stock and refrigerate overnight.

The next day, remove fat layer on stock. Add remaining ingredients; cover and simmer 1 hour. Uncover and simmer about 2 hours longer, stirring frequently to prevent sticking. Burgoo is ready when it reaches the consistency of a thick stew. Yield: about 1 gallon.

Belle Air Plantation in Charles City, Virginia, is the setting for these traditional Southern dishes (clockwise): Old-Fashioned Stack Cake (page 266), Country Ham (page 270), Piccalilli (page 288), Kentucky Burgoo (page 262), Okra and Tomatoes (page 272), Country Biscuits (page 61), Southern Cornbread (page 88), Red Beans and Rice (page 280), and Pecan Pie (page 271).

SEAFOOD GUMBO

1 cup salad oil or bacon drippings
1 cup all-purpose flour
2 large onions, chopped
2 stalks celery, chopped
1 large green pepper, chopped
6 cloves garlic, minced
1 gallon warm water
4 cups sliced okra
3 tomatoes, peeled and chopped
2 tablespoons salt
   Red and black pepper to taste
1 pint oysters, undrained
1 dozen cleaned fresh crabs* with claws
   or 1 pound fresh or frozen crabmeat
1½ to 2 pounds fresh or frozen medium
   shrimp, peeled and deveined
½ cup chopped parsley
½ cup chopped green onion tops
   Hot cooked rice
   Gumbo filé (optional)

Combine oil and flour in a heavy pot over medium heat; cook, stirring constantly, until roux is the color of a copper penny (about 10 to 15 minutes). Add onion, celery, green pepper, and garlic to roux; cook, stirring constantly, until vegetables are tender. *Do not let roux burn* as it will ruin gumbo; reduce heat if necessary.

Gradually add 1 gallon warm water to roux, in small amounts at first, blending well after each addition; add okra and tomatoes. Bring mixture to a boil. Reduce heat; simmer, stirring occasionally, at least 20 minutes (1 to 1½ hours is better as the roux develops more flavor at this point). Stir in salt, pepper, and seafood.

Bring gumbo to a boil, and simmer 10 minutes. Add parsley and green onion; simmer 5 minutes longer. Remove from heat, and serve the gumbo over hot rice.

Gumbo can be further thickened, if desired, by adding a small amount of filé to each serving. Yield: 12 to 14 servings.

To clean fresh crabs: Pour scalding water over crabs to kill them; remove large claws, and wash thoroughly. Turn crab upside down and lift the long, tapered point (the apron); pull off shell and remove the soft, spongy mass. Remove and discard legs. Wash crab thoroughly, and break body in half lengthwise; add to gumbo along with claws.

Note: Almost any kind of meat, poultry, or game can be substituted for the seafood in this recipe. Just cut it into pieces and brown it before adding to the roux.

PICKLED OKRA

   Hot peppers (1 for each jar)
   Garlic (1 clove for each jar)
3½ pounds small okra pods
   Dillseeds (1 teaspoon for each jar)
1 pint white vinegar
4 cups water
⅓ cup salt

Place hot pepper and garlic in hot sterilized jars. Remove part of stem from each okra pod. Pack okra into jars. Add dillseeds.

Combine vinegar, water, and salt in a saucepan; bring to a boil, and simmer about 5 minutes. Pour over okra. Adjust lids; process in boiling-water bath at simmering temperature (180° to 200°) for 10 minutes. Let pickles stand several weeks before opening. Yield: 4 to 5 pints.

Seafood Gumbo is one of the most popular gumbos in South Louisiana. Full of fresh crab, shrimp, and oysters, it's a meal all by itself.

CORN FRITTERS

    1 cup all-purpose flour
    1 teaspoon baking powder
    ¾ teaspoon salt
    ¼ teaspoon paprika
    2 eggs, separated
    2 tablespoons milk
    2 cups cooked, drained corn
      Hot salad oil

Combine flour, baking powder, salt, and paprika. Add egg yolks and milk, mixing well; stir in corn. Beat egg whites until stiff, and fold into batter.

Heat 2 inches of oil to 375°. Drop batter by teaspoonfuls into hot oil, and fry until golden brown. Drain well. Yield: about 2 dozen.

OLD-FASHIONED STACK CAKE

    ⅓ cup shortening
    ¾ cup firmly packed dark brown sugar
    ½ cup molasses
    2 eggs
    2⅔ cups all-purpose flour
    1 teaspoon baking powder
    1 teaspoon soda
    1 teaspoon salt
    ½ teaspoon ground cinnamon
    ½ teaspoon ground ginger
      Apple Filling

Combine shortening, sugar, molasses, and eggs; cream until light and fluffy. Combine dry ingredients; add to creamed mixture, blending well. Cover and chill at least 1 hour.

Divide dough into 5 parts, and pat into 5 well-greased and floured 9-inch cakepans (or pat each part into a 9-inch circle and place on greased cookie sheets). Bake at 400° for 8 to 10 minutes. Spread Apple Filling on warm layers; stack layers. Yield: one 5-layer cake.

Apple Filling:

    2 (8-ounce) packages dried apples
    1½ cups firmly packed brown sugar
    ¾ cup sugar
    2 teaspoons ground cinnamon
    ½ teaspoon ground allspice

Cover apples with water, and cook until tender (about 20 minutes); drain. While apples are hot, add remaining ingredients; stir until sugar dissolves. Yield: about 4 cups.

For the best baked sweet potatoes, select potatoes of the same size; place on rack in the middle of oven. Do not wrap; bake at 400° for 15 minutes. Then, reduce heat to 375°; bake medium potatoes for 45 minutes and large ones for 1 hour. Turn off heat, and let potatoes remain in oven about 30 minutes.

For a quick way to peel tomatoes, hold tomato over flame or heat for 1 minute. You may prefer to dip tomato in boiling water for 1 minute, and then plunge it into cold water. The skin should slip off easily by either method.

Southern Barbecue Special

(Dinner for Six)

Breezy Barbecued Chicken or Barbecued Spareribs
Corn-on-the-Cob   Garden Potato Salad
Zucchini Pickles
Corn Lightbread
Sweet Potato Pie or Peach Fried Pies
Fresh Mint Tea

BREEZY BARBECUED CHICKEN

　1 cup salad oil
　⅓ cup white vinegar
　3 tablespoons sugar
　3 tablespoons catsup
　1 tablespoon grated onion
1½ teaspoons salt
　1 teaspoon dry mustard
　1 tablespoon Worcestershire sauce
　1 clove garlic, minced
　　Dash of hot sauce
　3 (2-pound) broiler-size chickens, halved

Combine first 10 ingredients, and mix well; add chicken, and marinate in refrigerator overnight. Grill chicken over medium heat about 45 minutes, turning often and basting frequently with marinade. Yield: 6 servings.

BARBECUED SPARERIBS

　4 to 6 pounds spareribs
　　Salt
　　Pepper
　1 cup catsup
　½ cup dark corn syrup
　½ cup cider vinegar
　¼ cup finely chopped onion
　¼ cup Worcestershire sauce
　¼ cup prepared mustard
　2 teaspoons salt
　¼ teaspoon hot sauce

Sprinkle ribs with salt and pepper, and place in large kettle. Add water to cover, and bring to a boil. Reduce heat and simmer, covered, 1 to 1½ hours or until ribs are fork tender.

Combine remaining ingredients. Bring to a boil over medium heat, stirring constantly; reduce heat and let simmer 5 minutes.

Drain ribs. Brush both sides generously with sauce. Grill about 6 inches from heat, basting frequently, about 10 minutes on each side or until browned. Cut into serving-size pieces. If desired, heat remaining sauce and serve with ribs. Yield: 6 servings.

GARDEN POTATO SALAD

4 cups cubed cooked potatoes (4 to 5
    medium potatoes)
1 cup chopped celery
1 cup chopped zucchini
½ cup chopped green onion
½ cup vinegar
½ cup salad oil
1 teaspoon salt
¼ teaspoon garlic salt
    Lettuce
2 medium tomatoes, quartered

Combine first 8 ingredients; toss gently to mix.
Chill several hours. Spoon salad into a lettuce-
lined bowl, and garnish with tomato. Yield: 6
servings.

ZUCCHINI PICKLES

2 pounds fresh, firm zucchini
2 small onions
¼ cup pickling salt
2 cups sugar
1 teaspoon celery salt
1 teaspoon turmeric
2 teaspoons mustard seeds
3 cups cider vinegar

Wash zucchini, and cut in thin slices. Cut onions
into quarters; then slice very thin. Combine zucchini and onion; cover with 1 inch of water,
and add pickling salt. Let stand 2 hours; drain.
    Combine remaining ingredients and bring to
a boil. Pour over zucchini and onion, and let
stand 2 hours. Bring mixture to a boil, and simmer 5 minutes. Pack while hot into sterilized jars,
leaving ⅛-inch headspace. Process in boiling-
water bath 15 minutes. Yield: about 3 pints.

CORN LIGHTBREAD

2 cups cornmeal
1 cup all-purpose flour
½ cup sugar
1 teaspoon soda
1 teaspoon salt
2 cups buttermilk
3 tablespoons salad oil or bacon drippings

Combine dry ingredients; blend in buttermilk
and salad oil. Spoon into a lightly greased 9-
x 5-inch loafpan; let stand 10 minutes.
    Bake at 375° for 35 to 40 minutes. Let cool
5 minutes before removing from pan. Yield: 1
loaf.

SWEET POTATO PIE

2 cups cooked, mashed sweet potatoes
½ cup butter or margarine, softened
2 eggs, separated
1 cup firmly packed brown sugar
¼ teaspoon salt
¼ teaspoon ground ginger
½ teaspoon ground cinnamon
½ teaspoon ground nutmeg
½ cup milk
¼ cup sugar
1 unbaked 9-inch pastry shell
    Additional spices (optional)
    Whipped cream
    Orange rind

Combine sweet potatoes, butter, egg yolks,
brown sugar, salt, and spices; mix well. Add milk,
blending until smooth.
    Beat egg whites until foamy; gradually add ¼
cup sugar, beating until stiff. Fold into sweet
potato mixture. Pour filling into pastry shell;
sprinkle with additional spices, if desired. Bake
at 400° for 10 minutes. Reduce heat to 350°,
and bake 30 additional minutes. When cool,
garnish with whipped cream and orange rind.
Yield: one 9-inch pie.

PEACH FRIED PIES

2 (8-ounce) packages dried peaches
½ to ¾ cup sugar
2 tablespoons lemon juice
½ teaspoon ground cinnamon
½ teaspoon ground nutmeg
  Egg Pastry
  Salad oil

Cover peaches with boiling water, and cook over medium heat until very tender (about 30 minutes). Drain, reserving ¼ cup liquid; cool. Mash peaches, and combine with reserved liquid, sugar, lemon juice, and spices; set aside.

Roll out Pastry on waxed paper, one-third at a time. Cut out Pastry circles, using a 5-inch saucer as a measure.

Place about 3 tablespoons of peach mixture on half of each Pastry circle. To seal pies, dip fingers in water, and moisten edges of circles; fold in half, making sure edges are even. Using a fork dipped in flour, press Pastry edges firmly together.

Heat 1 inch of salad oil to 375°. Cook pies until golden brown on both sides, turning only once. Drain well on paper towels. Yield: about 1½ dozen pies.

Egg Pastry:

3 cups all-purpose flour
1 teaspoon salt
1 cup shortening
1 egg, beaten
4 tablespoons water
1 teaspoon vinegar

Combine flour and salt; cut in shortening until mixture resembles coarse cornmeal. Combine egg and water; sprinkle over flour mixture. Add vinegar, and lightly stir until mixture forms a ball.

Wrap pastry in waxed paper; chill at least 1 hour or until ready to use. Yield: pastry for about 1½ dozen 5-inch pies.

FRESH MINT TEA

4 tea bags
12 large, fresh mint leaves
3 cups boiling water
1 cup orange juice
¼ cup lemon juice
1 cup sugar
6 cups water
  Sprigs of mint
  Orange slices

Put tea bags and mint in a 3-quart pitcher; add 3 cups boiling water, and steep until cool. Discard tea bags and mint leaves.

Add orange juice, lemon juice, sugar, and 6 cups water to tea mixture; stir until sugar is dissolved. Serve over ice; garnish with mint sprigs and orange slices. Yield: about 3 quarts.

Down Home Dinner

(Dinner for Eight)

Country Ham
Sweet Potatoes in Apricot Sauce   Fried Green Tomatoes
Bread and Butter Pickles
Mississippi Spoonbread
Bread Pudding or Pecan Pie
Iced Tea

COUNTRY HAM

  1 (12- to 14-pound) country ham
  1 cup firmly packed brown sugar
  1 tablespoon whole cloves
    Sherry, apple cider, or fruit juice
    Spiced peaches
    Parsley

Soak ham in cold water overnight to remove excess salt; drain. Scrub ham thoroughly with a stiff brush, and rinse well.

Place ham, skin side down, in a large pot, and cover with cold water. Cover and simmer (do not boil) 20 to 25 minutes per pound or until internal temperature registers 160° on meat thermometer. Add hot water as necessary to keep ham completely covered during cooking.

Ham is done when shank bone pulls loose from meat. Remove ham from water; cool slightly; remove skin carefully; trim fat, leaving a ½-inch layer. Score fat; sprinkle with brown sugar, and stud with cloves. Bake at 375° for 20 minutes or until browned, basting frequently with sherry, cider, or fruit juice.

Remove to serving platter, and garnish with spiced peaches and parsley. Yield: about 20 servings.

SWEET POTATOES IN APRICOT SAUCE

  3 pounds sweet potatoes
  1 cup firmly packed brown sugar
1½ tablespoons cornstarch
  ¼ teaspoon salt
  ⅛ teaspoon ground cinnamon
  1 cup apricot nectar
  ½ cup hot water
  2 teaspoons grated orange rind
  2 tablespoons butter or margarine
  ½ cup chopped pecans

Boil sweet potatoes in salted water until tender; drain and cool. Peel potatoes, and cut in half lengthwise; place in a 2-quart shallow casserole.

Combine sugar, cornstarch, salt, and cinnamon in a saucepan. Add apricot nectar, water, and orange rind; bring to a full boil, stirring constantly. Remove from heat; stir in butter and pecans.

Pour sauce over potatoes so that all are glazed. Bake, uncovered, at 350° for 25 minutes or until sauce is bubbly. Yield: 8 servings.

FRIED GREEN TOMATOES

6 large, firm green tomatoes
   Salt and pepper to taste
1 cup cornmeal
   Bacon drippings or shortening

Cut tomatoes into ¼-inch slices. Season with salt and pepper; dredge in cornmeal. Heat bacon drippings in a heavy skillet; add tomatoes, and fry slowly until browned, turning once. Yield: 8 servings.

BREAD AND BUTTER PICKLES

6 quarts sliced cucumbers
6 medium onions, thinly sliced
1 cup salt
   Ice water
1½ quarts vinegar
6 cups sugar
¼ teaspoon cayenne pepper
1 tablespoon celery seeds
½ cup mustard seeds

Combine cucumber, onion, and salt; cover with ice water and let stand for 3 hours. Drain. Combine vinegar and seasonings in a large saucepan; bring to a boil. Add cucumber and onion; heat to simmering (do not boil). Pack pickles in hot, sterilized jars; cover with vinegar mixture and seal. Process pints for 5 minutes in boiling water bath. Yield: about 6 quarts.

MISSISSIPPI SPOONBREAD

1 cup cornmeal
2 cups milk
3 tablespoons butter or margarine
1 teaspoon salt
3 eggs
   Additional butter

Place cornmeal in a saucepan; gradually add milk, stirring until smooth. Bring to a boil over medium heat, stirring constantly. Remove from heat; add 3 tablespoons butter and salt, stirring until butter is melted. Cool. Add eggs, one at a time, beating well after each addition.

Pour batter into a well-greased 1½-quart casserole. Bake at 350° for 40 to 50 minutes. Serve immediately with butter. Yield: 8 servings.

BREAD PUDDING

   Softened butter or margarine
6 slices white bread
4 eggs
1 cup sugar, divided
1 teaspoon vanilla extract
   Dash of salt
3 cups milk
1 teaspoon ground cinnamon
1 (8-ounce) package cream cheese,
   softened

Butter bread and cut into 1-inch squares; place in a lightly greased 11¾- x 7½- x 1¾-inch baking dish.

Slightly beat 3 eggs. Add ½ cup sugar, vanilla, and salt; mix well. Heat milk; slowly add to egg mixture, mixing well. Pour over bread squares; sprinkle with cinnamon.

Combine cream cheese and ½ cup sugar; blend until smooth. Add 1 egg, beating well; spread mixture evenly over soaked bread. Bake at 350° for 45 minutes or until firm. Cool slightly. Yield: 8 servings.

PECAN PIE

½ cup melted butter or margarine
1 cup sugar
1 cup light corn syrup
4 eggs, beaten
1 teaspoon vanilla extract
¼ teaspoon salt
1 unbaked 9-inch pastry shell
   About 1 cup chopped pecans

Combine butter, sugar, and corn syrup; cook over low heat, stirring constantly, until sugar is dissolved. Cool. Add eggs, vanilla, and salt; blend well.

Pour filling into pastry shell, and top with pecans. Bake at 325° for 50 to 55 minutes. Yield: one 9-inch pie.

Pork Chop Dinner, Country-Style

(Dinner for Four)

Pork Chops and Old-Fashioned Gravy
Okra and Tomatoes or Turnip Greens
Skillet Corn or Black-Eyed Peas with Ham Hock
Beet Pickles
Favorite Southern Cornbread
Country Peach Dumplings or Yellow Squash Pie
Iced Tea

PORK CHOPS AND OLD-FASHIONED GRAVY

3 tablespoons all-purpose flour
½ teaspoon salt
½ teaspoon seasoned salt
4 small pork chops
2 tablespoons melted shortening
1¼ cups water, divided
¾ cup evaporated milk

Combine flour and salt. Dredge chops in flour mixture, reserving remaining flour mixture for gravy. Brown chops on both sides in hot shortening. Add ½ cup water; cover and simmer about 20 to 30 minutes or until tender. Remove chops from skillet and keep warm.

Discard all drippings except 2 tablespoons. Add 2 tablespoons reserved flour mixture to reserved drippings, blending until smooth.

Combine milk and remaining ¾ cup water; slowly add to flour mixture, stirring until smooth. Cook over low heat until smooth and thickened, stirring constantly. Serve gravy with chops. Yield: 4 servings.

OKRA AND TOMATOES

1 pound fresh okra
¼ cup bacon drippings
1 onion, chopped
1 green pepper, chopped
12 peeled fresh tomatoes or 1 (28-ounce) can whole tomatoes, drained
1 teaspoon sugar
1 teaspoon salt
½ teaspoon pepper
1 lemon, cut in wedges
1 tablespoon all-purpose flour
1 tablespoon water

Cover okra with water, and cook until tender; drain. Heat bacon drippings in a saucepan; add onion and green pepper, and sauté until tender. Add tomatoes, sugar, salt, pepper, lemon, and okra. Cover and simmer 15 minutes.

Combine flour and 1 tablespoon water, blending until smooth; add to okra and tomatoes. Cook until thickened, stirring constantly. Remove lemon wedges before serving. Yield: 4 servings.

TURNIP GREENS

2 pounds fresh turnip greens, kale,
    mustard greens, or spinach
    Water
¼ pound salt pork, ham, or bacon,
    chopped
    Salt to taste
¾ cup self-rising cornmeal
1 egg, beaten
¼ cup milk
1 tablespoon melted shortening

Wash greens thoroughly; cover with cold, salted
water and let soak 1 hour; drain. Bring about
2 cups of water to a boil; add greens and salt
pork and return to a boil. Cover, reduce heat,
and simmer about 1 hour or until greens are
very tender. Add salt to taste.

Combine cornmeal, egg, and milk; mix well.
Stir in shortening. Drop batter by teaspoonfuls
on top of simmering greens. Cover and simmer
20 minutes longer. Yield: 6 servings.

SKILLET CORN

3 cups fresh corn cut from cob
½ teaspoon salt
⅛ teaspoon pepper
1 tablespoon sugar
¼ cup butter
½ cup water
1 tablespoon all-purpose flour
¼ cup milk

Combine corn, salt, pepper, sugar, butter, and
water in a 10-inch skillet. Cover and simmer 15
minutes over medium heat, stirring occasionally.

Combine flour and milk, blending until
smooth; stir into corn. Cook an additional 5
minutes over low heat, stirring constantly. Yield:
4 to 6 servings.

BLACK-EYED PEAS WITH
HAM HOCK

1 pound dried black-eyed peas
5 to 6 cups water
1 small ham hock
1 to 3 teaspoons salt
1 large onion, whole

Put dried peas in colander in sink of cold water
or wash under cold running water; wash well
and remove faulty peas. Drain and place in heavy
6- to 8-quart kettle. Cover and soak 12 hours
or overnight.

The next day, add ham hock to kettle (add
more water if water does not cover peas) and
bring to a boil. Reduce heat and add 1 teaspoon
or more salt (it is better to start with a smaller
amount if salty ham hock is used). Add whole
onion; cover kettle and simmer about 1 hour
or until peas are tender. To avoid excessive
breaking of peas, do not stir during cooking; add
more salt if needed. Yield: 4 servings.

BEET PICKLES

3 quarts peeled, cooked, small beets
2 cups sugar
1 tablespoon whole allspice
1½ teaspoons salt
2 sticks cinnamon
3½ cups vinegar
1½ cups water

To cook beets, first wash and drain. Leave 2
inches of stems and taproots. Cover with boiling
water and cook until tender, about 35 to 45
minutes. Combine all ingredients except beets;
simmer for 15 minutes. Pack beets into hot sterilized jars, leaving ½-inch headspace. (Cut larger
beets in half if necessary.) Remove cinnamon.
Bring liquid to boiling. Pour, boiling hot, over
beets, leaving ½-inch headspace. Seal and process
in hot water bath for 30 minutes. Yield: about
6 pints.

FAVORITE SOUTHERN CORNBREAD

2 cups self-rising cornmeal
2 cups buttermilk
2 eggs
½ teaspoon soda
4 tablespoons bacon drippings

Combine cornmeal, buttermilk, eggs, and soda; mix well. Heat bacon drippings in a heavy 10-inch skillet; pour half of hot drippings into cornmeal mixture, and mix well. Pour batter into hot skillet, and bake at 425° for 30 minutes. Yield: 8 servings.

COUNTRY PEACH DUMPLINGS

1½ cups all-purpose flour
2 teaspoons baking powder
½ teaspoon salt
5 tablespoons shortening
½ cup milk
6 large, ripe peaches, peeled and pitted
¾ cup plus 2 tablespoons sugar
  Ground nutmeg
2 tablespoons honey
  Milk
2 tablespoons melted butter

Combine flour, baking powder, and salt; cut in shortening with 2 knives or a pastry blender until mixture resembles coarse cornmeal. Add ½ cup milk, mixing well.

Roll dough to ⅛-inch thickness on a lightly floured surface; cut into six 7-inch squares.

Place a peach in center of each square; top each with 2 tablespoons sugar, dash of nutmeg, and 1 teaspoon honey. Moisten edges of dough with milk; pull corners of square over peach. Pinch dough together, sealing all seams.

Place in a lightly greased 13- x 9- x 2-inch baking dish. Drizzle each dumpling with 1 teaspoon butter; sprinkle all with remaining 2 tablespoons sugar. Bake at 400° for 35 to 40 minutes. Yield: 6 servings.

YELLOW SQUASH PIE

5 medium-size yellow squash, sliced
¼ cup melted margarine
¾ cup sugar
1 tablespoon lemon extract
1 tablespoon all-purpose flour
2 egg yolks, beaten
  Dash of salt
1 baked 9-inch pastry shell

Cook squash in a small amount of boiling water until tender; drain well and mash. Combine margarine, sugar, lemon extract, flour, eggs, and salt; add squash, stirring well.

Spoon squash mixture into pastry shell, and bake at 375° for 20 to 25 minutes or until firm. Yield: one 9-inch pie.

Bake potatoes in half the usual time: Let them stand in boiling water for 15 minutes before baking in a very hot oven.

Avoid purchasing green-tinted potatoes. The term used for this condition is "light burn," which causes a bitter flavor. To keep potatoes from turning green once you have bought them, store in a dark, cool, dry place.

Fresh-from-the-Garden Supper

(Supper for Eight)

Collard Soup
Dried Peas with Rice and Tomatoes or Dirty Rice
Fried Okra
Garden Stuffed Yellow Squash
Sweet Potato Biscuits   Fig Preserves
Corn Relish
Blackberry Cobbler
Iced Tea

COLLARD SOUP

  1 **bunch collard greens**
  4 **slices bacon**
  3 **tablespoons melted butter or margarine**
½ **cup chopped onion**
  1 **green pepper, sliced**
  1 **chicken bouillon cube**
  1 **cup boiling water**
    Half-and-half or milk
    Salt and pepper to taste

Check leaves of greens carefully; remove pulpy stems and discolored spots on leaves. Wash thoroughly in several changes of warm water; drain. Cut greens crosswise in narrow strips.

Cook bacon in butter in a large saucepan; drain and crumble. Set aside.

Sauté onion and green pepper in bacon drippings 2 minutes. Dissolve bouillon in water; add to sautéed vegetables along with greens. Cover and simmer until greens are tender. Drain well.

To every 2 cups cooked greens, add 2 cups half-and-half; puree in electric blender. Add salt and pepper to taste. Heat thoroughly, and sprinkle with bacon. Yield: 10 to 12 servings.

DRIED PEAS WITH RICE AND TOMATOES

1½ **cups dried peas**
1¼ **cups cooked rice**
  4 **medium onions, sliced**
1½ **cups cooked or canned tomatoes**
 ¾ **teaspoon salt**
    Dash of black pepper

Soak peas overnight in 2 quarts water. Cook peas until tender in same water. Add cooked rice, onions, tomatoes, salt, and pepper. Spoon into a 2½-quart casserole and bake, covered, at 350° about 30 minutes. Yield: 8 servings.

DIRTY RICE

1 pound chicken livers or giblets,
   chopped
1 pound bulk sausage
½ cup butter or margarine
1 cup chopped onion
½ cup chopped celery
1 bunch green onions, chopped
2 tablespoons chopped parsley
1 clove garlic, minced
½ teaspoon thyme
½ teaspoon basil
3 cups cooked rice
   Salt and pepper to taste
   Hot sauce to taste
1 (10¾-ounce) can chicken broth

Sauté chicken livers and sausage until browned; remove from skillet, and set aside.

Melt butter in skillet. Add onion, celery, green onion, parsley, and garlic; sauté until tender. Add thyme, basil, rice, chicken livers, and sausage; mix well. Stir in salt, pepper, hot sauce, and chicken broth. Cook over medium heat until rice is hot, stirring constantly. Yield: about 8 servings.

FRIED OKRA

1½ to 1¾ pounds okra
3 quarts water
¾ cup salt
   Cornmeal
   Salad oil

Wash okra well; drain. Cut off tip and stem ends; cut okra crosswise into ½-inch slices.

Combine water and salt; pour over okra. Soak 30 minutes; drain, rinse well, and drain again. Roll okra in cornmeal, and fry in hot oil until golden brown. Drain on absorbent towels. Yield: 8 to 10 servings.

GARDEN STUFFED YELLOW SQUASH

8 to 10 medium-size yellow squash
½ cup chopped green pepper
1 medium tomato, chopped
1 medium onion, chopped
2 slices bacon, fried crisp and crumbled
½ cup shredded Cheddar cheese
½ teaspoon salt
   Dash of pepper
   Butter or margarine

Wash squash, and simmer in water 8 minutes or until just tender; drain, and cool slightly. Cut a thin slice from side of each squash; remove seeds.

Combine remaining ingredients except butter; mix well, and spoon into squash shells. Dot each with a pat of butter, and bake at 400° for 20 minutes. Yield: 8 to 10 servings.

SWEET POTATO BISCUITS

1 cup all-purpose flour
3 teaspoons baking powder
½ teaspoon salt
⅓ cup margarine
1 cup mashed, cooked sweet potatoes
   (1 large sweet potato)
   About 3 tablespoons milk

Combine dry ingredients. Cut in margarine with 2 knives or a pastry blender. Add sweet potatoes and enough milk to make a soft dough. Knead lightly, if desired.

Roll dough to ½-inch thickness; cut in rounds and place on a lightly oiled baking sheet. Bake at 425° for 15 to 20 minutes. Yield: 12 medium or 15 small biscuits.

FIG PRESERVES

7 cups sugar
¼ cup lemon juice
1½ quarts hot water
2 quarts firm, ripe figs, peeled
2 lemons, thinly sliced

Combine sugar, lemon juice, and hot water in a large saucepan; cook over medium heat until sugar dissolves. Add figs and cook over high heat 10 minutes, stirring occasionally. Add lemons and continue cooking rapidly 10 to 15 minutes or until figs are clear. (If syrup becomes too thick before figs become clear, add boiling water, ¼ cup at a time.)

Cover; let stand 12 to 24 hours in a cool place. Pack into sterilized jars, leaving ¼-inch headspace; seal jars with metal lids. Process jars in a boiling-water bath for 30 minutes. Yield: about 10 half pints.

Note: Figs may be preserved without peeling, although the product will not be as high in quality. If unpeeled, figs should be covered with water, boiled for 15 to 20 minutes, and drained before adding to syrup.

CORN RELISH

½ cup sugar
½ teaspoon salt
½ teaspoon celery seeds
¼ teaspoon dry mustard
⅛ teaspoon white pepper
½ cup cider vinegar
1 (17-ounce) can whole kernel corn, drained
2 tablespoons diced green pepper
1 (4-ounce) jar pimiento, diced
1 tablespoon instant minced onion

Combine sugar, salt, celery seeds, mustard, pepper, and vinegar in a 1-quart saucepan; bring to a boil. Boil 2 minutes, and remove from heat. Stir in corn, green pepper, pimiento, and onion. Cool. Pour into a pint jar. Cover tightly, and refrigerate several days before serving. Yield: 1 pint.

BLACKBERRY COBBLER

Pastry for double crust pie
4 cups fresh blackberries
2 cups sugar
½ teaspoon ground nutmeg
4 teaspoons apple cider vinegar
½ cup hot water
4 tablespoons butter or margarine, divided

Roll out half of pastry, and cut into 1-inch wide strips. Place on a cookie sheet, and bake at 450° about 8 minutes or until lightly browned.

Combine blackberries, sugar, nutmeg, vinegar, and water; spoon half into a 3-quart baking dish, and dot with 2 tablespoons butter. Place baked pastry strips on top. Cover with remaining berry mixture, and dot with remaining 2 tablespoons butter.

Roll out remaining pastry, and cut into 1-inch wide strips; arrange lattice-fashion on top of cobbler. Bake at 425° for 15 to 20 minutes or until lightly browned; reduce heat to 300° and bake 1 hour. Yield: 8 servings.

Chicken in a Pie

(Dinner for Six to Eight)

Chicken Pot Pie with Cheese Crust
Lemony Carrots or Fresh Collard Greens
Tossed Green Salad   Buttermilk Salad Dressing
Squash Pickles   Watermelon Rind Pickles
Old-Fashioned Gingerbread with Lemon Sauce
Iced Tea   Coffee

CHICKEN POT PIE WITH CHEESE CRUST

2 (2½-pound) chickens, cut up
2 quarts water
2 chicken bouillon cubes
1 cup diced onion, divided
½ cup diced celery
½ cup chopped parsley, divided
1 medium tomato, peeled and quartered
1 cup sliced mushrooms
½ cup melted margarine
½ cup all-purpose flour
1½ teaspoons salt
⅛ teaspoon pepper
   Cheese Crust

Combine chicken, water, bouillon cubes, ½ cup onion, celery, ¼ cup parsley, and tomato in a large saucepan; bring to a boil. Reduce heat; simmer, covered, 30 minutes. Cool. Reserve broth; bone chicken, and chop meat.

Sauté ½ cup onion and mushrooms in margarine until tender; add flour, blending until smooth. Gradually add 3 cups broth; cook, stirring constantly, until smooth and thickened. Add salt, pepper, and remaining parsley.

Place chicken in a greased 1½-quart casserole; add sauce. Top with Cheese Crust, and crimp edges to seal. Decorate with pastry cutouts, if desired. Cut vents in pastry. Bake at 400° for 30 to 35 minutes. Yield: 6 to 8 servings.

Cheese Crust:

1 cup all-purpose flour
½ teaspoon salt
⅓ cup margarine, softened
1 egg, beaten
1 tablespoon water
¼ cup shredded Cheddar cheese

Combine flour and salt in a mixing bowl; cut in margarine with 2 knives or a pastry blender. Add egg and water, blending well. Stir in cheese.

Roll dough to about ¼-inch thickness on a lightly floured board; shape to fit top of casserole. Yield: pastry for single crust pie.

LEMONY CARROTS

¼ cup lemon juice
¼ cup honey
1 cup water
4 cups sliced carrots
¼ cup melted margarine
¼ cup minced fresh mint

Combine lemon juice, honey, and water in a saucepan. Add carrots and bring to a boil; cover and simmer until tender. Drain carrots; dot with margarine, and sprinkle with mint. Yield: 8 servings.

FRESH COLLARD GREENS

1½ to 2 pounds fresh collard greens or 2 (10-ounce) packages frozen chopped collard greens
3 cups water
1½ teaspoons salt
½ cup diced salt pork

Check leaves of collards carefully; remove pulpy stems and discolored spots on leaves. Wash leaves thoroughly; drain well, and chop. Combine collards, water, and salt in a Dutch oven. Bring to a boil; reduce heat to low. Simmer, uncovered, for 25 minutes or until tender. Drain well.

Sauté salt pork in a skillet until golden brown; do not drain. Add collards, stirring lightly. Cook over low heat 5 minutes. Yield: 6 to 8 servings.

BUTTERMILK SALAD DRESSING

2 cups mayonnaise
1 (16-ounce) carton commercial sour cream
2 tablespoons instant minced onion
2 tablespoons dehydrated parsley flakes
2 tablespoons freeze-dried chopped chives
½ teaspoon celery salt
½ teaspoon garlic powder
1 teaspoon monosodium glutamate
1 teaspoon chervil
½ teaspoon pepper
1 teaspoon salt
2 cups buttermilk

Combine all ingredients except buttermilk, blending well. Slowly stir in buttermilk. Refrigerate at least 2 hours. Yield: about 6 cups.

SQUASH PICKLES
(see Index)

WATERMELON RIND PICKLES
(see Index)

OLD-FASHIONED GINGERBREAD WITH LEMON SAUCE

½ cup shortening
½ cup sugar
1 egg
1 cup molasses
2½ cups all-purpose flour
1½ teaspoons soda
1 teaspoon ground ginger
1 teaspoon ground cinnamon
½ teaspoon salt
½ cup hot water
Lemon Sauce

Combine shortening and sugar, and cream until light and fluffy; add egg and molasses, beating well.

Combine flour, soda, spices, and salt; add to creamed mixture alternately with water, beating well after each addition. Pour batter into a greased 9-inch square baking pan. Bake at 350° for 45 minutes or until done. Cool in pan on rack. Serve with Lemon Sauce. Yield: 9 servings.

Lemon Sauce:

Grated rind and juice of 2 lemons
2 eggs
2 cups sugar
¼ cup butter or margarine, melted
½ cup water

Combine all ingredients in a saucepan; cook, stirring constantly, over low heat until mixture thickens. Yield: about 2 cups.

Cajun Red Beans and Rice

(Dinner for Four)

Red Beans and Rice
Tossed Green Salad   Zesty French Dressing
Piccalilli
Colonial Cornbread
Coconut Supreme Cream Pie or Pecan Pralines
Iced Tea

RED BEANS AND RICE

1 pound dried red beans
1 large ham bone
1 large onion, chopped
1 large clove garlic, chopped
1 bay leaf
⅛ to ¼ teaspoon red pepper
2 teaspoons salt
1 pound smoked mild or hot link sausage,
    cut into 2-inch pieces
    Hot cooked rice

Wash beans thoroughly, cover with water, and soak overnight.

Drain beans, and place in a heavy saucepan; cover with water. Add ham bone, onion, garlic, bay leaf, and red pepper; bring to a boil. Reduce heat; cover and simmer 2 hours or until beans are tender. Add more water during cooking, if necessary.

Add salt and sausage to beans. Simmer, uncovered, until a thick gravy forms; stir occasionally. Remove bay leaf before serving. Serve over hot rice. Yield: 4 servings.

ZESTY FRENCH DRESSING

1 (15-ounce) can tomato sauce
1½ cups salad oil
½ cup vinegar
1 cup sugar
1 tablespoon prepared mustard
1 teaspoon pepper
1 teaspoon salt
1 tablespoon paprika
1 tablespoon celery seeds
3 cloves garlic

Combine all ingredients in blender; cover and blend thoroughly. Yield: about 3½ cups.

PICCALILLI

8 quarts green tomatoes, finely chopped
1 head cabbage, finely chopped
8 large onions, finely chopped
3 green peppers, finely chopped
1 cup pickling salt
2 quarts cider vinegar
1 (1-pound) package brown sugar

1 tablespoon mustard seeds
1 tablespoon ground cinnamon
2 tablespoons black pepper
¼ teaspoon red pepper
1 tablespoon ground allspice
2 tablespoons ground ginger

Combine vegetables and salt; cover with water, and soak overnight. Drain and rinse vegetables.

Combine remaining ingredients, and bring to a boil; add drained vegetables, and return to a boil. Simmer 30 minutes or until vegetables are tender.

Pack hot mixture into sterilized jars; seal. Process in boiling-water bath 5 minutes. Yield: 16 pints.

COLONIAL CORNBREAD

1 cup self-rising cornmeal
2 eggs, beaten
1 teaspoon salt
1 cup commercial sour cream
1 cup cream-style corn
½ cup bacon drippings or melted shortening

Combine first 5 ingredients, mixing well. Heat bacon drippings in a 10-inch heavy skillet; pour all but 2 tablespoons of hot drippings into cornmeal mixture, and mix well. Pour batter into hot skillet, and bake at 400° for 30 minutes or until golden brown. Yield: 6 to 8 servings.

COCONUT SUPREME CREAM PIE

¼ cup cornstarch
⅔ cup sugar
½ teaspoon salt
3 cups milk
3 eggs, separated
1 teaspoon vanilla extract
¾ cup flaked coconut
1 baked 9-inch pastry shell
6 tablespoons sugar
¼ cup flaked coconut

Combine cornstarch, ⅔ cup sugar, and salt in top of a double boiler. Gradually add milk, stirring until smooth. Cook over boiling water, stirring constantly until thickened. Cover; cook 10 minutes longer, stirring occasionally.

Beat egg yolks. Blend a small amount of hot mixture into egg yolks, mixing well; stir egg yolks into remaining hot mixture. Cook over boiling water 2 minutes, stirring constantly. Remove from water; stir in vanilla and ¾ cup coconut. Cool; pour into pastry shell.

Beat egg whites until foamy. Gradually add 6 tablespoons sugar; continue beating until stiff peaks form. Spread meringue over pie; sprinkle ¼ cup coconut over top. Bake at 425° for 5 minutes. Yield: one 9-inch pie.

PECAN PRALINES

2 cups sugar
1 teaspoon soda
1 cup buttermilk
⅛ teaspoon salt
2 tablespoons butter or margarine
1 tablespoon light corn syrup
2½ cups pecan halves

Combine sugar, soda, buttermilk, and salt in a heavy 4-quart saucepan; cook over medium heat to 210° (about 5 minutes), stirring constantly. Add butter, syrup, and pecans; continue cooking until candy reaches 234° (soft ball stage) or about 5 minutes more, stirring constantly.

Remove from heat; beat with a wooden spoon for 2 to 3 minutes, just until mixture begins to thicken. Working rapidly, drop tablespoonfuls onto lightly buttered waxed paper; let cool. Wrap pralines in waxed paper and store in airtight container. Yield: about 18 (3-inch) pralines.

APPENDICES

Handy Substitutions

Even the best of cooks occasionally runs out of an ingredient she needs and is unable to stop what she is doing to go to the store. At times like those, sometimes another ingredient or combination of ingredients can be used. Here is a list of substitutions and equivalents that yield satisfactory results in most cases.

Ingredient called for	Substitution
1 cup self-rising flour	1 cup all-purpose flour plus 1 teaspoon baking powder and ½ teaspoon salt
1 cup cake flour	1 cup sifted all-purpose flour minus 2 tablespoons
1 cup all-purpose flour	1 cup cake flour plus 2 tablespoons
1 teaspoon baking powder	½ teaspoon cream of tartar plus ¼ teaspoon soda
1 tablespoon cornstarch or arrowroot	2 tablespoons all-purpose flour
1 tablespoon tapioca	1½ tablespoons all-purpose flour
2 large eggs	3 small eggs
1 egg	2 egg yolks (for custards)
1 egg	2 egg yolks plus 1 tablespoon water (for cookies)
1 cup commercial sour cream	1 tablespoon lemon juice plus evaporated milk to equal 1 cup; or 3 tablespoons butter plus ⅞ cup sour milk
1 cup yogurt	1 cup buttermilk or sour milk
1 cup sour milk or buttermilk	1 tablespoon vinegar or lemon juice plus sweet milk to equal 1 cup
1 cup fresh milk	½ cup evaporated milk plus ½ cup water
1 cup fresh milk	3 to 5 tablespoons nonfat dry milk solids in 1 cup water
1 cup honey	1¼ cups sugar plus ¼ cup liquid
1 square (1 ounce) unsweetened chocolate	3 tablespoons cocoa plus 1 tablespoon butter or margarine
1 clove fresh garlic	1 teaspoon garlic salt or ⅛ teaspoon garlic powder
1 teaspoon onion powder	2 teaspoons minced onion
1 tablespoon fresh herbs	1 teaspoon ground or crushed dry herbs
¼ cup chopped fresh parsley	1 tablespoon dehydrated parsley
1 teaspoon dry mustard	1 tablespoon prepared mustard
1 pound fresh mushrooms	6 ounces canned mushrooms

Equivalent Weights and Measures

Food	Weight or Count	Measure
Apples	1 pound (3 medium)	3 cups, sliced
Bacon	8 slices cooked	½ cup crumbled
Bananas	1 pound (3 medium)	2½ cups, sliced, or about 2 cups, mashed
Bread	1 pound	12 to 16 slices
Bread	About 1½ slices	1 cup soft crumbs
Butter or margarine	1 pound	2 cups
Butter or margarine	¼-pound stick	½ cup
Butter or margarine	Size of an egg	About ¼ cup
Candied fruit or peels	½ pound	1¼ cups, cut
Cheese, American	1 pound	4 to 5 cups, shredded
cottage	1 pound	2 cups
cream	3-pound package	6 tablespoons
Chocolate morsels	6-ounce package	1 cup
Cocoa	1 pound	4 cups
Coconut, flaked or shredded	1 pound	5 cups
Coffee	1 pound	80 tablespoons
Cornmeal	1 pound	3 cups
Cream, heavy or whipping	½ pint	2 cups, whipped
Dates, pitted	1 pound	2 to 3 cups, chopped
Dates, pitted	7¼-ounce package	1¼ cups, chopped
Eggs	5 large	about 1 cup
Egg whites	8 large	about 1 cup
Egg yolks	12 large	about 1 cup
Flour		
all-purpose	1 pound	4 cups, sifted
cake	1 pound	4¾ to 5 cups, sifted
whole wheat	1 pound	3½ cups, unsifted
Graham crackers	16 to 18 crackers	1⅓ cups crumbs
Lemon juice	1 medium	2 to 3 tablespoons
Lemon rind	1 medium	2 teaspoons, grated
Macaroni	4 ounces (1 cup)	2¼ cups, cooked
Milk		
evaporated	6-ounce can	¾ cup
evaporated	14½-ounce can	1⅔ cups
sweetened condensed	14-ounce can	1¼ cups
sweetened condensed	15-ounce can	1⅓ cups
Miniature marshmallows	½ pound	4½ cups
Nuts, in shell		
almonds	1 pound	1 to 1¾ cups nutmeats
peanuts	1 pound	2 cups nutmeats
pecans	1 pound	2¼ cups nutmeats
walnuts	1 pound	1⅔ cups nutmeats
Nuts, shelled		
almonds	1 pound, 2 ounces	4 cups
peanuts	1 pound	4 cups
pecans	1 pound	4 cups
walnuts	1 pound	3 cups
Orange, juice	1 medium	⅓ cup

Equivalent Weights and Measures *(Continued)*

Food	Weight or Count	Measure
Orange, rind	1 medium	2 tablespoons, grated
Potatoes	2 pounds	6 medium
Potatoes	4 to 5 medium	4 cups cooked and cubed
Raisins, seedless	1 pound	3 cups
Rice	1 cup	about 4 cups cooked
Spaghetti	7 ounces	about 4 cups cooked
Sugar		
brown	1 pound	2¼ cups firmly packed
powdered	1 pound	3½ cups unsifted
granulated	1 pound	2 cups
Whipping cream	1 cup	2 cups whipped

Equivalent Measurements

Use standard measuring cups (both dry and liquid measure) and measuring spoons when measuring ingredients. All measurements given below are level.

3 teaspoons	1 tablespoon
4 tablespoons	¼ cup
5⅓ tablespoons	⅓ cup
8 tablespoons	½ cup
16 tablespoons	1 cup
2 tablespoons (liquid)	1 ounce
1 cup	8 fluid ounces
2 cups	1 pint (16 fluid ounces)
4 cups	1 quart
4 quarts	1 gallon
⅛ cup	2 tablespoons
⅓ cup	5 tablespoons plus 1 teaspoon
⅔ cup	10 tablespoons plus 2 teaspoons
¾ cup	12 tablespoons
Few grains (or dash)	less than ⅛ teaspoon
Pinch	as much as can be taken between tip of finger and thumb

COOKING MEASURE EQUIVALENTS *(page 182)*

Metric Cup	Volume (Liquid)	Liquid Solids (Butter)	Fine Powder (Flour)	Granular (Sugar)	Grain (Rice)
1	250 ml	200 g	140 g	190 g	150 g
¾	188 ml	150 g	105 g	143 g	113 g
⅔	167 ml	133 g	93 g	127 g	100 g
½	125 ml	100 g	70 g	95 g	75 g
⅓	83 ml	67 g	47 g	63 g	50 g
¼	63 ml	50 g	35 g	48 g	38 g
⅛	31 ml	25 g	18 g	24 g	19 g

GLOSSARY

à la Mode—Food served with ice cream

Al dente—The point in the cooking of pasta at which it is still fairly firm to the tooth; that is, very slightly undercooked

Aspic—A jellied meat juice or a liquid held together with gelatin

Bake—To cook food in an oven by dry heat

Barbecue—To roast meat slowly over coals on a spit or framework, or in an oven, basting intermittently with a special sauce

Baste—To spoon pan liquid over meats while they are roasting to prevent surface from drying

Beat—To mix vigorously with a brisk motion with spoon, fork, egg beater, or electric mixer

Béchamel—White sauce of butter, flour, cream rather than milk, and seasonings

Bisque—A thick, creamy soup usually of shellfish, but sometimes made of pureed vegetables

Blanch—To dip briefly into boiling water

Blend—To stir 2 or more ingredients together until well mixed

Blintz—A cooked crêpe stuffed with cheese or other filling

Boil—To cook food in boiling water or liquid that is mostly water (at 212°) in which bubbles constantly rise to the surface and burst

Boiling-water-bath canning method—Used for processing acid foods, such as fruits, tomatoes (with high-acid content), pickled vegetables, and sauerkraut. These acid foods are canned safely at boiling temperatures in a water-bath canner.

Borscht—Soup containing beets and other vegetables, usually with a meat stock base

Bouillabaisse—A highly seasoned fish soup or chowder containing two or more kinds of fish

Bouillon—Clear soup made by boiling meat in water

Bouquet Garni—Herbs tied in cheesecloth which are cooked in a mixture and removed before serving

Bourguignon—Name applied to dishes containing Burgundy and often braised onions and mushrooms

Braise—To cook slowly with liquid or steam in a covered utensil. Less-tender cuts of meat may be browned slowly on all sides in a small amount of shortening, seasoned, and water added.

Bread, to—To coat with crumbs, usually in combination with egg or other binder

Broil—To cook by direct heat, either under the heat of a broiler, over hot coals, or between two hot surfaces

Broth—A thin soup, or a liquid in which meat, fish, or vegetables have been boiled

Capers—Buds from a Mediterranean plant, usually packed in brine and used as a condiment in dressings or sauces

Caramelize—To cook white sugar in a skillet over medium heat, stirring constantly, until sugar forms a golden-brown syrup

Casserole—An ovenproof baking dish, usually with a cover; also the food cooked in it

Charlotte—A molded dessert containing gelatin, usually formed in a dish or a pan lined with ladyfingers or cake

Chill—To cool by placing on ice or in a refrigerator

Chop, to—A cut of meat usually attached to a rib

Chop—To cut into pieces, usually with a sharp knife or with kitchen shears

Clarified butter—Butter that has been melted and chilled. The solid is then lifted away from the liquid, and discarded. Clarification heightens the smoke point of butter. Clarified butter will stay fresh in the refrigerator for at least 2 months, much longer than regular butter.

Coat—To cover completely, as in "coat with flour"

Cocktail—An appetizer. Either a beverage or a light, highly seasoned food, served before a meal

Compote—Mixed fruit, raw or cooked, usually served in "compote" dishes

Condiments—Seasonings that enhance the flavor of foods with which they are served

Consommé—A clear broth made from meat

Cool—To let stand at room temperature until food is no longer warm to the touch

Court Bouillon—A highly seasoned broth made with water and meat, fish or vegetables, and seasonings

Crackling Bread—Cornbread baked with chopped cracklings added

Cracklings—The crunchy, crisp bits of pork left after the fat is rendered for lard

Cream, to—To blend together, as sugar and butter, until mixture takes on a smooth creamlike texture

Cream, whipped—Cream that has been whipped until it is stiff

Crème de Cacao—A chocolate-flavored liqueur

Crème de Café—A coffee-flavored liqueur

Crêpes—Very thin pancakes

Croquette—Minced food, shaped like a ball, patty, cone, or log, bound with a heavy sauce, breaded, and fried

Croutons—Cubes of bread, toasted or fried, served with soups, salads, or other foods

Cruller—A doughnut of twisted shape, very light in texture

Cube, to—To cut into cube-shaped pieces

Curaçao—Orange-flavored liqueur

Cut in, to—To incorporate by cutting or chopping motions, as in cutting shortening into flour for pastry

Demitasse—A small cup of coffee served after dinner

Devil, to—To prepare with hot seasoning or sauce

Dice—To cut into small (about ¼-inch) cube

Dissolve—To mix a dry substance with liquid until the dry substance becomes a part of solution

Dot—To scatter small bits of butter over top of a food

Dredge—To coat with something, usually flour or sugar

Filé—A powder made of sassafras leaves and used for seasoning and thickening foods

Filet—Boneless piece of meat or fish

Flambé—To flame, as in Crêpes Suzette or in some meat cookery, using alcohol as the burning agent; flame causes some caramelization, enhancing flavor

Flan—In France, a filled pastry; in Spain, a custard

Florentine—A food containing, or placed upon, spinach

Flour, to—To coat with flour

Fold—To add a whipped ingredient, such as cream or egg white to another ingredient by gentle over and under movement

Frappé—A drink whipped with ice to make a thick, frosty consistency

Fricassee—A stew, usually of poultry or veal

Fritter—Vegetable or fruit dipped into, or combined with, batter and fried

Fry—To cook in hot shortening

Garnish—A decoration for a food or drink, for example a sprig of parsley

Glaze (To make a shiny surface)—In meat preparation, a jelled broth applied to meat surface; in breads and pastries, a wash of egg or syrup; for doughnuts and cakes, a coating with a sugar preparation

Grate—To obtain small particles of food by rubbing on a grater or shredder

Gratin, au—A food served crusted with breadcrumbs or shredded cheese

Grill—To broil under or over a source of direct heat, such as charcoal

Grits—Coarsely ground dried corn, served either boiled, or boiled and then fried

Gumbo—Soup or stew made with okra

Herb—Aromatic plant used for seasoning and garnishing foods

Hollandaise—A sauce made of butter, egg, and lemon juice or vinegar

Hominy—Whole corn grains from which hull and germ have been removed

Jardiniere—Vegetables in a savory sauce or soup

Julienne—Vegetables cut into long thin strips or a soup containing such vegetables

Jus, au—Meat served in its own juice

Kahlua—A coffee-flavored liqueur

King, à la—Food prepared in a creamy white sauce containing mushrooms and red and/or green peppers

Kirsch—A cherry-flavored liqueur

Knead—To work a food (usually dough) with the hands, using a folding-back and pressing-forward motion

Marinade—A seasoned liquid in which food is soaked

Marinate, to—To soak food in a seasoned liquid

Meringue—A whole family of egg white-sugar preparations including pie topping, poached meringue used to top custard, crisp meringue dessert shells, and divinity candy

Mince—To chop into very fine pieces (about ⅛-inch)

Mornay—White sauce with egg, cream, and cheese added

Mousse—A molded dish based on meat or sweet whipped cream stiffened with egg white and/or gelatin (if mousse contains ice cream, it is called bombe)

Panbroil—To cook over direct heat in an uncovered skillet containing little or no shortening

Panfry—To cook in an uncovered skillet in a shallow amount of shortening

Parboil—To partially cook in boiling water before proceeding with final cooking

Pasta—Any of a large family of flour paste products, such as spaghetti, macaroni, and noodles

Pâté (French for paste)—A paste made of liver or meat

Petit Four—A small cake, which has been frosted and decorated

Pilau or pilaf—A dish of the Middle East consisting of rice and meat or vegetables in a seasoned stock

Poach—To cook in liquid held below the boiling point

Pot Liquor—The liquid in which vegetables have been boiled

Pot Roast—To cook larger cuts of meat with liquid added

Preheat—To turn on oven so that desired temperature will be reached before food is inserted for baking

Puree—A thick sauce or paste made by forcing cooked food through a sieve

Reduce—To boil down, evaporating liquid from a cooked dish

Remoulade—A rich mayonnaise-based sauce containing anchovy paste, capers, herbs, and mustard

Render—To melt fat away from surrounding meat

Rind—Outer shell or peel of melon or fruit

Roast, to—To cook in oven by dry heat (usually applied to meats)

Roux—A mixture of butter and flour used to thicken gravies and sauces; the color may be brown (if mixture is browned before liquid is added) or white

Sangría—A beverage based on dry red wine and flavored with various fruit juices (and sometimes brandy) and served cold

Sauté—To fry food lightly over fairly high heat in a small amount of fat in a shallow, open pan

Scald—(1) To heat milk just below the boiling point (2) To dip certain foods into boiling water before freezing them (also called blanching)

Scallop—A bivalve mollusk of which only the muscle hinge is eaten; also to bake a food in a sauce topped with crumbs

Score—To cut shallow gashes on surface of food, as in scoring fat on ham before glazing

Sear—To brown surface of meat over high heat to seal in juices

Set—Term used to describe gelatin when it has jelled enough to unmold

Shred—Break into thread-like or stringy pieces, usually by rubbing over the surface of a vegetable shredder

Simmer—To cook gently at a temperature below boiling point

Singe—To touch lightly with flame

Skewer—To fasten with wooden or metal pins or skewers

Sliver—A fine thin slice, as in slivered almonds

Soak—To immerse in water for a period of time

Soufflé—A spongy hot dish, made from a sweet or savory mixture (often milk or cheese), lightened by stiffly beaten egg whites

Steam—To cook food with steam either in a pressure cooker, on a platform in a covered pan, or in a special steamer

Steam-pressure canning method—Used for processing low-acid foods, such as meats, fish, poultry, and most vegetables. A temperature higher than boiling is required to can these foods safely. In this method, the food is processed in a steam-pressure canner at 10 pounds' pressure (240°) to ensure that all spoilage microorganisms are destroyed

Steep—To let a food stand in not quite boiling water until flavor is extracted

Stew—A mixture of meat or fish and vegetables cooked by simmering in its own juices and liquid, such as water and/or wine

Stir—To mix with a steady, circular motion with a spoon, whisk, or beater

Stir-fry—To cook quickly in oil over high heat, using light tossing and stirring motions to preserve shape of food

Stock—The broth in which meat, poultry, fish, or vegetables has been cooked

Syrupy—Thickened to about the consistency of egg white

Toast, to—To brown by direct heat, as in a toaster or under broiler

Torte—A round cake, sometimes made with breadcrumbs instead of flour, which may contain dried fruits and nuts

Tortilla—A Mexican flat bread made of corn or wheat flour

Toss—To mix together with light tossing motions, in order not to bruise delicate food, such as salad greens

Triple-Sec—An orange-flavored liqueur

Veal—Flesh of a milk-fed calf up to 14 weeks of age

Velouté—White sauce made of flour, butter, and a chicken or veal stock, instead of milk

Vinaigrette—A cold sauce of oil and vinegar flavored with parsley, finely chopped onions and other seasonings and served with cold meats or vegetables

Whip—To beat rapidly to increase air and increase volume

Wok—A round bowl-shaped metal cooking utensil of Chinese origin used for stir-frying and steaming (with rack inserted) of foods

INDEX

N

O

P